LANGUAGE IN AFRICA
An Introductory Survey

AFRICAN LANGUAGE GROUPS

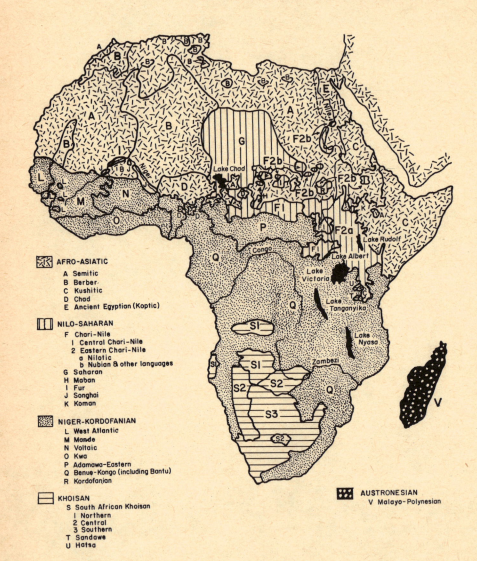

AFRO-ASIATIC
- A Semitic
- B Berber
- C Kushitic
- D Chad
- E Ancient Egyptian (Koptic)

NILO-SAHARAN
- F Chari-Nile
  - 1 Central Chari-Nile
  - 2 Eastern Chari-Nile
    - a Nilotic
    - b Nubian & other languages
- G Saharan
- H Maban
- I Fur
- J Songhai
- K Koman

NIGER-KORDOFANIAN
- L West Atlantic
- M Mande
- N Voltaic
- O Kwa
- P Adamawa-Eastern
- Q Benue-Kongo (including Bantu)
- R Kordofanian

KHOISAN
- S South African Khoisan
  - 1 Northern
  - 2 Central
  - 3 Southern
- T Sandawe
- U Hatsa

AUSTRONESIAN
- V Malayo-Polynesian

Figure 1

LANGUAGE IN AFRICA

An Introductory Survey

Edgar A. Gregersen

GORDON AND BREACH
New York Paris London

Copyright © 1977 by
Gordon and Breach Science Publishers Inc.
1 Park Avenue
New York, N.Y. 10016

Editorial office for the United Kingdom
Gordon and Breach Science Publishers Ltd.
41-42 William IV Street
London, W. C. 2

Editorial office for France
Gordon & Breach
7-9 rue Emile Dubois
Paris 75014

Library of Congress catalog card number 72-78389. ISBN 0 677 04380 5.

To
Joseph H. Greenberg

Introduction to the Series

As editor of a new series I am uncomfortably aware of the recent outpouring of anthropological books, a number of which comprise the "series" genre. Some people may feel that a new anthropology series is simply redundant and can contribute little to our understanding of human behavior. Yet, I would argue, there are enough very talented anthropologists with excellent professional backgrounds and diverse orientations to meet the needs of many more series.

One of the notable objectives of the *Library of Anthropology* is to provide a vehicle for the expression in print of new, controversial and seemingly "unorthodox" theoretical, methodological, and philosophical approaches to anthropological data. Another objective follows from the multidimensional or holistic approach in anthropology which is the discipline's unique contribution toward understanding human behavior. The books in the series will deal with such fields as archaeology, physical anthropology, linguistics, ethnology and social anthropology. Since no restrictions will be placed on the types of cultures included, a New York or New Delhi setting will be considered as relevant to anthropological theory and methods as the highlands of New Guinea.

The *Library* is designed for a wide audience and, whenever possible, technical terminology will be kept to the minimum required. In some instances, however, a book may be unavoidably somewhat esoteric and consequently will appeal only to a small sector of the reading population—advanced undergraduate students and graduate students in addition to professional social scientists.

My hopes for the readers are two fold: first, that they will enjoy learning about people; second, and perhaps more important, that the readers will come to experience a feeling of oneness with humankind.

New York City   *Anthony L. LaRuffa*

Preface

This book developed out of a survey course on African languages that Uriel Weinreich invited me to teach at Columbia University. The focus of the course changed considerably in the years that I did teach it (1964–1968), in large part to accommodate the interests of many students without a background in linguistics who registered for it. These interests lay outside detailed analyses of any one language and tended towards linguistically peripheral topics such as history, anthropology, and education. The present work shows the effects of such an accommodation. I hope it will prove to be useful to both linguists and non-linguists alike.

Various kinds of stimuli and aid have enabled me to write this book. The Anthropology Department and the African Studies Program of Yale University—in particular Leonard W. Doob and John Buettner-Janusch—provided financial assistance that permitted me to do field work in Kenya in 1959, my first field-trip to Africa. The Social Science Research Council awarded me a post-doctoral research training fellowship for 1961–1962 at Columbia University where I studied under Joseph H. Greenberg and began learning Swahili under David W. Crabb and Lugo Mtagwaba. My interest in Africa had been stimulated previously at Yale by G. P. Murdock; Professor Greenberg encouraged me to continue research in African linguistics, which I did during my teaching appointment at Columbia from 1963 to 1968. In 1964, the U.S. Department of Health, Education, and Welfare awarded me an NDEA-related Fulbright Hays travel grant, which permitted me to do research in Nigeria, Tanganyika, Zanzibar, and Kenya in 1964. W. H. Whiteley and the East African Swahili Committee provided generous assistance to me during my stay in Dar es Salaam.

Many thanks to the Bibliothèque Nationale, the library of the École Nationales des Langues Orientales Vivantes, the library and faculty of the School of Oriental and African Studies, and various other centers of scholarship for their invaluable aid. Special acknowledgment must be given to the Forty-Second Street Library (New York Public Library, Central Branch) and the various libraries of Columbia University where most of the library research for this book was done.

Illustrations in this book are reproduced with the permission of the following:

News and Publication Service, Stanford University (the photograph of Joseph H. Greenberg).

Routledge & Kegan Paul, Ltd, London (the photographs of 19th century Africanist linguists from Robert Needham Cust, *A Sketch of the Modern Languages of Africa*).

The American Museum of Natural History (the photographs of a woman with large lip plugs).

I. J. Gelb and the University of Chicago Press (the line drawing of the Narmer palette, from Gelb, *A Study of Writing*).

The Metropolitan Museum of Art, New York (the photograph of a statue of Thoth).

The Trustees of the British Museum (the photograph of the Rosetta stone, from E. A. Wallis, *The Rosetta Stone*).

Professor E. Bolaji Idowu and Longman Nigeria Limited (the photograph of the statue of Èṣù, from Idowu, *Olódùmarè: God in Yoruba belief*).

The Nigerian Consulate of New York (the photograph of a Yoruba drummer).

Reinaldo de Almeida and the Companhia de Diamantes de Angola, Lisboa (the photograph of a Shinje with filled teeth, from Almeida, *Mutilações dentárias nos negros da Lunda* [DIAMANG Publicações culturais, no 33])

A. Schmitt and Otto Harrassowitz Verlag, Wiesbaden (the photograph of King Nʒoya, from Schmitt, *Die Baum-Schrift*, with the signature of the king in his own script).

Joseph H. Greenberg (modified form of the map of language distributions).

The photographs of Chief Sikalenge and a Tonga headman, both taken by Professor Doke himself, are reproduced from C. M. Doke, *A Comparative Study in Shona Phonetics* (Johannesburg, University of Witwatersrand Press, 1931) figures 25 and 26, with the permission of the author and of the Witwatersrand University Press, Johannesburg.

The photograph of Carl Meinhof is reproduced from Boas, *et al.*, *Festschrift Meinhof* (L. Friederichsen and Co.); that of Diedrich Westermann from Johannes Lukas, ed., 1955, *Afrikanistische Studien*, Berlin: Akademie-Verlag (Deutsche Akademie der Wissenschaften zu Berlin, Institut für Orientforschung, Veröffentlichung Nr 26).

Gary S. Vescelius expertly drew (or redrew) the maps of language distribution and language diffusion. James Nazarian helped with photographic services.

The invidious job of typing was done by a number of people, but primarily by the secretarial services of Queens College, the members of which have requested to remain anonymous.

Joseph H. Greenberg, William E. Welmers, Kay Williamson, Robert Austerlitz, Abraham Rosman, Judith Timyan, Phillip Ravenhill, and Robert L. Ross read the book in manuscript and made many helpful suggestions and corrections.

Patricia Sullivan checked bibliographical references. Phyllis Rafti compiled the index. Many thanks for all this aid. I fear I did not make enough use of it: any errors still found are of course my own.

Edgar A. Gregersen
New York

Table of Contents

List of Figures

Part One   INTRODUCTORY CHAPTERS

CHAPTER I

Introduction

The one thing African languages have in common, setting them off from all the other languages in the world, is the fact that they are spoken in Africa.

Even so minimal a characterization has to ignore awkward facts such as the European and Indian languages widely spoken in Africa (e.g. English, French, Portuguese, Gujarati) and the African languages transplanted elsewhere (e.g. Yoruba surviving in Cuba as a ritual language, Lucumí; Hausa formerly spoken in Brazil; Swahili sometimes to be found in parts of India). But what the characterization is meant to imply is that Africa does NOT represent some sort of natural linguistic area. It is not linguistics, but a variety of nonlinguistic considerations—notably geographical, political, and anthropological—that has focused interest on the 1000 or so African languages as a group.

These nonlinguistic considerations prove to be the ultimate justification for any work of the present kind. Here, they have also helped determine the overall approach: not only are the implications of the study of African languages discussed for historical reconstruction and educational policy (among other fields), but no linguistic training is assumed of the reader. In point of fact much of this book can be regarded as an introduction to general linguistic method using examples drawn from African languages. Such an approach is possible because African languages differ in no essential way from the languages of Europe, Asia, or the Americas; and linguistic techniques developed for non-African languages are applicable to African languages—if valid at all. Although some scholars seem to be unwilling to go along with this conclusion, it will here be taken as axiomatic.

Although considerably weaker, a linguistic justification for a book devoted solely to language in Africa is also possible. In the first place, some of the important findings from the African linguistic field can be summarized and brought into perspective for general linguistic theory. In light of what has already been said it should be clear that African languages are as relevant and important to a general study of languages as English, French, or Chinese. As a specific example we may mention that a recent survey study of the phonetics of various West African languages by Peter Ladefoged has helped bring about a number of revisions of an important general theory of phonology, the subdivision of linguistics dealing with pronunciation.

Secondly, the language families of Africa are, with one major exception (the Semitic family), confined within the boundaries of the continent—at least to our present knowledge. Even if larger groupings including non-African languages could eventually be demonstrated beyond doubt, the extensiveness, variety, and time depth involved in the African subgroups would more than warrant a continued study of them independently. For example, Swahili, spoken on the east coast of Africa, can be shown to be related to Zulu in South Africa, and probably also to Fulani in the westernmost portions of the continent. This is a language family spoken in an area larger than all of Europe, and the constituent languages of this family are often so divergent that many scholars still question the validity of setting them up in a single grouping.

A third justification lies in the fact that certain features of pronunciation, idiom, or structure are found over a wide area in Africa or seem to be restricted entirely to Africa. Precisely how many of the similarities should be accounted for remains unclear. Some writers have assumed that they point to the common origin of all African languages, or possibly parallel developments from a similar mentality—explanations that are highly dubious. Quite likely borrowings of various kinds and of a prolonged and fairly intensive sort are involved in many of these similarities. With regard to specific idioms and phrases, a similar cultural background in many instances seems to permit a pooling of metaphors. Consider for example a common West African expression that means *things are not going well.* In Pidgin English (a form of English that has developed on the west coast) the expression is **wota don pas gari** [water done pass gari] *there is more water than gari* (a kind of flour). The phrase refers to the difficulty of eating mush or gruel with the fingers unless it has a properly firm consistency: too much water and the result is mess. A phrase such as this would likely be developed or borrowed only by people who eat with their fingers in the first place—a pan-African custom.

Among the nearly exclusively African or pan-African traits are the following.

Pronunciation

The few sound types that seem to be largely restricted to Africa include: (1) a "flapped" **v** apparently found only in certain languages in Nigeria and Congo; (2) click sounds on the order of the interjection written *tut-tut* or *tsk-tsk* in English or the sound made to gee-up horses, their use as fulfledged consonants in normal words being restricted to certain languages in southern and eastern Africa; (3) combinations such as **kp**, **gb** (more rarely **pt**, **bd**), i.e. simultaneously pronounced **k** plus **p**, etc., are widely scattered over the western Sudan (outside of Africa, they have been reported only from a small part of Melanesia); (4) lip trills, like the English *brrr* to indicate the sensation of being cold, found in a few

African languages as normal consonants (also reliably reported in at least one instance from Central America).

Quite commonly throughout Africa, words and syllables normally end on vowels, and words often may begin with **ng** (as in *king*) or with combinations such as **mb** or **nd** (other consonant combinations are unusual). Nearly all languages south of the Sahara and some others are total, using pitch distinctions to differentiate otherwise similar words.

Idiom

A number of idioms and metaphors have a wide but by no means universal distribution over the continent. The following list should be suggestive: *to be with* meaning *to have*; *thing of eating—food*; *he and his head—he himself* and *he killed his head—he killed himself*; *she has a belly—she is pregnant*; *skin of mouth—lip*; *mouth of house—door*; *neck of arm—wrist*; *to eat* (or *drink*) *tobacco —to smoke*; *don't touch my ear—great-grandchild*. Names of body parts are generally used to denote positional relationships; *belly of—in*(*side*); *head of—*(*up*)*on*; etc. The expression *son of* or *child of* is common to indicate diminution (*son of book—small book*) or agent (*son of law—lawyer*), sometimes both in the same language; *child of tree* is a common expression for *fruit*. The right and left hands are often designated as the *male hand* (or *hand of eating*) and *female hand*, respectively. Quite frequently one term is used for both sun and day, moon and month, eye and face, finger and toe, hand and arm, hair and feather, (wild) animal and meat, eat and conquer (sometimes also copulate), hear and understand (sometimes also feel, perceive). Of course, similar usages can sometimes be found even in European languages; thus, in French **doigt** can refer to either the finger or toe (although a special word for toe also exists, **orteil**); and in Russian **ruká** refers to either the hand or the whole arm.

In some instances similar words with generally the same meaning are used across language families; thus, **nama** or **nyama** is practically a pan-Africanism for *animal*, *meat*. Such examples are fairly rare, however, but some scholars are more willing to accept similarities of this kind than others; thus, Hausa **mùtûm** *man*, *person* has been compared to Swahili **mtu** with the same meaning.

Structure

A few grammatical constructions may be noted as widespread and even typically (but not necessarily exclusively) African.

Adjectival constructions are frequently absent or avoided in favor of constructions with verbs or abstract nouns; thus, *the man is tall* may correspond to *the man has height* or a construction involving a verb we can represent as *to tall* (meaning *to be tall*): *the man talls*. Comparison is nearly everywhere expressed by means of a verb *to surpass*: *the man is taller than the boy* is usually *the man surpasses the boy in height* or *the man is tall, surpasses the boy*.

Possessive phrases such as *the man's knife* are very often constructed on the order of *knife* (*of*) *man*.

Doubling (technically, reduplication) of a word or of part of a word is commonly used to form plurals both of nouns and verbs and occurs also in the formation of adverbial and other construction. Pidgin English **smol-smol** [small-small] *a little*, **sisi-sisi** *six pence* [sisi] *a piece*, **fos-fos taym** [first-first time] *the very first time* are representative of some of the common uses of reduplication.

Quite a widespread feature of African languages rare elsewhere is an extensive system of verbal derivation. In Bantu languages, for example, a sentence such as *that woman cooked the food for the boy* would be construed along the lines of *that woman cook-for-ed the boy the food*, where *cook-for-ed* represents one word. That is, African languages sometimes indicate in the form of the verb a relationship expressed in other languages merely by position, or by a separate word (as in English with the preposition *for*), or by a special form of another word in the sentence (in German or Russian the word *boy* would be in the dative case).

Elaborate noun class systems are characteristic of a large number of languages in Africa. These systems may be compared with the gender systems of many European languages where nouns fall into groups traditionally labeled as masculine, feminine, and neuter. However in African languages, the division is somewhat different: as a rule nouns denoting both men and women are lumped into one class, and nouns devoting neuter objects fall into a variety of classes. The result is that English *he* and *she* may correspond to a single term in a particular African language, but *it* may have as many as ten corresponding forms. It should be pointed out, however, that such a system is not exclusively African: similar ones are found in various Australian, New Guinea, Caucasian, and North American Indian languages.

In addition to these features, widespread vocabulary borrowings from Arabic and other languages have helped to create at least a superficial similiarity among several African languages. Literally hundreds of words based on Arabic denoting trade goods and religious and other cultural innovations are shared by languages otherwise unrelated. Thus, words based on Arabic **qalam** *pen* or *pencil*, **kitaab** *book*, **maala'ika** *angels* (but with singular meaning) **sanduuq** *box*, **bunduuq** *gun*, **faras** *mare* (but usually with the meaning *horse*) have spread to an enormous number of languages even where direct contact with Arab traders did not take place. Words denoting European or New World importations have similarly spread and forms based on English *tobacco*, *cigar*(*ette*), *whiskey*, *hospital*, *motor* (*car*) are well-nigh universally known.

The present book is organized into three main sections. Part one introduces basic linguistic notions and terminology; a sketch of the techniques of description, classification, and reconstruction; and a survey of the history of the study of African languages. Part two discusses in some detail the language families of Africa and special problems involving particular languages. Part three is concerned with topics related to the general field but not strictly linguistic, such as nonlinguistic inferences from linguistic information, African writing systems, and problems in language planning, and policy. No attempt is made at providing and encyclopaedic coverage of every language, or even a complete listing. Cust, in his monumental *A Sketch of the Modern Languages of Africa*, attempted such a coverage in 1883 and even at that time of embryonic knowledge of the field two volumes were required. Now, ten times that number would prove inadequate. For example, the several volumes of *The Handbook of African Languages*[1] contain, with a few notable exceptions, mostly lists of languages with population data, and fairly comprehensive bibliographies. In this introductory survey the emphasis is more on methodology and problem areas than on particular languages.

The term Africa is here used in its broadest geographical sense and will even include the island Madagascar. Some Africanist linguists feel that their subject matter is properly the language of "Black Africa". Such a decision is as arbitrary as any other since some languages of Black Africa are related to languages spoken elsewhere, e.g. Hausa spoken by blacks is related to Arabic, Somali, and Berber spoken by people usually classified as white.

Certain African languages have been referred to in the literature by more than one name, e.g. Tiv is sometimes referred to as Munchi. As far as possible I have tried to use either the most common form or a form recommended by leading scholars, with reference to variants when these are also widely used. Names of Bantu languages and a few others are elsewhere found sometimes with a prefix and sometimes without; thus, Kiswahili (also spelt kiSwahili or KiSwahili) or Swahili. The practice of most English-speaking Africanists of dropping such prefixes in an English context has been followed here, with few exceptions. Hence, the forms Zulu, Rwanda, Ganda, Kongo, Luo will be found—not isiZulu, runyaRwanda, Luganda, Kikongo, Dholuo.[2]

Throughout the book, languages will be identified not only by where they are spoken but also in terms of the most recent classification of African languages by Greenberg (1963). Although much of it remains at present on the level of plausible hypothesis and has not been subject to the rigorous techniques developed elsewhere, this classification bids fair to become as valid and commonplace in linguistic thinking as Indo-European. Changes of detail, particularly as more (and more accurate) data become available, are inevitable. But the general structure will probably remain. In anticipation of a discussion of the methodological problems involved, here is a brief résumé of that classification together with particular examples of some of the more common or important African languages.

I) Niger-Kordofanian, including the important Niger-Kongo division comprised of Bantu and the former Western Sudanic; e.g. Zulu, Swahili, Bulu, Yoruba, Igbo (Ibo), Mende (Malinke) Fulani (Fula, Peul, Fulfulde).

II) Afro-Asiatic, including the former Hamito-Semitic in addition to Chadic; e.g. Ancient Egyptian, Berber, Amharic, Arabic, Somali, Hausa.

III) Nilo-Saharan, comprised of a number of distantly related subgroups such as Songhai, Kanuric, Fur, and Chari-Nile (including Nilotic and Central Sudanic); e.g. Maasai (Masai), Luo, Nubian, Mangbetu, Kanuri.

IV) Khoisan, including Bushman, Hottentot, and two isolated languages in East Africa: Sandawe and Hatsa (Kindiga, Hadza, Hadzapi.)

V) Austronesian or Malayo-Polynesian, the only relevant example for our purposes being Malagasy (Malgache) spoken on the island of Madagascar.

Notes and References

A number of general studies of African languages has appeared, many of them now historical interest only. The following are among the more important items, arranged chronologically; those preceded by an asterisk are suggested readings.

Robert Needham Cust, 1883, *A sketch of the modern languages of Africa*, London.

Carl Meinhof, 1910, *Die moderne Sprachforschung in Afrika*, Berlin. (Translated, 1915, as *Introduction to the study of African languages.)*

Alice Werner, 1925, *The language families of Africa*, London. 1930, *The structure of African languages*, London.

O. Assirelli, 1938, *Africa polyglotta*, Bologna.

Lilias Homburger, 1940, *Les langues négro-africaines et les peuples qui les parlent*, Paris.

*Diedrich Westermann, 1949, *Sprachbeziehungen und Sprachverwandtschaft in Afrika* (Sitzungsberichte der Deutschen Akademie der Wissenschaften, Philosophisch-historische Klasse No. 1), Berlin.

Joseph H. Greenberg, 1949—54, [A series of articles with the general title:] Studies in African linguistic classification, *South-western Journal of Anthropology*. (A revised version of these articles, issued as a separate monograph, has appeared: *1963, *The Languages of Africa,* Bloomington: *International Journal of American Linguistics* 29.I.II.) *1959, Africa as a linguistic area, in Bascom and Herskovits (eds), *Continuity and Change in African Culture*, 15-27, Chicago.

*Archibald N. Tucker, 1957, Philology and Africa, *Bulletin of the School of Oriental and African Studies*, 20-541-554.

C.F. and F.M. Voegelin, 1964, *Languages of the world: African fascicle one.* (Anthropological Linguistics 6.5).

István Fodor, 1966, *The problems in the classification of the African languages*, Budapest.

Maurice Houis, 1966, *Aperçu sur les structures grammaticales des langues négro-africaines*, Lyon.

Pierre Alexandre, 1967, *Langues et langage en Afrique noire*, Paris.

Jack Berry and Joseph H. Greenberg, eds., 1971, *Linguistics in Sub-Saharan Africa* (*Current trends in linguistics*, Vol. 7), The Hague.

*Wm. E. Welmers, 1973, *African language structures*, Berkeley and Los Angeles.

1) The Handbook of African Languages is published by Oxford University Press for the International African Institute. Ten volumes have so far appeared; some are particularly informative and quite comprehensive, e.g. C.M. Doke, 1954, *The Southern Bantu languages* .

2) Similarly, a single term is used to denote both a people and the language they speak, following normal English usage for other areas, e.g. French, Russian, Japanese. Thus, the terms Fulani, Mossi, and Tuareg are used instead of special language names (Fula, Mo:ré, Tamasheq respectively). (I have modified the spelling of certain of Greenberg's labels to bring them more nearly in line with the Africa Alphabet Conventions by using k instead of his c (Niger-Kongo instead of Niger-Congo, Kushitic instead of Cushitic, etc.).

CHAPTER II

Clearing the Bush

This chapter begins our introduction to linguistic method by trying to clear away possible misconceptions, as well as tidying up some basic terminology.

To start with, it should be noted that linguistics, like all sciences, is not normative: it makes no value judgments about its subject matter, except perhaps for the implicit judgment that all languages are worthy of study in the first place. The layman's concern about the relative beauty or ugliness of a language falls outside the province of linguistics. Hence, statements of untrained travelers in Africa to the effect that this or that language encountered on their journeys is variously "beautiful", "harsh", "musical", "guttural", "pleasing", "expressive", or the like, are simply of no consequence. Everyone remains free to cultivate his own prejudices in such matters, of course. But prejudices of this sort are undoubtedly worthless for, if not actually detrimental to, linguistic analysis.

Much the same can be said for the idea of "correctness", which has permeated so much of traditional language teaching. Correctness in the traditional sense is invariably a characteristic of upper class speech only, or of a literary norm, if it exists. In some instances grammarians in their codifications of grammatical rules have actually abandoned normal usage on the pretext of supplying a more "logical" or "pleasing" form. The conception of what is grammatical thus can become divorced from what is really used. An extreme example of this is found in the Arabic speaking world, which includes most of North Africa. Here, "correct" Arabic is regularly identified with a literary norm based on the spoken language of the early middle ages as recorded in the Koran; no one speaks this form of Arabic natively, and in most informal contexts it would be completely inappropriate, but every other kind of Arabic is, in native tradition, held to be a "grammarless" corruption. The modern linguist normally takes a completely different view. All languages and dialects—even those spoken by uneducated, illiterate, or technologically primitive peoples—have highly involved rules for constructing sentences. For the linguist, by definition, these rules constitute the grammar of a language. That the rules may not as yet be explicitly formulated or codified is beside the point. Furthermore, the linguist accepts as correct for any given language the usage that is natural and acceptable to native speakers of that language. A normal native speaker, merely by virtue of the fact that he has internalized the usage of his speech community throughout his childhood, must be said to speak his own "dialect" perfectly. Of course, people may make slips of the tongue in actual conversation (we are all familiar with spoonerisms such as "queer old dean" for "dear old queen", and other anomalies); but these are matters of performance, not necessarily of competence on the part of the speaker, who would undoubtedly correct himself if the slip were brought to his attention.

For these reasons, a linguist would be quite willing in many instances to write up a grammatical analysis of the speech of a single illiterate native speaker. It goes without saying that certain nonlinguistic considerations might sway the choice of which speaker to use as an informant, e.g. whether a man's dialect was widely used or spoken by only a handful of people, or whether the dialect was socially acceptable or substandard. The important point here, to use an English example, is that the speaker who normally says "I ain't got none" speaks "perfectly" in the linguistic sense, although in some social contexts he may be guilty of a *faux pas*. Labels such as "substandard" are ultimately sociological, not linguistic.

The question of the relative difficulty of African languages represents another kind of nonlinguistic problem that can be answered only with reference to the learner's previous language background and training. In all language communities, normal children achieve reasonable fluency in their first language by the time they are five. Nowhere do we find children unable to master their mother tongue before, say, adolescence, because of some unusual intricacy of the grammar. The acquisition of a second language by an adult is a different matter. As far as English-speaking people are concerned, Swahili, for example, would probably be relatively easier than Somali, Kanuri, or Zulu if only because Swahili is not tonal and the others are; but for a speaker of Chinese, tones would presumably not present much difficulty since Chinese itself is tonal but even this requires empirical verification twice the tonal systems are so different. We might perhaps note, however, that some languages in at least some respects have proved to be less tractable than others to the professional linguist—among these, some of the Nilotic languages of East Africa, e.g. Dinka ("Dinka", says William F. Welmers in a memorable phrase, "is a stinka"). But then, much of the analysis of English remains incomplete or disputed.

Nonsophisticated people approaching the study of African languages often expect to find simple languages with minuscule vocabularies—unsuitable, as older commentators might have put it, for the expression of profound or noble sentiments. In short, languages that might have been dreamt up by Hollywood script writers for a Tarzan movie.[1] R. C. Abraham, one of the great field workers in the African field and himself the author of numerous grammars and dictionaries, is reported[2] to have believed before he started work on Yoruba that its grammar could be written on the back of a postage stamp. He soon discovered otherwise, however, and later declared that Yoruba was "an endless ocean".

In point of fact, all languages everywhere in the world for which we have adequate information prove to have complicated grammars and vocabularies with well in the tens if not hundreds of thousands of words (an exact number is impossible to quote, in part because a universally accepted definition of "word" does not exist at present). Reports of languages with total vocabularies of only a few hundred words, so inadequate that natives have to "eke out their words with gestures", making communication impossible in the dark, have turned out to be gross distortions of fact. Probably the only people (other than deaf mutes) who must resort to gesture to make up for vocabulary deficiencies are tourists in a foreign country—not excluding English-speaking tourists.

Not only is the word stock of every language considerable and apparently adequate for the culture it is used in, but the vocabularies of all languages share certain universal characteristics.[3] For example, there are always words to express the notions of true or false and hence every language is able to handle the basic concepts of propositional logic. All languages have words for dealing with time, space, and number. Personal pronouns constitute a linguistic universal; without exception they have at least three persons (e.g. I, you, he) and two numbers (singular and plural). Kinship terms and proper names are universally present categories. At least some parts of the vocabulary, notably words dealing with sex and excretion but sometimes others as well, are tabued or avoided with euphemisms everywhere. Idioms and metaphors can be found in all languages. And it may be added that a small number of words everywhere tend even to have similar forms—not only imitative, onomatopoetic words on the order of *cuckoo*, but also kinship terms such as *mama*, *papa*, and a few other items like *me*; cf. Swahili **kuku** *fowl*, **mama** *mother*, **mi(mi)** *I/me*.[4]

Attempts to set off some contemporary languages as more "primitive" than others have proved to be unsuccessful. Although full-fledged language in the present sense could hardly have developed overnight, and rudimentary speech of one sort or another must have existed at one point in the evolution of man, no reliable report exists of a surviving primitive language. It is true that even today a few people survive with a primitive technology, such as the Hatsa of Tanzania near Lake Eyasi, and the Naron Bushmen of the Kalahari Desert in South Africa (both speakers of Khoisan languages): they are hunters and gatherers without domesticated animals, metallurgy, pottery, or writing. Nevertheless, from the point of view of structure, their languages are the equal of any of the languages of industrialized Europe or America. Edward Sapir, the eminent linguist and anthropologist, put it this way: "The lowliest South African Bushman speaks in the forms of a rich symbolic system that is in essence perfectly comparable to the speech of the cultivated Frenchman".[5] Of course, the technical jargon of, say, nuclear physics would hardly occur in the language of a preliterate group, but it could be developed either from the derivational resources of the language itself or borrowed wholesale from English; such jargon represents specialized vocabulary with a peripheral status in any language anyway.

With regard to grammatical structure, languages are, to be sure, remarkably diverse. But what languages seem to have in common is equally if not more remarkable. For example, in all languages there are means for making statements, asking questions, giving commands, and reporting what other speakers have said. Specific rules always obtain for the construction of phrases and clauses and for joining clauses together. In no language can one discover a "longest" sentence: a still longer one could always be produced. Although noun-like words and verb-like words may not be distinguished by some external formal characteristic, they probably must be posited in accounting for the syntax of every language, as must such distinctions as subject, predicate, and object. Even with regard to fairly specific details of word order in a sentence, a considerable number of universals or near universals exist: in most languages of the world a subject normally precedes an object; an *if*-clause normally precedes the *then*-clause; etc. As a matter of fact, one of the main interests in contemporary linguistic theory is the question of linguistic universals and how to account for them.

Another universal characteristic of languages, but of another kind, is change. We all know that the standard English of Shakespeare's time is not exactly the same as that of today; for earlier periods such as the time of Chaucer or of King Elfred, the differences are even clearer. Wherever written records exist they demonstrate the fact of change over and over again. It is sometimes alleged that certain dialects have nevertheless remained unchanged and intact, that the English spoken in the Kentucky hills, for example, is pure Elizabethan English or that French Canadian preserves the French of the 17th Century. Examination of the facts reveals that although some features of these dialects may represent an earlier form no longer preserved elsewhere, other changes have taken place, changes that may not have occurred in other dialects. Change occurs, but not always in the same way or in the same area of the language. Thus, statements to the effect that Pigmies of Equatorial Africa, for example, speak an older or even archaic version of the languages of their neighbors (a common allegation) must be taken with a grain of salt. Just as there are no truly primitive languages around so also are there no "archaic" or "pure" ones.

The relationship between language and race[6] represents another area where a considerable number of patently false beliefs occur. For example, some people have seriously maintained that the size of the jaws, the degree of eversion of the lips, the extent of protusion of the teeth, and so on, can produce a "racial accent" (we are of course not concerned here with nonracial abnormalities on the order of cleft palates). The experience of people in the English-speaking world should belie such an assertion. Certainly the racial attributes of a Sidney Poitier or Sammy Davis can hardly be guessed from their pronunciation. Examples of white people brought up speaking African languages flawlessly are many among missionary families and European settlers who have engaged African nurses for their children. L.S.B. Leakey, the renowned archeologist, was such an example and spoke both English and Kikuyu, reportedly without a trace of an accent in either.

As for other possible correlations between language and race, the following facts are pertinent in the African situation. The Herero, who are negroid, speak a language related to the languages spoken by bushmanoid peoples. The various Pigmy groups speak the languages of their non-Pigmy neighbors and have no distinctive language of their own. Rwanda, a Bantu language, is spoken by Bantu, Nilotic, and Pigmy peoples. The Chadic languages are all spoken primarily by blacks but are genetically related to Semitic and Berber associated with whites.

The only reasonable conclusion is surely that language and physical type are independent of each other in any necessary way (although general correlations do in fact exist).

I should like to end this chapter by introducing certain technical terms that might cause some difficulty because of their meanings in informal use.

In informal usage, the terms "language" and "dialect" often imply some sort of social or cultural judgment. In a discussion of a European or American situation, "language" would probably refer to the official upper-class literary norm, and dialect would be the label for substandard or regional varieties. For other areas, dialect is frequently used for all forms of speech that are unwritten; for this reason, one sometimes finds references to "African dialects" where "African languages" would be linguistically more appropriate.

In formal technical usage, a dialect is usually taken to mean merely a variety or subdivision of a language. The speech of an individual member of a language community is an "idiolect". Highly similar idiolects constitute a dialect. Mutually intelligible dialects constitute a language.[8] Dialects do not necessarily exhibit clear-cut boundaries but tend to merge imperceptibly. Even the criterion of intelligibility remains vague since the required degree of intelligibility has never been agreed on and would undoubtedly be dependent on subjective judgments in the last analysis.

The term dialect in linguistic jargon implies no value judgment about social acceptibility at all: one speaks, therefore, of "standard dialect", "substandard dialect", "prestige dialect", etc. In point of fact a language can have several standard dialects (as in English, "standard Southern British English", "standard General American English", etc.); in some instances these have developed into separate literary norms, which in informal usage are referred to as languages. The Skandinavian situation in Europe presents a striking example: all the continental

Skandinavian "languages" are in fact interintelligible, hence by definition dialects of a single language; yet four literary norms exist (standard Danish and Swedish, and Norwegian *riksmål* and *landsmål*), established essentially for nationalistic reasons. In some African languages, a similar situation has been brought about in several instances by rival missionary groups working in neighboring areas. In this way, two main literary dialects have been developed for Twi, a Niger-Kongo language spoken in Ghana; and both are sometimes called separate languages: Twi and Fante.

The amount of variation between dialects can be slight or considerable. The informal distinction between "accent" and "dialect" is, however, not normally made in linguistic discussion, since "dialect" would be used to cover all sorts of differences as well as all degrees; the distinction between variation in pronunciation as opposed to vocabulary or grammatical forms is simply a bit too tenuous to be justified in most instances.

Quite clearly the distinction between language and dialect often proves to be hard to apply in a practical situation. In many instances it will not do merely to ask a group whether they can understand the speech of a neighboring community. Cultural and social considerations will often be the basis for the answer, rather than strictly linguistic ones. Wolff reports, for example, that the Nembe of the Eastern Niger Delta say they understand the closely related Kalabari; but the latter maintain that Nembe is unintelligible except for an occasional word. In this instance, a matter of prestige is partially involved. The Kalabari are prosperous, the Nembe not so. It is of some advantage for the Nembe to understand Kalabari but not the other way round. The Kalabari are presumably psychologically unreceptive to the notion of intelligibility, whereas the Nembe are quite eager. Apparently desire influences performance.[9]

In the Africanist literature many examples of disagreement can be found concerning the status of speech varieties. Thus, Malinke (with about 1,200,000 speakers), Bambara (about 900,000) and Dyula (about 1,140,000) spoken throughout the western portions of West Africa are variously cited as separate languages, e.g. by Greenberg, or dialects of a single language, e.g. by Westermann and Bryan, and by Delafosse. (The number of speakers involved and the fact that they are presently to be found in several different countries has, of course, no bearing on the problem.) Since a high degree of mutual intelligibility is reported among the three, we are undoubtedly dealing with dialects of a single language in this particular case.[10]

The definition of "language" (as opposed to "dialect") suggested above does not necessarily require all the dialects of a language to show complete interintelligibility. All that is necessary is an unbroken chain of intelligibility. Thus, in any given language, we might find a chain of dialects A, B, C, D, . . . Dialects A and B are mutually intelligible, and so are B and C, and C and D. But D and A are not

Figure 2   THOTH (JHWTY)

In Ancient Egyptian religion, the god Thoth was regarded as the Divine Word through whom all creation came into existence. He is the patron of scribes, the Master of the words of the gods, the Lord of writing, and the Creator of all languages.

Courtesy of the Metropolitan Museum of Art
Rogers Fund, 1946.

or are understood with considerable difficulty. Nevertheless, A, B, C, D still would be said to constitute a single language. Such a situation characterizes, for example, the German and Italian language communities; dialects at the geographical extremes are barely interintelligible (nowadays recourse can always be made in these communities to the official national language, really a second language). Similar examples can be found in agreat many of the languages of Africa.

It should not be difficult to see why it is hardly possible at present to quote an exact number of languages spoken in the African continent.

If any rigorous attempt at classification were to be made, many well established language-dialect labels would undoubtedly have to be modified—several of the so called Nilotic "languages" probably becoming dialects of a single language, and at least some of the Berber "dialects", separate languages.

In all events, the usual number of languages cited for the whole of the African continent—800—seems too low. An estimate of at least a 1000 would probably be more realistic, and this probably represents one-fifth or even as much as one quarter of the total number of languages in the world.

Figure 3   ÈṢÙ

A statue of the god Èṣù (Èṣù Ilare), Ile-Ifè, Nigeria. In Yoruba religion, this trickster god (like the god Legba in the belief of neighboring Fon speakers) is the divine messenger with a knowledge of all languages.

Notes and References

1) Tarzan, as even the casual reader of Edgar Rice Burroughs's series knows, has been hopelessly mispresented by moviemakers. Tarzan spoke not only Ape and various other subhuman languages, but was fluent—and elegant—in French, English, German, and "West African" (Apparently to be identified with Swahili!). He also knew a smattering of Arabic. By a curious accident, he first learned to speak French although he had previously taught himself to read and write English, and retained a French accent in his other human languages. See *Tarzan of the Apes* (1912).

2) Reported by Robery G. Armstrong, 1963, Vernacular languages and cultures in modern Africa,, page 68 (in John Spencer, ed., *Language in Africa*, Cambridge, 64—77).

3) For a discussion of language universals, see Joseph H. Greenberg, ed., 1963, *Universals of language*, Cambridge; and E.H. Lenneberg, 1967, *The biological bases for language*, New York.

4) See G.P. Murdock, 1959, Cross-language parallels in parental kin terms, *Anthropological Linguistics* 1, 1—6; Roman Jakobson, 1962, Why "mama" and "papa"?, *Selected writings* I, The Hague.

5) *Language*, New York, 22.

6) Many physical anthropologists reject the traditional notion of race as untenable on biological grounds. In the present discussion, older terminology is retained primarily as a point of departure.

7) For this reason, Mark Twain's otherwise contrived plot for *Pudd'nhead Wilson* is at least partially plausible: if a white infant and a black one were switched and each brought up as the other, nothing in their acquired speech habits would betray the switch. In Twain's story, the real identities are eventually revealed on other grounds, and at the end of the story the white boy, who had been raised as a negro slave in antebellum days

> "Found himself rich and free, but in most embarassing situation. He could neither read nor write, and his speech was the basest dialect of the Negro quarter."

(Throughout the story, the real black boy was able to "pass" both from the point of view of complexion and language, and the other social graces as well.)

8) In *The handbook of African languages*, a difference is made between a DIALECT CLUSTER (i.e., in the terminology used here, a language comprised of a number of dialects no one of which appears to be dominant) and a LANGUAGE (a language either without dialect variation or with a dominant dialect). The distinction seems to me to be specious and impractical. It is not used here or normally by linguists outside of the African field. Note that the preferred form of the adjective derived from "dialect" is "dialectal", not "dialectical". A somewhat different approach to the language/dialect problem has been suggested by various generative linguists in terms of the number of rules shared by different forms of speech, but the practical problems here seem at least as great as those involving the notion of intelligibility.

9) Hans Wolff, 1959, Intelligibility and interethnic attitudes, *Anthropological Linguistics*, 1 : 34—41. See also David L. Olmsted, 1954, Achumawi-Atsugewi non-reciprocal intelligibility, *International Journal of American Linguistics* 20, 181—184.

10) See Charles S. Bird, 1970, The development of Mandekan (Manding): a study of the role of extra-linguistic factors in linguistic change, in Davis Dalby (ed.), *Language and history in Africa*, New York, pp. 146—159.

CHAPTER III

Basic Linguistic Methodology and Theory

The job of the linguist, no matter what language he deals with, is to: (1) find out the pertinent facts about that language; (2) present some sort of analysis of these facts; (3) relate his findings to a general theory of language. A considerable amount of practical agreement exists about how to accomplish the first goal, but serious disagreement exists about the last two.

The kind of information the linguist seeks may be summed up in a rough and ready fashion under the following rubrics: (a) the sounds of a language (technically its *phonology*); (b) the stock of words and other elements with meaning (*lexicon*); (c) the analysis of words into their constituent meaningful elements (*morphology*); (d) the arrangement of words into sentences (*syntax*). The study of the meaning of words and sentences (*semantics*) has proved to be particularly elusive and has sometimes—perhaps out of desperation—been excluded from the domain of linguistic inquiry, but it of course belongs there.

Language basically involves vocal communication, and hence such devices as writing systems, sign language, and the like have played only a marginal role within linguistics. Traditionally, linguists have tended to ignore even some aspects of vocal communication such as interjections (like English *tut-tut, whew*) and hardly ever include these sounds in a discussion of phonology. Certain paradoxical statements and others which a native speaker may actually say—on the order of *"sringg* is not an English word"—are also ignored, if not dismissed, on the grounds of being metalinguistic, i.e. a special language used to talk about language.

Present day linguistics has reached such a stage of professionalism and sophistication that the layman finds it difficult even to follow articles written in the technical jargon. The Africanist field, however, has suffered from a considerable degree of amateurishness, which still can sometimes be found. In the field of phonology, for example, we find egregious errors of all kinds, very much on the level of an unsophisticated German or Frenchman who might record that the English word *sin* has two main meanings: (1) transgression of a religious rule; (2) slim, slender—confusing *sin* and *thin* because of the absence of a *th*-sound in his native language. Examples of this sort are legion in the Africanist literature, and of course in actual practise. Thus it is reported that a certain Anglican bishop, an Englishman, preaching in Igbo made the following *faux pas*. He apparently wanted to say **Jɛ́sù Krístì nwὲrè ǹnúkù íkɛ̀** *Jesus Christ has great power*, but his pronunciation of the final word was perceived as íkὲ by the Igbo congregation (with the final syllable pronounced on a lower pitch than in the word **íkɛ̀** *power*), the sentence then meaning *Jesus Christ has big buttocks*—a statement not necessarily heretical but hardly conducive to serious prosetylization.[1]

Mistakes of this sort are possible even for people who have otherwise acquired a language fairly well and have spoken it for quite a while. When contact with a language is fleeting or short ranged, errors can become even more grotesque. In the accounts of early travelers, the pronouns for *I* and *you* are often confused: the traveler asks "How do you say 'I'm going'? " and receives a reply meaning "You're going". Another source of confusion stem from the fact that in many African areas, people normally do not point with their index fingers, but rather with their chin and pursed lips. The investigator who does point with a finger is quite likely to elict the word for *finger* when what he really wants is *bird*, *tree*, or the like. A similar sort of misunderstanding must be the reason that one of the early investigators of Luo, the Rev. Mr. M. Wakefield writing in 1887, included in his word list an item **arío** glossed as *ears*—the word must be **arιyɔ** *two*.[2] Taylor has pointed out that many towns on early maps of Nigeria had the same name presumably because when cartographers went to a town they must first have gone to the market, and when they asked where they were, were given the appropriate answer: "market".[3] Pierre Alexandre notes an even more remarkable instance of confusion: on an old map of Gabon he found a number of rivers called *Silo*, *Dilo*, or *Sidilo*—apparently answers in pidgin French (Français-tiraillou) to the question "what's that", the answer being "it's water" (cf. standard French *c'est de l'eau*).[4]

Most of the mistakes just mentioned are due to carelessness and can easily be corrected by even cursory checking. But other mistakes such as those involving tone pose more fundamental problems. Consider the following situation.

A linguist is to analyze the sound system of Swahili and Maasai, languages spoken by neighboring groups in East Africa. In both he finds a number of consonants so similar he can use the same single phonetic symbols for each. Let us examine one set of these consonants, which occurs in the two languages:

ɓ   b   p   v

[The ɓ represents a "gulped" (technically, imploded) b; we shall assume our linguist has been properly trained in phonetics and can distinguish ɓ from b—a skill too often lacked by early investigators.]

These sounds are phonetically the same in the two languages, but the linguist notices that they function differently. In Swahili, p and v can occur at the beginning of a word, between vowels, and after m. Words can be distinguished

by these consonants alone; thus **pita** *pass* is different from **vita** *war*, and clearly separate symbols are needed to represent them. But a special relationship obtains between ɓ and b: ignoring a few details, ɓ can occur in the beginning of a word and
between vowels, but NOT after m, whereas b occurs ONLY after m. Furthermore,
both are phonetically similar. These facts suggest that only a single symbol is needed in Swahili for both ɓ and b, say (tentatively) B. How a B is actually pronounced
is predictable from the sounds surrounding it—in technical jargon, the environ-
ment of ɓ. For example, in **BamBa** *catch*, the first B will be realized as ɓ since it
occurs at the beginning of a word, the second B as b since it follows m. For
Swahili, then, the four original sounds can be represented by only three symbols,
for which we can conveniently use p, v, and b (to cover both ɓ and b).

In Maasai, a completely different system for the same sounds exists. In
Maasai, only ɓ occurs in all the possible positions for a consonant: at the
beginning of a word, between vowels, and after m. The sound b can occur only
after m; p only at the beginning of a word; v only between vowels. This means
that words cannot be distinguished in Maasai by b, p, or v. In technical terms,
they do not contrast, and show noncontrastive distribution: they function as a
single unit and can be represented by one symbol. Hence, only two symbols are
needed for the series where Swahili needed three (and other languages might
need other representations): in the official spelling of Maasai b is used for ɓ, p is
used for b p v. As a matter of fact, the Maasai word ɛ-nàɪpɔ́cà *lake* with written
p has been borrowed into English as a place name *Naivasha* with v, in accordance
with actual pronunciation.

Clearly—on one level at least—the important thing is not the sounds themselves, but how they are organized into a system of contrasts. A unique sound
without reference to a phonological system is a PHONE. A unit of sound contrast within a phonological system is a PHONEME, which has traditionally been
thought of as a class of phonetically similar and noncontrastive phones. The
phones that are the constituent members of a phoneme are ALLOPHONES of
that phoneme, e.g. [b p v] are the allophones of the Maasai phoneme /p/.

Swahili Phonemes		Phones		Maasai Phonemes
/b/	{	ɓ		/b/
		b	}	
/p/		p		/p/
/v/		v		

The development of the phoneme concept at the turn of the century has led
to a fairly important theoretical distinction, applied to other parts of language
besides phonology and even to other aspects of human behavior, usually with

less notable success. This distinction is usually referred to as etic (from "phone-*tic*") vs. emic (from "phon*emic*"), i.e., raw data as recorded blind so to speak by an intrusive observer, versus a system of units meaningful to the speaker or culture bearer.

Some schools of linguistics extend the emic analysis to most if not all parts of language, and with it the *x - x-eme - allo-x* terminology. Most American linguists, for example, use MORPHEME to designate the basic linguistic form with mean-ing. In English, the word *bakers* "people who bake" is usually analyzed as containing three such units: *bake* (an action) + *er* ("one who does") + *s* (pro-nounced as z; meaning: "plural"). The various forms of realizations of morpheme are its ALLOMORPHS. Thus, the English morpheme indicating "plural" has a variety of shapes: *z* in *bakers*; *s* in *books*; *ez* in *watches*; *en* in *oxen*; a change of vowel in *men*; *ren* plus a change of vowel in *children*; no overt mark, or "zero" (symbolized by ϕ in linguistic formulas) in *sheep*, *fish*, etc. The same sorts of phenomena occur in all languages. In Bantu languages the allomorphs of "plural" are quite complicated; thus, in Swahili, for **mtu** *person* the plural is **watu** with a **wa** prefix and a dropping of the singular **m**: for **kikapu** *basket*, **vitabu**; for **tembo** *elephant*, **tembo** with zero marker.* Obviously, then, a single morpheme can be realized in a variety of ways: by a long string of phonemes or by none, or by resources not available in English, e.g. tonal differences as in the Hausa **yá tàfí** *and then he went* vs. **yà tàfí** *let him go*, where the contrast is shown on the forms of **ya** *he*.

Morphemes can be spelt out phonemically—*dogs*, *books* being then symbol-ized by spellings on the order of *dog-z*, *buk-s*. Or else a morpheme can have invariant spellings no matter what its actual pronunciation is; *books* might be spelt as { buk } + { ez } or even { buk } + { Pl }. Such spellings are called MORPHOPHONEMIC. The Swahili plurals given above could be indicated as {Pl } + { m } + {tu } (or the like) for **watu**, etc. Obviously a fairly abstract representation can be produced in this way, and patterns emerge that are not necessarily clear-cut in phonemic representations.

Linguists working within the emic tradition are essentially concerned with producing a rigorous, nonmentalistic, behavioristic analysis, whereby the tech-niques for discovering linguistic structures are in effect made synonymous with linguistic theory and the general goals of linguistic analysis. Usually such lin-guists have concentrated almost exclusively on phonology and morphology and have rarely produced anything approaching a comparable study of syntax. The treatment of phonology in particular—emphasizing as it frequently does the

---

* In East Africa native speakers of English talk about *many lion, elephant, giraffe*, i.e. use a common form for both singular and plural of African game animals (cf. normal *deer*, pl. *deer*). In Swahili, animal names are normally also invariable for number. The usages are historically independent of each other but represent an interesting example of convergence.

incommensurability of different phonemic systems—has the added drawback of making it difficult to see how dialects with different phonological systems could be mutually intelligible (some dialects of Twi, for example, reportedly have 7, others 9, still others 10 vowels but all these dialects are interintelligible).

Since the publication in 1957 of Noam Chomsky's *Syntactic Structures*, much of this emic approach has been challenged. Chomsky proposed that the grammar of a language should be formulated as a kind of computer program that will generate all the acceptable sentences in the language. This position is known as "generative" or "transformational" (the terms are not completely synonymous) and was perhaps influenced (although this has been officially denied) by attempts at creating a method for the machine translation of foreign languages.

The traditional emic approach assumes that one knows nothing intuitively about the languages being investigated and that every step in the description must be obvious in some way from the data. The data themselves are usually taken to be a limited (but, one hopes, representative) corpus of texts. The generative approach is almost totally different. It assumes—in fact requires— omniscience about the total linguistic facts. It is not concerned with labeling and cataloging details of a limited corpus. And it tries to provide a theory of the possible sentences of a language by means of a series of ordered rules on the order of a probability tree in computer programing, a procedure which invariably involves completely hypothetical steps.

As a very small example of what is meant by an ordered rule and the kind of approach that characterizes generative analysis, consider again the problem of phonemic analysis given earlier for Swahili. Earlier it was concluded that a phoneme b had allophones [ɓ] and [b], which by definition could not contrast. In point of fact, however, ɓ and b do contrast, but the contrast is very limited and occurs in positions entirely predictable from grammatical information. Thus, the adjective written **mbaya** in the official spelling (stem -**baya** *bad*) is pronounced with [b] when referring to things, but with [ɓ] when referring to persons. In the traditional emic analysis, grammatical predictability is counted, as it were, of no avail: a contrast has been established, hence the separate phonemic statuses of ɓ and b. The generative approach would exploit the grammatical information and skip over a purely phonemic level altogether so that in some rules one would have only b, in other rules, both b and ɓ. The kind of argument used might run as follows: the exception to the general rule that only b occurs after m, not ɓ, involves only nouns and adjectives referring to persons, and here the m is really a prefix, e.g. the plural of **mbaya** *bad* is **wabaya**. Now with other words denoting persons whose stems begin with vowels, not consonants, **mw-** is the form of the prefix, not **m-** alone: **mw-oga** *coward*, plural **wa-oga**. The most economical description would probably posit **mu-** as a hypothetical form for the prefix, and say that the u becomes w before vowels, and is dropped before consonants. Given these details we can explain the two forms of mbaya in the following steps.

1) We can posit **mbaya** for things, *__mubaya__ for persons, as the underlying forms.

2) It is then possible to account for the distribution of ɓ, which occurs between vowels and hence occurs in **muɓaya**.

3) The final step would delete the u, producing **mɓaya**.

Quite obviously in the generative approach there is no clear cut level of description that corresponds to the phonemic level of other schools. Indeed, generative grammarians have persistently argued against the necessity or even desirability of such a level of description, and recognize only morphophonemic and phonetic (actually subphonetic) levels, with intervening stages in the various rules.

The generative approach tries to account for the possible life history of any sentence, as it were, from its simplest and most undifferentiated state (usually symbolized as S, for "sentence"), observing how it is chugged through the machinery of rules until it finally emerges as a realized sentence. The final stages of this life history constitute the surface structure of the sentence; the earlier stages, the underlying or deep structure. By using sufficiently abstract formulations, one can make many of the rules for all languages identical or nearly so, and an interesting attempt has in fact been made to present rules for the deepest part of the underlying structure which would constitute linguistic universals. In one variant of the generative models now available it is maintained that only two parts of speech need be set up for any language: nouns and verbs. Everything given other labels in schoolbook grammers (adjectives, adverbs, conjunctions, etc.) ultimately may be viewed as one or the other. For example, in this scheme, adjectives turn out to be a kind of verb. Such an analysis is motivated for English grammar by a number of reasons that need not concern us here, but the interesting thing is that many African languages such as Kongo, Dinka, and Yoruba (as well as many non-African languages such as Japanese), words that correspond to English adjectives actually do behave like verbs and take verbal inflection. As was pointed out earlier in the brief discussion of pan-Africanisms, the English construction *the book is red* would be rendered as *the book reds* in such languages.

On an even deeper level of analysis, it has been proposed that declarative sentences in English are introduced by *I say that*, which is eventually deleted. That is, a sentence such as *He went* has an underlying structure on the order of *I say that he went*. This hypothetical stage for English has been posited largely to account for several otherwise irregular uses of *myself* as in *This is a picture of myself* (otherwise, *myself* occurs only in sentences with *I*, as in *I hit myself*). Interesting enough, such an analysis may account for a curious detail in Arabic, where there are three words roughly equivalent to the English conjunction *that*:

ʔan used after verbs such as "want", "command"; ʔanna used after all other verbs. But nearly all declarative sentences in Arabic can be optionally introduced by ʔinna. It has been suggested that this usage can best be explained by positing an underlying *I say*.

The developments in some parts of linguistics are at present so rapid that it is difficult even for the professional linguist to keep up to date. In generative theory especially, change has been almost frenetic. There, however, it is the actual "programing" that changes; the underlying notions persist that at least some rules in the grammer must be ordered, as well as the notion that some sentences are "related" (e.g. that *John killed Mary* and *Mary was killed by John* are both derivable from some hypothetical stage, say **John killed Mary by*-[*passive*] or *killed by-John ϕ-Mary* plus transform rules to account for word order and the like).

Despite the great interest in theory that has characterized linguistics in recent decades, in the African field much linguistic work has been remarkably rudimentary usually in an old-fashioned school book tradition based on the old models for Latin and Greek. Some attempts have been made to create "African" models—as though African languages were unique and inscrutable except to the African. As a rule, analyses of this sort turn out to be even less adequate than others. However, a considerable number of sophisticated studies written from a wide variety of schools of thought have already appeared, and are steadily piling up, using, for example, theoretical frameworks such as tagmemics or Firthian contextural analysis—approaches not considered here. Unfortunately, the diversity of approach is often accompanied by highly divergent jargon. For example, French scholars tend to use the term *moneme* for *morpheme*, and use *morpheme* to mean an affix or inflection. In this book, jargon will be kept to a minimum. But some technical terms have been presented to make it easier to talk about basic concepts.

Notes and References

1) Chukwujindu Ezenekwe (personal communication).
2) M. Wakefield, 1887, *Vocabulary of the Kaviróndo language,* London.
3) F.W. Taylor. I have misplaced the exact reference but believe it occurred in the *Journa of the African Society*, sometime in the 1920's.
4) Pierre Alexandre, 1967, *Langues et language en Afrique noire*, Paris, p. 38 fn 2.

PART TWO   LINGUISTIC REPERTOIRE

(The general reader may want to skip this section until later, even though it is written in a very nontechnical way. The more adventurous should not wait.)

CHAPTER IV

Phonology

Only a very few aspects of the sounds and sound systems found in African languages will be discussed here. In particular, detailed phonetic descriptions will not be attempted for the most part, because such descriptions are tedious at best for the nonlinguist (more often than not unintelligible), superflous for the linguist.

As for the matter of transcription: an alphabet proposed by the International African Institute will be used (with few modifications), the socalled Africa Alphabet.[1] This is really a modified form of the alphabet of the International Phonetic Association, which may already be familiar to the reader from French textbooks and other language learning materials. As a matter of fact, the Africa Alphabet has been the basis for the official spellings of several African languages and a movement exists to extend its use to all languages of the world.

Of course, phones, phonemes, morphophonemes can be represented by any symbol one likes since the value of the symbol is arbitrarily determined. For example a sound much like that written *sh* in English spelling is represented by *x* in Portuguese, *ch* in French, ш in Russian, ‏ش‎ in Arabic, ▭ in Ancient Egyptian hieroglyphs; one could just as well draw palm tree or star depending on aesthetic prejudices, and by fiat, let it have the value *sh*. On the other hand, in deference to established reading habits and ease of printing, a more nearly conventional kind of representation is normal and preferable. An early account of Malagasy should show the problems inherent in unusual transcriptions. For quite a while, the Malagasy material was believed to be a hoax, but finally it was discovered that the author, an English sailor, was recording Malagasy words with standard English spellings but eighteenth century Cockney values! [2]

Although the Africa Alphabet is now almost universally used by Africanists, earlier writers often used a form of the "Lepsius Alphabet".[3] In it, the resources of normal Roman letters were increased by the use of diacritics so that ń represented an *ny* sound, n the *ng* of king, š an *sh* sound, s̩ the *th* of *thin* (considered as a "lisped" *s*). The serious student of African languages must be familiar with these conventions because some of the classic writers in the field use it, e.g., Meinhof and Westermann. The official orthography of Venda is still based on the Lepsius alphabet.

The Africa Alphabet avoids diacritics as much as possible and tries to provide new letters for sounds not represented by the usual Roman letters; e.g., *sh* is

28

represented as ʃ ; *ng* as ŋ (but *ny* is usually ny, although the International Phonetic Association uses ɲ).

No language makes use of all the sounds that the human ear can discriminate. The great majority of languages have fewer than 40 consonant and vowel phonemes. Consonants, for example, are often defined as those sounds produced by blocking off or narrowing at some point of the vocal track the stream of air produced during speech. An infinite number of points of production or articulation are conceivable, but a considerably smaller number actually is used in any given language: always fewer than 10, but more than 1.

In many languages, stops (consonants that block off the air stream in the mouth completely) and nasals (stops that are released through the nose) form a symmetrical subset convenient for a discussion of patterns of articulation. In English, for example, we have the stops p t k paralleled by the nasals m n ŋ, as well as by another group of stops b d g (p t k are voiceless, b d g are voiced; during the production of voiced sounds, the vocal cords vibrate, which they do not do for voiceless sounds). To my knowledge, no African language has been reported with fewer than three points of articulation. In world wide distribution a one-way pattern doesn't occur at all; a two-way pattern is rare but does occur in certain Pacific languages such as Hawaiian. A three-way pattern is not uncommon in African languages, e.g., many Bantu languages, as well as Geʿez. But a four-way pattern is perhaps the most common, where in addition to the labial (p), dental or alveolar (t), and velar (k) positions, there is also one other position. The most usual four way set up is p t c k (with a palatal c, something like English *ch*). This has been reported for Dyula, Twi, Lango, and an enormous number of other languages. Four other four-way patterns have been reported, but are much rarer: p t k q (with a uvular q, a kind of retracted "k") reported for Arabic, Iraqw, and certain dialects of Swahili; p ṭ t k (where a dental [ṭ] and alveolar [t] series have been distinguished) reported for a few languages such as Temne, Limba, and Venda; p t t̩ k (with a "retroflex series", the t being an r-colored, retracted t) reported for at least one language, Bangando. The fourth series is wholly unique to my knowledge, reported for only a single language in the world, Loma: b ʙ d g (the ʙ represents a b-like sound produced by lower lip against upper teeth; b is produced by both lips; the complete series occurs only for voiced stops).[4]

Five position systems involve almost the maximum number of stop/nasal positions anywhere in the world, and are quite rare on any continent. In Africa, such systems are found almost exclusively in the eastern portions, primarily in the Sudan and Lake regions, and occur in a number of languages not necessarily related. The pattern is perhaps mostly clearly found in Nilotic languages such as Nuer, Dinka, and Shilluk, where we have the following symmetrical pattern:

p·	ṭ	t	c	k
b	ḍ	d	j	g
m	ṇ	n	ɲ	ŋ

Similar but occasionally defective systems occur in Temein (lacking c), Nyimang and Luo (lacking ɲ)—all Nilo-Saharan languages; and also in Katla, Koalib, and Kadugli-Krongo—all Niger-Kordofanian languages. Another five-position system is reported for two West African languages, Serer and Wolof: p t c k q. In both the system is defective because q is the only uvular consonant. A third system, familiar from languages spoken in India, with p ṭ t c k, seems not to occur in Africa (although Ewe approaches it). Six-position systems reported from Australia are not reported from Africa at all.

In our survey we have not considered double stops such as k͡p, which are found in a great many west African languages of various language families. Such double stops involve a simultaneous articulation of k and p, etc., although they function as a single phoneme. Languages with double stops frequently have corresponding double nasals such as ŋ͡m but these occur almost exclusively in combination with double stops, e.g. Efik ŋ͡mk͡pa *death*. In a very few languages such as Gã, Idoma, and Urhobo, ŋ͡m occurs separately, e.g., Gã èŋ͡mɔ̀ *he laughed*. As we have seen, the most common double consonants are k͡p, g͡b and n͡m; but others exist. And in Margi, with one of the most elaborate consonant systems in the world (something on the order of 50 distinct consonant phonemes), p͡t, b͡d, m͡n occur, but NOT k͡p, etc.; m͡n occurs independently: m͡nà *mouth*.

Some consonants can be prolonged audibly during one breath released through the mouth; e.g., s z f v x (the *ch* of *Bach*). These are called spirants. Very few languages in the world lack spirants altogether. A handful from the Pacific, such as Hawaiian, Kapauku, Marshallese, and Arunta, are reliably reported as devoid of them. In Africa, only the Nilotic languages tend to lack spirants—most are at least devoid of s-like sounds (sibilants); e.g., Nuer, Dinka, Shilluk, Acoli, Lango. Why this should be so is not altogether clear, but may be a result of the apparently long established Nilotic custom of extracting the lower front teeth at puberty. On the other hand among the Sotho-Tswana speaking peoples of southern Africa, where the upper front teeth are removed, "whistling" s and z (ş ẓ) occur. In Chopi and Tswa a whistle is so prominent in the production of these sounds that a definite musical note is heard; in other dialects very little whistling is detectible. The absence of teeth may not be a sufficient explanation for the development of ş and ẓ because they contrast with and do not supplant nonwhistling s and z. In Manyika, as a matter of fact, the contrasts s ş sw şw are found. Similar sounds occur in neighboring languages: Venda, Thonga, Nyungwe, Sena. They are not reported from another area in the world.

A number of trilled and flapped consonants occur throughout the continent, usually represented by r. A uvular trill, R, found in a few European languages, is almost nonexistent in Africa except in some dialects of Sotho in words where other dialects use an alveolar trill. It has been thought that French missionaries may have introduced this variant, but Tucker doubts this, "having heard natives use the uvular trill in parts of Basutoland as yet unaffected by contact with missionaries".[5] A very few African languages use a lip trill, (symbol suggested, ρ or ʀ) which occurs in English in the interjection to express the sensation of cold, *brrr*. Its use as a normal phoneme is recorded for (Niger-Kordofanian) Ngwe, and (Nilo-Saharan Mangbetu and Baka where a voiced and voiceless variety occur as well as the Comorro Island dialect of Swahili, where it corresponds to standard Swahili **bw**.[6] Such a trill is recorded for only one or two languages outside of Africa.

A lip flap—a flap produced by the lower lip striking the upper teeth, symbol ⱱ-occurs exclusively in Africa, generally in a fairly small area in West Africa in neighboring but not necessarily related languages; e.g. Margi, Tera (Afro-Asiatic), Ngwe, Ngbaka, Ngbaka Mabo, Ndogo-Sere (Niger-Kordofanian), Kresh, Mangbetu (Nilo-Saharan). It also occurs to a more limited extent in southeastern Africa, e.g., in various Shona dialects. In most of these languages, the sound is commonly or exclusively used in a special category of word, often phonemically anomalous, called *ideophones* (English examples include *wham*, *thud*, *kerplunk, boom)*. Occasionally ⱱ does occur as a normal consonant, e.g., Ngaba Mabo:ⱱíìná *nine*.

Throughout the present discussion, it has been assumed that the sounds discussed have been produced with air expelled from the lungs through the mouth as they normally are in all languages. Sounds can of course be produced other ways, and at least three other basic air-stream mechanisms exist. Air can be gulped in while the vocal cords are closed. The ɓ mentioned in chapter 3 is an example of such a "gulped" sound or IMPLOSIVE. An imploded g is actually used by some speakers of English in the word *gulp* itself—at least when used as an interjection in the manner of Li'l Abner. On a popular American television program one character habitually used an implosive d (ɗ) in the phrase *Mr. Dillon*. It has been reported that certain Negro as well as certain Southern dialects of American English always implode b d g, perhaps an African survival. In African languages implosives and corresponding explosives (e.g., both ɓ and b) frequently contrast. Implosives—and acoustically similar sounds with slightly different articulations—occur not only in Swahili and Maasai, but in many other languages such as Zulu, Iraqw, Bagirmi, Hausa, Margi, Igbo, and Fulani.

If a sound is produced while the vocal cords are closed but air is not gulped, the result is an EJECTIVE. When an ejective is correctly made, the speaker's Adam's apple can often be seen to move upward; with an implosive, it moves downward. Ejectives are normally symbolized as k' s' etc. They are rare in West and North African languages but common in African Semitic, Kushitic, and

Bantu. In Amharic, for example, the ejective series p' t' c' k' s' contrasts with nonejective p t c k s.

Clicks represent yet another air stream mechanism. Air from the lungs is cut off not at the vocal cords, but higher up by the back of the tongue against the roof of the mouth, as in the production of k. Another closure is made in the front of the mouth, and during the click, mouth air is compressed. Probably all languages use clicks for interjections. In English we have ʇ (e.g. ʇʇ written *tsk-tsk* or *tut-tut*), and ʗ, the sound used to gee up a horse. Nor should it be forgotten that a kiss—all romantic misconceptions to the contrary—involves basically only a lip click (or two), symbol ʘ . In some Bushman languages ʘ actually occurs as a phoneme. A click often compared to the sound of the popping of a cork, and used in English in imitation of a baseball making contact with a bat, or a jaw with a gloved fist, is represented as ᗡ, technically, a palato-alveolar. Alveolar ǂ and retroflex Ψ are less commonly used click types, and have no usual English equivalent.[7]

The largest number of unmodified clicks used in a language is reportedly five. In !Kung Bushman we find ʇǂᗡΨʗ; in Cape Bushman,ʘʇǂᗡʗ. All Khoisan languages contain such click phonemes (at least ʇᗡʗ), but Bushman languages are said to be more prolific in their use than the others. Doke notes for example that "in Hottentot whole sentences are common without the use of a single click. In Bushman this is rare".[8] In a number of Southern Bantu languages bordering on Khoisan, clicks are also found as ordinary phonemes. In Zulu, Swazi, Xhosa, Yeye we find ʇᗡʗ; in Southern Sotho only ᗡ. The consensus is that the Bantu clicks represent borrowings from Khoisan. For a single Kushitic language, Sanye (or Dahalo) spoken on the Kenya coast, Damman reported 2 clicks, ʇ and ǂ. In a study undertaken little more than a decade later, Tucker found only one, ʇ .[9]

As far as the world-wide distribution of clicks goes, Southern Africa is unquestionably the major area. Elsewhere, they seem not to occur, but clicks (or rumors of clicks) are reported from one or two languages in Central and South America.

Vowels, like consonants, can be set up as comprising a subsystem of their own. In languages with both nasal and oral (= nonnasal) vowels, the nasal vowels never exceed and almost invariably are fewer in number than the oral vowels, e.g., Yoruba has 7 oral vowels ieɛaɔou but only 4 nasal vowels ĩɛ̃õũ. A more striking example is provided by Ngwe with 14 oral and 6 nasal vowels or Dan with 12 oral vowels and 8 nasal ones.

By far the most common oral vowel patterns in African languages contain 5 or 7 vowels; as shown in patterns (1) and (2) in Figure 4 the vowels are arranged according to the height of the tongue during the production of the vowel (e.g., the tongue is closer to the roof of the mouth for *i* as in *machine*, than for *a* in *father*) and what part of the tongue is highest (for *i*, the front part of the tongue is at the highest point; for *u,* the back). Values of symbols are given at the end of the chapter.

Pattern (1) is reported for Swahili, Zulu, Hausa, Ganda, and a great many other languages; (2) for Kikuyu, Bulu, Efik, some dialects of Twi (others have as many as three additional vowel phonemes), and several others. The simplest vowel system used in an African language is probably (3), found in Malagasy and perhaps no other African language. A slightly different four vowel system with a central vowel (ə) is reported for most Berber dialects (4). The three-vowel scheme associated with Classical Arabic (5) seems not to occur in the various colloquial forms of Arabic spoken in Africa. Two (or fewer) vowel systems, which may occur in some Caucasian languages are unreported in Africa. So also are vowel systems without a front-back distinction (again as in some Caucasian languages). The most complicated African system reported to date is (6), found in Ngwe, where vowel types otherwise quite rare in African languages are found: front vowels made with rounded lips (ɥøœ) and back vowels without (ɯɣʌ). Dan has an extensive series of centralized vowels (ɨɜə) (7).

Tongue height in vowel production could involve an infinite number of distinctions, but for African—and perhaps all the world's languages—no more than five heights have proved to be distinctive, as in the scheme of (8). Needless to say, such systems are rather rare. In Africa they are found in a few West African languages but are especially associated with Nilotic (and "Nilo-Hamitic") languages such as Luo, Acoli, Bari, Lotuho, Nandi—which is interesting because a five-position consonant pattern also occurs frequently in Nilotic, as though there were a common design underlying both vowel and consonant schemes.

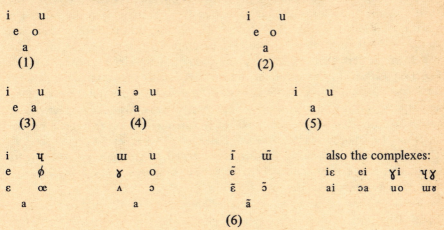

Figure 4　VOWEL PATTERNS

i	ɨ	u		ĩ	ũ
e	3	o			
ɛ	ə	ɔ		ɛ̃	ə̃	ɔ̃
æ	a	ɒ		æ̃	ã	ɒ̃

(7)

i	u
ɪ	℧
e	o
ɛ	ɔ
a	ɑ

(8)

In African languages with the ten-vowel systems of (8) and some others, the vowels can be broken up into 2 classes, e.g.,

A.	i	e	a	o	u
B.	ɪ	ɛ	ɑ	ɔ	℧

Phonetically, these classes may be characterized in a number of ways: A-vowels are usually higher and tenser than B-vowels, and may be accompanied by a different voice quality (A vowels being "breathy" or "baggy"; B vowels "hard" or "creaky"). [10] The interesting thing is that within a word or even a phrase, the vowels of the two classes cannot occur together. Thus, in Igbo the words íɓò Igbo and égò *money* contain only class A vowels, but in ɔ́b℧ *pit-trap* and ákw℧kwó *book* only class B vowels. The pronoun prefixes vary according to the vowels of the verb they precede; e.g., *he (past)·*is ó in ó-sìrì *he cooked*, but ɔ́ in ɔ́-sàrà *he washed*. In Luo, prefixes and suffixes usually follow the same pattern, but occasionally they are unchanging and the vowels of the verb or noun they accompany change; e.g. ɔ̀-cwɔ̂wɔ̀ *he speared*, but ò-cwówò-u *he speared you (pl)*, where the stem vowels are modified to agree with **u** *you(pl)*. Such restrictions on the co-occurrence of vowel classes is known as VOWEL HARMONY. The form of vowel harmony discussed here, based on alternating vowel heights essentially, is the only common one in African languages, but others occur—at least in languages outside the continent.

Various forms of consonant "harmony" also exist. In Alur and various other Nilotic languages, dentals and alveolars cannot both occur in the same word, e.g., ḍɔ̀ḍɔ̀ *to suck*, tìtɔ̀ *to arrange*, but* ḍɔ̀dɔ̀, etc.* tìṭɔ̀ do not exist.

What these facts of co-occurrence restrictions suggest is that we ultimately have to deal with components BELOW the phoneme level. Thus, rather than specify whether every vowel in a word showing vowel harmony belongs to class A or B by special symbols, a feature can be extracted from the whole word. We could set up such a feature say *tense*, and distinguish o from ɔ by saying the first is [+ tense], the second is [- tense]. The Luo examples given above could thus be rewritten as [-tense] **ò-cwôwò** and [+ tense] **ò-cwówò-u**. No information is lost, and a feature that permeates the whole word is specified once. Obviously, a level of abstraction is thereby reached with enormous implications for phonological theory. A further application may be seen in the nasal stop clusters such as mb ṇḍ nd nj ŋg ŋ̂mg̑b. In Luo, the first five combinations occur, including **ṇ̣d**—but there is no independent ṇ, and n never occurs before ḍ. In Ịjọ, the second and fourth do not occur, but ŋ̂mg̑b does, although ŋ̂m does not exist apart from this cluster. Now in one version of traditional phonemic analysis, parallel phonemic facts are explained in parallel ways. The consequences of such a procedural rule are to set up an ṇ phoneme for Luo and an ŋ̂m for Ịjọ. A simpler solution is suggested by the use of features. All these clusters can be uniquely specified merely by stating that a nasal precedes the b d g etc., since we do not find *mg or *ṇd. If we say [+ nasal] b, [+ nasal] gb, all the information is readily conveyed. The implication of such examples is that features such as [nasal], [tense], [stop], [vocalic] and the like are the systematic units of phonology, not the traditional phonemes. Distinctive feature analysis was first developed by Jakobson, who thought he could limit the actual number of features needed in all the languages of the world to twelve binary ones. This attempt proved inadequate to deal with 5-position stops, double stops, and various other phonological elements frequent in African languages. The theory has since been modified and made more nearly tenable by Halle and Chomsky.[12] Few works have been published on African languages using this approach, but many such studies will undoubtedly be forthcoming.

We have already singled out an area phonology that has often proved to be particularly difficult or elusive to the linguistically untrained: tone. The great majority of languages in Africa (other than Semitic and Berber) are tonal in the sense that some pitch distinctions are phonemic in some "normal" words. The exceptions include Swahili, Lunyoro, Nyakyusa, Makua (all Bantu); Fulani, Nubian, and possibly Teda. Some languages have been described as transitional and on the way to losing their tonality, e.g., Mende, Runyankore, and possibly Ịjọ and Maŵiha. It is generally asserted that trade languages and pidgins are toneless, and this is certainly true of Swahili[13] and Kitchen Kaffir. But on the other hand, a tonal system is quite firmly intrenched in Lingala; West Coast Pidgin English and Town Bemba (a pidginized Bantu language used in Rhodesia) are tonal for many and perhaps most speakers.

The importance of tone can hardly be overemphasized. A few examples have

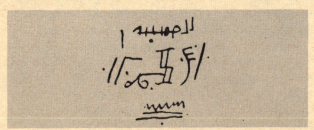

Figure 5   KING NƷOYA

Inventor and reformer of the Bamum script with a specimen of that script.

already been given of *faux pas* involving tonal mistakes. Carrington [14] has reported several delightful slips he recorded from Europeans speaking Kele, one being **álàmbákà bòìlì** *he watched the river bank* confused with **álámbáká bòílì** *he boiled his mother-in-law*. Worthy of the Adulterer's Bible was the missionary pronunciation of the Lord's Prayer where (since affirmative and negative constructions were differentiated by tone alone) the missionaries were understood as saying "may thy kingdom not come, may thy will not be done", etc. Of course, the degree to which tone is important in a language, its "functional load", varies. In Yoruba and Igbo failure to distinguish tones properly would lead to frequent and perhaps total incomprehensibility; in Hausa on the other hand, this is hardly the case and there are relatively few words distinguished solely by tone. [15]

Some linguists have tried to characterize tonal systems as either register or contour. A register system is one in which tone phonemes (or tonemes) are basically level in pitch throughout a syllable. When glides occur, they can often be analyzed as combinations, e.g., a falling tone could be analyzed in such a system as high plus low. Most if not all African tonal languages seem to be essentially of the register type. Contour systems have tones that usually glide, and may also involve nonpitch distinctions of tempo and intensity, among other features. Chinese and Vietnamese are the classic examples of contour tone languages. Such systems may not occur in Africa, but the eminent linguist Beach has attempted to describe Hottentot in such terms. Although he has been criticized for doing so, he may be right. For example, the six tonemes he posits are realized on monosyllables as: (1) high-rising (´Ꞓxai *cold*), (2) mid-rising (ʻŋꞓaī *blow*), (3) low-rising (ˌŋƅae *sing*), (4) high-falling (ˋꞠ ʔoa *work*), (5) mid-falling (ˎƅʔoa *kiss*), (6) low-mid level (ˏƅʔau *thick*). [16] In none of these can the tonal movements be conveniently analyzed in terms of end-points. If Beach is right, it seems possible to divide Africa as a whole into three large tonal areas: (a) Northern, nontonal, (b) Southwestern, contour, (c) Central, register. But Hagman has recently suggested that even Hottentot must be described as having a register system.

In African register systems, the number of pitch levels that are phonemic vary from two to five. Two (high-low) seem to be most common among Bantu languages and are quite frequent elsewhere, e.g., Hausa, Yaunde, Basa, Kanuri, Tubu, Mangbetu. Three are not uncommon, particularly in the geographical area called the Sudan, e.g., Yoruba, Moru, Ma'di, Lugbara, Zaghawa, Nilotic, Galla, Somali, Didinga-Murle. A four-register system (high-mid-norm-low) is rare and is reported only for Jabo (Gweabo) by Sapir, for one dialect of Bariba in Dahomey by Welmers, and for Koma by Burns; it may also occur in Igede. An even rarer system has five registers (extra high-high-mid-norm-low); only three examples of this are reliably reported in the entire linguistic literature; two of these are

American Indian (Trique and Ticuna); the third and most recently reported, a West African language spoken in Ivory Coast and Liberia, Dan.

A difficulty for tonal analysis found in some languages has been called by Guthrie "tonal crumbling", i.e. the tonal contrasts are maintained within a sentence, but when words are pronounced alone it is virtually impossible to distinguish tone. This is the case for Luo, but not for the closely related Acoli.

Another difficulty is that tonemes are not necessarily always realized completely in isolated words but rather on an adjacent word. Such a phenomenon has been called tonal displacement, a phenomenon particularly well documented by Richardson for Sukuma. [17] There, some words have a "dangling" high tone that must be realized on the second syllable of a subsequent word if it is to be realized at all. Words with such a displaced high could be marked +H in the lexicon, those without as -H. Contrast **akasɔla** (-H) *he chose* and **akabɔna** (+H) *he saw* when followed by the same word, **balemi** *farmers*:

> akasɔla balemi   *he chose farmers*
> akabɔna balémi   *he saw farmers,*

where the **balémi** shows the high tone.

All languages have sentence melody or intonation whether they are tonal or not. In tone languages, intonation acts something like one Chinese silk screen painting on another: it modifies, but does not obliterate the underlying patterns of tone contrast. A common tendency is for the general pitch of a sentence to sink, a phenomenon called down drift. With down drift, a high tone after a low is lower than before a low; thus, the sequence high-low-high would be realized as $[^-\_-]$. A high after a high, a low after a low would remain the same. In many African languages, a high after a high may be lowered in certain situations. Such a lowering is called tone slip or down step, and a symbol for this is $^!$. Down step is quite common in African languages, e.g., Maasai, Efik, Igbo, Tiv, Xhosa, but has rarely been reported elsewhere in the world. The situation is complicated by the fact that a down-step high, i.e. $^!$ ́, often behaves like a mid tone, and some linguists have therefore been led to interpret all mids as lowered highs.

Throughout this discussion we have focused on sounds in isolation. But all languages have rules whereby sounds are combined into syllables and words. For example, in normal standard English, words can begin with *tr-* (*tray, trip, tree*) but not *sr-, zr-, chr-, whr-, plr-*. Permitted sequences in a given language make up the canonical forms of that language. The general characteristics of syllable and word formation in African languages include the following:

1) Words normally end on vowels, and the favorite syllable patterns is consonant-vowel.

2) Consonant clusters are unusual except for combinations with w or y.

Nasal-stop combinations are fairly common, and some languages have combinations with **l** or **r** initially, but these are rare.

3) A nasal may constitute a syllable all by itself; e.g., Swahili **mtu** (syllables **ḿ + tu**) *person*. An initial ŋ is not uncommon.

These observations do not really set off African languages and one can even find similarities in English. I myself pronounce (occasionally, at least) *endeavor* with initial *nd-*, *inject* with *nj-*, *inquire* with *ŋg·* —all with initial syllabic nasals. Of course, there are many exceptions to these rules as far as African languages go. In at least one Bantu language, Faʔ, spoken in Zaïre, no vowels, only syllabic nasals occur in many words, thus violating the first statement, e.g. ɣ́ń *run*, **fnsm fǹ** *this knife*. Painter notes that in Gonja contrasts such as **krʷ** *grind* and **kŕ** *tie* occur. [18] But nothing anywhere in Africa approaches the consonantalism of the American Indian Language Bella Coola with words on the order of ɬkʼʷtχʷ *make it big* (although this particular transcription may mask a phonetic vowel).

The tempo of actual speech can modify phonemic realization considerably. Roger Wescott has noted for Bini that in rapid speech, several phonemes disappear altogether. [19] A common feature of normal quick speech is the elision and contraction of vowels, often with tonal complications—the tone of one syllable being dropped while the vowel is retained or vice versa, or else a compound tone develops. Pronunciations such as these—like the normal English pronunciation of *is she*? as 'iʃʃiy? rather than 'izʃiy? —cannot be dismissed as "bad" or "slovenly". On the contrary, they constitute an integral part of the native command of a language and hence play a significant role in the grammar of a language.

A closing note. The main differences between Africa Alphabet (AA) and that of the IPA involve the following:

I P A	A A
j	y
ɟ *or* dʒ	j
ɲ	ny
ʎ	ly
y	[nothing; ü sometimes used]
ʔ	'
Φ	f
β	v
ɩ	I
ɷ	ʊ

For IPA y (the value of *u* in French, *ü* in German) for which there is no AA equivalent, I suggest the compromise letter ɥ borrowed from the Russian alphabet. All vowel symbols would thus be of the same size and there would be no problem with diacritics.)

The general values of vowel signs are roughly as follows, with the equivalents set off in italics in the key words.

FRONT UNROUNDED

i   mach*i*ne
ι   p*i*t
e   (Scotch) d*ay*, French
     *é*té, German *Eh*re
ε   p*e*t
ae   p*a*t
a   (New England) f*a*ther,
     French p*a*tte [this symbol is
     often used for *a*]

FRONT ROUNDED

ɥ   French l*u*ne, German f*üh*len
Y   German f*ü*llen
φ   French p*eu*, German Höhle
œ   French p*eu*r, German Hölle

BACK ROUNDED

u   r*u*le
ɷ   p*u*t
o   (Scotch) g*o*, French *eau*,
     German R*o*se
ɔ   (British) l*aw*, German S*o*nne
ɒ   (British) h*o*t, General American
     l*a*w

BACK UNROUNDED

ɯ   [unrounded u]
ɣ   [unrounded o]
ʌ   c*u*p
ɑ   f*a*ther, (General American) h*o*t,
     French p*â*te [usually written a]

CENTRAL

ɨ   Russian s*y*n 'son' (in some
     dialects of American English
     pr*e*tty, j*u*st [adv], ros*e*s)
з   (Southern British) b*i*rd
ə   Chin*a*

NASAL

ɛ̃   French v*in*
ɔ̃   French b*on*
ã   French bl*anc*, etc.

Notes and References

Many of the descriptions given here are technically inadequate. The interested reader is advised to consult the following books for more nearly adequate treatment of such matters.

D. Westermann and Ida C. Ward, 1933, *Practical phonetics for students of African Languages*, Oxford.
Peter Ladefoged, 1968, *A phonetic study of West African languages*, Cambridge.
A. N. Tucker, 1929, *Comparative phonetics of the Suto-Chuana group of Bantu languages*, London.
C. M. Doke, 1926, *The phonetics of Zulu*, Witwatersrand.
W. H. T. Gairdner, 1917, *Egyptian colloquial Arabic*, Cambridge.
D. M. Beach, 1938, *The phonetics of the Hottentot language*, Cambridge.

1) See D. Westermann and Ida C. Ward, *op. cit.* Also *Practical orthography of African languages*, revised ed., Memorandum I, International Institute of African languages and Cultures, London 1930.
2) O. C. Dahl, 1951, *Malgache et Maanjan*, *Avhandlinger utgitt av Egede-Instituttet*, Oslo, 3.
3) For a detailed description of this, see C. Meinhof, 1932, *Introduction to the phonology of the Bantu languages*, Berlin.
4) As given by David Dalby, 2967, A Survey of the indigenous scripts of Liberia and Sierra Leone: Vai, Mende, Loma, Kpelle and Bassa, *African Language Studies*, 8
5) Tucker, 1929, *Comparative phonetics*, p. 49.
6) M. A. Bryant, Personal Communication.
7) Different symbols for clicks are used in the existing official orthographies. In Zulu c q x represent ʇ ʗ ʖ, respectively. In Nama Hottentot, / is used for ʇ, ≠ for ǂ, ! for ʗ, // for ʖ.
8) Doke, 1926, *Phonetics of Zulu*, 296.
9) Tucker, personal communication.
10) In Dinka and Nuer, the breathy-creaky distinction would seem to be phonemic, but the interpretation is not clear. See A. N. Tucker and M. A. Bryan, 1966, *Linguistic analyses: The non-Bantu languages of North-eastern Africa*, Oxford, 402–3.
11) There is no a-ɑ distinction in Igbo.
12) See Noam Chomsky and Morris Halle, 1968, *The sound pattern of English*, New York, Evanston, and London.
13) On the island of Pemba, native speakers of Swahili have a tonal dialect. A. N. Tucker, personal communication.
14) See J. F. Carrington, 1940, *The talking drums of Africa*, London.
15) See Joseph H. Greenberg, 1960, A method for measuring functional yield as applied to tone in African languages, *Report of the Tenth Annual Round Table Meeting on Linguistics and Language Studies*, ed. by Richard S. Harrell, Washington, D.C.
16) Beach, 1938.
17) Irvine Richardson, 1959, *The role of tone in the structure of Sukuma*, London.

18) Colin Painter, 1970, *Gonja: a phonological and grammatical study,* Bloomington.
19) Roger Wescott, 1965, Speech-tempo and the phonemics of Bini, *Journal of African Languages* 4.3: 182–190.

CHAPTER V

Syntax

Of all the aspects of grammatical analysis, syntax is the one least well represented for African languages.

The subject matter of syntactic analysis is the grammatical sentences of a
language (or of language in general). Higher levels than sentence might be set up,
such as paragraph, discourse, monolog—but these have usually been dealt with as
concatenations of sentences despite certain problems in such an approach. For
example, in all languages there are probably sentences that cannot function in
normal usage as the first utterance in a discourse because they by their form or
meaning depend on a preceding sentence. In a great many African languages, a
special "sequentive" form of the verb is used to indicate an "and then" idea
inappropriate for an initial sentence; e.g. (where glosses given are suggestive
rather than strictly accurate):

Igbo	ɛ́-gbu-ɛ-m	*and then I killed*	(ɛ́...m *I*, gbu *kill*, -ɛ- *and then*
Swahili	a-ka-sema	*and then he said*	(a *he*, ka *and then*, sema *say*)
Hausa	sú-kà gúdù	*and then they ran.*	(su *they*, kà *and then*, gudù *run*)

The notion of sentence used by modern linguists is commonly that of complete utterance, but even so a vague formulation entails several difficulties. Here
we shall assume we know what a sentence is, and what the grammatical sentences in the languages discussed are.

All languages have as a basic sentence type, the subject-predicate kind—like
John died yesterday, when *John* is the subject and *died yesterday* is the predicate. Other kinds of sentences also exist, of course. Interjections, exclamations,
vocatives, and the like make up universally found minor sentence types. So also
do responses and additions, such as the second parts of the following examples.

(1) Where did you go last night? Home.
(2) I want this one. The red one.

From the point of view of sentence types, African languages present no differences with other languages of the world.

43

One detail with regard to responses might be mentioned, however, and that is that throughout the continent the answers to negative yes-no questions require the reverse of the English construction. Thus, in English, the appropriate response to *he didn't go home?* is, if in point of fact he didn't go, *no*. In African languages, the answer would be *yes*, with the implication *yes, you're right, he didn't go home.* Of course, such usage is not restricted to Africa and occurs in a great many languages, including Russian.

In subject-predicate sentences, we have to deal with notions such as subject and object, among others, representing syntactic relationships that must be posited for all languages, but these notions are not easy to define rigorously. In the sentence *John killed Paul,* John is a subject and performs the action implied by the verb, and Paul is the object receiving the actions of the verb. But in *Paul was killed by John,* with the same truth value, *Paul* is said to be the grammatical subject although he is still perforce the recipient of the verbal action. These are matters of some theoretical importance, but once again we shall simply assume that notions such as subject are valid and in fact understood and not question them further.

The basic word order throughout Africa is Subject-Verb-Object (SVO). It is reported for most Niger-Kordofanian languages as well as for Chadic, Nilotic, and many other members of Nilo-Saharan. Specific languages with this word order include Fulani, Yoruba, Zulu, Luganda, Hausa, Shilluk, Songhai, Zande.

Another fairly common basic word order pattern is SOV. This occurs regularly in Kushitic languages, "African" Semitic, Kanuric, and Khoisan. Specific examples: Amharic, Galla, Kanuri, Sandawe, Nama Hottentot, Nubian.

In the north and northeastern parts of the continent another pattern is not uncommon: VSO. This is found regularly in three of the five branches of Afro-Asiatic, viz. Egyptian, Berber, and Semitic. The occurrence of SOV in African Semitic languages (i.e. Ethiopic) mentioned above may be due to the influence of neighboring Kushitic speaking groups. VSO is rare in Africa apart from Afro-Asiatic, and for this reason in part certain Nilotic languages with that ordering were formerly thought to be somehow closely related to Afro-Asiatic and labeled Nilo-Hamitic, e.g. Nandi, Maasai, and Lotuho. Clearly, there need be no genetic relationship between languages merely because they share the same basic word order. The Nilo-Hamitic controversy has generated a good deal of discussion and will be discussed in some detail in a later chapter (chapter 7).

Malagasy, a Malayo-Polynesian language, seems to be the only African language with an VOS order (but this is used when the object is indefinite; VSO is used when the object is definite).

Nowhere in Africa is a "free" word order such as that of Latin or Russian reported, where SVO, VSO, SOV, etc. are generally equivalent. This is true even for languages such as Kanuri or Awiya where elaborate case systems exist and the words that functions as subject or object are clearly marked by their shape rather than by position in a sentence. In Bilin, true enough, a rather great laxity of order is reported, but hardly of the degree associated with the traditional notion of "free".

The only exceptional pattern recorded for an African language, which is exceedingly rare from the point of view of worldwide distribution as well, occurs in Mamvu, a language of the Moru-Mangbetu group: OSV. Whether this order is neutral in style is not altogether clear, however.

In the great majority of languages in the world, the dominant order is almost always one where the subject precedes the object.

Even in those languages where (part of) the predicate precedes the subject in a verb-object construction, eg. in the VSO and the rare OSV pattern, in socalled equational sentences (sentences of the type *X is Y*: *John is a good boy*, etc), the subject nevertheless precedes the predicate.

Mamvu:	íní	àndú	*you are big*
	you	big	
Arabic:	ır-raagil	tawíil	*the man is tall*
	the man	tall	

A variety of ways of realizing equational sentences occur, particularly in a present tense situation. There may be a verb (as in English), or none, as in the two examples just given. Usually a verb on the order of *be* is dropped in the present, but not in other forms, eg. Swahili **Mohammedi seremala** *Mohammed is a carpenter* but **Mohammedi alikuwa seremala** *Mohammed was a carpenter*. In Hausa no verb at all occurs. A curious but apparently superficial resemblance in the equative occurs in a large number of African languages, namely the occurrence of a particle of some sort that is monosyllablic and contains an n plus a vowel like i or e, eg. Hausa **nèe**, Luo **nı**, Yoruba **ni**, Swahili **ni** (the sentence given above is really a reduction of **Mohammedi ni seremala**). Whatever their ultimate origin, at present these elements are clearly different in function. Hausa **nèe** for example, has a corresponding feminine form **cèe**; in the other languages mentioned the forms are invariable. Yoruba **ni** is a predictable morphophonemic alternant of a verb **li** *be*. Swahili **ni** seems to be a neutralized subject marker and Luo **nı** a kind of particle.

The basic word order patterns have been correlated with other aspects of word order. For example, from a worldwide sample of languages, a correlation has been established between VSO order and the use of prepositions, whereas SOV order is generally associated with postpositions. Of course, we must speak rather loosely in using these terms since "prepositions" in African languages commonly turn out to be transparent noun forms, e.g. *head-of* for *on*, etc.; or else postpositions may in fact be case endings rather than separate particles. Such looseness is not intolerable if we consider all these devices as ways of indicating syntactic relationships; what is important for us is whether the relationship is marked before the noun (stem) or after. Examples of the correlation suggested are provided by Arabic, with VSO and prepositions; and Kanuri with SOV and postpositions, e.g. **lèn** *on*; **fɔr lèn** *on the horse*; **mbên** *through*; **tàgà mbên** *through the window*. Amharic is sometimes cited as exceptional because it is now SOV and has both prepositions and postpositions. But work done by Ferguson suggests that the prepositions are fossilized remnants from a VSO stage, thus supporting the correlation even more strikingly.[1] It is clear from many languages that prepositions and postpositions may come from the same element historically. For example, the prepositions of the Bongo-Bagirmi group seem to be etymologically related to the postpositions of Moru-Mangbetu: Bongo **dɔ-ma** *on me* (head my) but Lendu (a Moru-Mangbetu language) **ma-dʒɔ̀**, where **dɔ** and **dʒɔ** are presumably related.

Languages with prepositions, in turn, almost always have possessive phrases (such as *John's book*) where the possessor (*John*) follows the thing possessed (*book*), while in languages with postpositions the possessor almost always precedes. Examples of these correlations for African languages include the following: (1) with prepositions and possessor following possessed: Berber, Fulani, Shilluk, Hausa, Efik, Kresh, Iraqw; (2) with postpositions and possessor preceding possessed: I̩jo, Nubian, Ewe, Nupe, Songhai, Twi, Nama Hottentot. A somewhat less tidy correlation between possessive phrase order and basic word order can be formulated: both VSO and SVO tend to have possessed-possessor ordering, and SOV possessor-possessed. SOV is often associated, as we have seen, with a mirror-image construction of SVO. In many other instances—not all directly associated with basic word order, however—variant constructions tend to involve mirrored orderings. We shall discuss some of these later.

In African languages as well as in most of, if not all, the languages of the world, possessives indicate more than mere possession whatever their form. Some of the additional categories include: material (e.g. *a table of wood*), description (*a man of courage*), origin (*a woman of*[English *from*] *the north*), contents (*a bottle of water*), and others as well, some not so frequent outside of Africa such as the indication of ordinal numbers. Thus, *second book* is quite widely construed as *book of two*. The indication for *first* is frequently somewhat irregular, not normally **book of one* but rather *book of beginning* or the like (Swahili **kitabu cha kwanza** [kwanza *to begin*]).

In several African languages variants of possessive phrases occur quite frequently with a distinction in meaning so that one form is used for "intimate" possession (e.g. indicating attachment to parts of the body), vs. "nonintimate" possession (objects in temporary possession). In Lango, both forms have the same ordering, but the nonintimate form doubles the final consonant of the possessed and requires a linking element à: **pyèn léê** *skin of animal* vs. ᴘʏèɴɴ à ᴅáɴɔ *skin of person* (i.e. animal skin belonging to person). Various other ways of noting such a distinction exist. As a rule, the intimate form involves mere juxtaposition.

A linking element found in African possessive phrases frequently involves an -a. Despite its wide distribution across language families, this trait must surely be a superficial and accidental similarity only.

Bantu	-a	(preceded by concordial element e.g. y-a, z-a)
Hausa	ná	(masculine, plural),
	tá	(feminine)
Lango	à	
Acholi	pà	
Ndunga	ta	
Krongo	-a	
Tima	ka	

In many languages, some nouns—mostly kinship terms—can only occur in a possessive phrase. In Luo and Dinka, for example, the word for *father* occurs only in phrases such as *my father, his father, John's father*, etc. Such words are said to take inalienable possessives. They have posed some difficulty for Christian missionaries who are doctrinally obliged to deal in terms of the Father and the Son *in abstracto*; the translations are not always linguistically commendable.

The two main subdivisions within a sentence are noun phrases and verb phrases.

In noun phrases, there are powerful constraints that limit word order. For example, when any or all of the following items—demonstrative (e.g. *this, that*), numeral (*two, second*), descriptive adjective (*red, tall, big*)—precede the noun they modify, they are nearly always found in that order, as in English: *these two red books*. This order is reported for Ijo, Efik, Amharic, Sidamo, and Nama Hottentot. But it is quite rare for a discriptive adjective to precede the noun it modifies in African languages in the first place. The main exceptions to this statement are the Kushitic and Ethiopic languages.

In languages where the elements in question follow the modified noun—the usual situation in Africa—they are found in one of two orders: either (a) *books these two red* or (b) *books red two these*. Type (a) is rare in Africa, while (b) is the most common pattern and occurs in Fulani, Swahili, and Yoruba. Of course, variations exist; demonstratives may precede a noun and descriptive adjectives follow (although the reverse is rarely if ever the case), as in Maasai.

The verbal phrase shows considerable complexity in all languages. Only a few points will be covered here.

Although verbs and nouns may not be formally distinguished—that is, nothing in their shape gives a clue as to whether they are one or the other—their syntactic use is hardly ever ambiguous.

The distinction between transitive verbs (those taking an object, as in *John read the book*) and intransitive (without an object, as in *John runs*) seems to be universal. In some African languages, there is a class of transitive verb that not only can take an object, but must—and that, commonly a noun similar in form to the verb. In English, we find such "cognate" object constructions in *to dream a dream*, *to sing a song*, but in English the object is optional, one may just as well say *he's singing* as *he's singing a song*. In Yoruba, on the other hand, the object must be included, and one not only *sings a song*, but also *sleeps a sleep*, *works a working*, *beats a beating, laughs a laughter*, etc. Similar constructions exist in a great many other languages such as Igbo, Arabic, and Luo. In Ewe, if an object is indeterminate, a kind of dummy object *someone* or *something* is obligatory: **ma ŋlo nú** *I shall write (something* [**nú**]).

An indirect object (*John* in *he gave John the book* or *he showed John the letter*) is realized in many ways. Although such objects are traditionally associated *par excellence* with the verb *give* in European languages—hence the term *dative*, the case of "giving"— in many African languages the indirect object of the verb give is treated differently from that of other verbs such as *show* or *tell*. In Hausa, for example, we find **yáa núunàa wà Mùhámmádù wásíikàa** *he showed Mohammed a letter* where the indirect object involves a phrase with **wà** *to, for*, but **yáa báa Mùhámmádù líttáafìi** *he gave Mohammed a book* where the indirect object is indicated only by position. A similar situation obtains in Swahili and other Bantu languages: verbs normally take an **i** or **e** before an indirect object, but **pa** *give* never does so, e.g. **nilim-som-e-a Mohammedi kitabu** *I read* (**soma**) *a book to Mohammed* but **nilimpa Mohammedi kitabu** *I gave* (**pa**) *Mohammed a book*.

The indirect object may, then, be realized in a number of ways: merely by position, by some sort of introductory word such as the Hausa **wà** or Luo **nι** or by a word that seems to be related to the word for *give* if that is not the main verb: *I show it give him*, a common pattern in West Sudanic languages. Or else there may be a change in the noun itself (case distinction) as in Galla and Kanuri (although here we may be dealing with postpositions rather than case in the traditional sense); or by a modification in the verb as exemplified by Swahili and other Bantu languages but also to be found in some Nilotic languages such as Nuer, Shilluk, Bari, Lotuho, and Maasai.

In some languages it is possible to transform an underlying object so that it becomes the grammatical subject; such a transformation is known as the passive, e.g. *John killed Bill* becoming *Bill was killed by John.* Sometımes the "agent" or "logical subject" (here *John*) is not expressed, e.g. *Bill was killed.* In many African languages only such an indefinite passive is possible, as is true for Arabic. In a considerable number of African languages the closest thing to a passive is an indefinite subject construction, i.e. *John was killed* would be construed as *they killed John* or *one killed John.* Such is the case in Koptic, Hausa, and Luo.

To my knowledge, the passive is never formed in any African language with an auxiliary verb like the English *be.* The commonest device is to change word order and modify the verb itself: in Ijo there are tonal changes in the verb, e.g. **kòri-mi** *catch*–**korí-mí** *be caught*; in Shilluk, tone changes plus a distinctive suffix, e.g. **yá cwɔlá** *I call*–**yâ·cwɔlɔ** *I am being called*; in Arabic, change in the vowels, **kataba** *wrote*–**kutiba** *was written*; in Swahili and many Bantu languages an element -w- e.g. **soma** *read*–**som-w-a** *be read.*

Sometimes the passive as used in African languages is not altogether in accord with English idiom. For example in Ijo, even locative expressions where there are no real objects have passive-like transformation, e.g. **indií, wári-bi-ò, emí** [fish, house-X-in, is] *there is fish in the house*; the passive, **wári-bi, indi emí,** is difficult if not impossible to convey in English.[2] In languages such as Swahili or Maasai with "dative" forms of the verb (in Bantuist jargon, the applied or prepositional form), the corresponding passive transform has a somewhat unexpected ring to speakers of English, perhaps, because the indirect object, not the direct one, must be made into the grammatical subject, as in the following Swahili example.

ACTIVE   Mohammedi alimsomea Ali kitabu.
        Mohammed read the book to Ali.
PASSIVE   Ali alisomewa kitabu na Mohammedi.
        Ali was read-to the book by Mohammed.

Although auxiliaries do not occur in forming the passive in African languages, they have a wide use in many other contexts. As a matter of fact, these auxiliaries often have uses taken up by adverbial constructions in English; e.g., auxiliaries with the meaning [*to do*] *first* (*he sang first*), [*to do*] *again* (*he sang again*), [*to do*] *often, not* [*to do*], [*to have*] *previously* [*done*], etc. are quite common and are exemplified in part by Hausa and Maasai.

The auxiliaries are closely associated with tense or aspectual distinctions, and in point of fact many tense-aspectual forms seem ultimately derivable from separate auxiliaries or verbs. Thus, the particle **záa** in Hausa used to mark the future must be related to a verb stem **z**-found in the words for *come, go* (cf. English *I am going to do it*); similarly in Nilotic. In Bantu, on the other hand, the future marker (generally **ta**) is related to the verb *to want* (cf. English *will*, which may indicate both volition and futurity).

A distinctive feature of many West African languages is a multiple verb construction, known in the literature as serial verbs. The following Yoruba sentence is a good example:[3] **Dàda rà màluu Kpajɛ** *Dada bought a cow and slaughtered it for food*, literally *Dada bought* [rà] *cow killed* [Kpa] *ate* [jɛ]. Such constructions have been analyzed as a reduction or compression of a number of clauses, the subjects and objects of which are the same. We can perhaps set up a rule whereby the underlying structure is said to be:

Dada bought a cow + Dada killed a cow + Dada ate a cow

and both *Dada* and *cow* are dropped after the first occurrence. In Yoruba and Ewe the dropping rule begins at the right. In Ijo with an SOV basic pattern, the dropping starts from the left: *Dada a cow bought killed ate.*

A comparable example of elision in combining clauses is the dropping of verbs in compounds such as *John ate a banana, Bill* [ate] *a mango, Joe* [ate] *a pawpaw*. Resources for such "gapping" as the phenomenon is known, are probably available in many languages, but not in Ijo.

These compounds constitute part of the larger topic of how sentences are joined together to form larger sentences. Two basic kinds of joining exist; co-ordinate (*John worked and Mary slept*) or subordinate (*John worked while Mary slept, John worked because Mary slept,* etc.). A special type of subordination is embedding, i.e. inserting one sentence within another to form, among other things, relative clauses: from two basic sentences such as *John was working* and *John saw Mary* we can create *John, who saw Mary, was working*, etc. All these devices and many more are found in probably all African language. By and large, however, despite the availiability of many sorts of devices for subordination—producing a Chinese-box kind of sentence—the preferred stylistic device in African languages is the stringing along of seperate short sentences or co-ordinate clauses (technically, PARATAXIS). Thus, instead of something on the order of *I saw a man who was working*, the more stylistically common form in most instances would probably be *I saw a man, he was working*. However, the degree to which such constructions rather than others are used varies considerably from language to language, and from context to context within a language.

An important function of embedding in African languages is the signaling of emphasis. In English, in a sentence such as *Mumbo went to the market yesterday*, nearly every element can be stressed not by changing the word order or construction in any way, but merely by pronouncing the emphatic word with greater prominence or loudness: MUMBO *went to the market yesterday, Mumbo went to the market* YESTERDAY, etc. In African languages, although some phonological stress or intonational possibilities exist, a widespread and stylistically common way of emphasizing is the use of constructions along the lines of *it was Mumbo who went to market yesterday, it was yesterday Mumbo went to market*. Welmers has investigated this kind of construction in some detail for Kpelle and from the basic sentence

Sumo è wɛɛ wúru tèe à yuɔ̂ ǹɔɔi sû
(Sumo he yesterday sticks cut with ax in forest)
Yesterday Sumo cut sticks in the forest with an ax,
he produces 6 emphatic sentences with **ɓé** *it is*: **sumo ɓé wɛɛ wúru tèe à yuɔ̂
ǹɔɔi sû** *It was Sumo . . .* ; and so similarly: *it was yesterday, it was in the
forest . . .* , etc.).[5] In Hausa, since pronoun and aspectual particles have differing
forms in relative as opposed to nonrelative clauses, it is possible to delete much
of such emphatic constructions without loss of information, e.g. **Bènjí yánàa
áykìi** *Benji is working* could be emphasized as **Bènjí nèe wândà yá kèe áykìi**
Benji is the one who is working. The possible reductions include:

> Bènjí nèe yá kèe áykìi
> Bènjí yá   kèe áykìi
> Bènjií kèe áykìi

where **kèe** is the alternate of **nàa** in a relative clause; the presence of **kèe** alone is
enough of a signal to set off emphasis.

Questions involving question words in African languages often involve a
similar construction; thus *who went*? is normally construed as *who is it who
went*? This is usual in Hausa, Kpelle, and Swahili. So similarly, *where is it he
went*?, *when is it he went*? But even in European languages one sometimes finds
similarities, e.g. French *qui est-ce qui est venu*?

In joining and embedding sentences various kinds of adjustments often occur.
If we were to join the two sentences *John₁ bought a cow₁* + *John₂ slaughtered a
cow₂* to produce a single sentence, and *John₁ = John₂*, *cow₁ = cow₂* (i.e. we're
talking about the same John and cow in the two sentences), we must eliminate
redundant items (*John₂, cow₂*) by dropping or substitution, both processes
comprising PRONOMINALIZATION: *John bought a cow and ate it.* Pronominalization is found in all languages and it would seem that most of the specific rules
for pronominalization are the same for all languages. Nevertheless there are
occasional divergences. In the Yoruba example of serial verbs quoted above, a
pronoun corresponding to English *it* (referring to *cow*) was not used at all;
pronominalization involved zeroing out altogether. Even the pronominal resources of languages differ, though slightly. In a very few African languages,
there are two kinds of third person pronoun,—one being an obviative, having no
clear parallel in English. In such languages which include Moru, Ma'di, Lugbara,
Kresh, Bongo, Ndogo, Zande, Lango (but to my knowledge no Bantu or Afro-
Asiatic language), a sentence such as *he₁ said he₂ is beating the child* is not
ambiguous because the obviative pronoun would be used for *he₂*, if *he₁*, and *he₂*
do not refer to the same person. In Moru, and Logbara there is also an obviative
form for *you* (sg), so that two forms would be used in *you₁ will do this and*

you₂ will do that. An obviative form for *I* has not been reported from any language in the world, and would seem to be (on nonlinguistic grounds) fairly farfetched, appropriate mostly in schizophrenia. Some other dimensions of pronoun systems are mentioned in the next chapter.

Perhaps the most important syntactic element that cuts across phrase boundaries in a sentence is agreement, whereby some word in a sentence—adjective, demonstrative, verb pronoun—shows its syntactic relationship or dependence on some other word, almost invariably a noun. The phenomenon should be quite familar to the reader from French, German, or Russian as well as other European languages he may have studied. There, nouns belong to two or more essentially arbitrary classes or genders, normally labeled masculine and feminine (and for some also neuter), and articles, adjectives, and pronouns normally have distinct forms to agree with each class of noun; thus in French we find masculine **stylo** *pen* and feminine **plume** also *pen* (or *feather*) modified differently: **le stylo vert**—**la plume verte**. In such systems the noun has an inherent characteristic or feature of gender and the other words have derived gender. Sometimes the shape of the noun itself indicates its gender, or there may be semantic clues. The important thing is that the modifying words have alternate forms to indicate agreement—often in a way not unlike the displaced high tone of Sukuma, mentioned in the previous chapter. Gender systems need not be based on categories that correspond to the European sex-linked ones—although many Africanists restrict the word "gender" to languages that have noun classes based at least possibly on natural sex distinctions, other systems involving classes, not genders.

In point of fact, sex—gender systems are relatively rare in Africa apart from Afro-Asiatic languages, which normally have masculine and feminine, but no neuter; a similar set-up is found in some Khoisan languages, viz. Nama Hottentot, Naron Bushman, Sandawe, and Hatsa. The sole examples of gender systems with natural sex correlations in Niger-Kordofanian are Ịjọ, with masculine-feminine-inanimate, and Ma, with an additional gender referring to animals. The four-way system reported for Ma seems to be unique in Africa.

A masculine-feminine-neuter division is quite rare in Africa and is found mostly in Kadugli-Krongo languages. In Maasai, a masculine-feminine-place division exists, but the place gender reportedly has only one member, the noun for *place* itself, **e-wwéjì**. In Teso, another three-way division is reported, masculine-feminine-common, the latter gender denoting small or young objects, and terms used in a general as well as a pejorative sense.

Of course, the terms masculine and feminine are used somewhat loosely, and allocation of nouns to the particular classes may vary from language to language. In Lotuho, for example, all nouns are feminine except those denoting males. In Hausa, nouns ending on -aa , and those denoting females, towns, countries, and numbers are feminine; others are usually masculine. In Bari nouns denoting males as well as big, strong, long objects or objects used as active agents or instruments are masculine; feminine nouns include those denoting females, also small, weak, soft, round, hollow, flat, objects, or objects used in a passive sense. In this language, the universal sex symbolism posited by Freud seems quite consistently worked out, but the consistency is hardly so obvious elsewhere.

The most spectacular gender systems are found in Niger-Kordofanian languages, interestingly enough at either end of the geographical extremes, e.g. Bantu and West Atlantic. In Fulani, a West Atlantic language, there are something like 20 genders, in Swahili about 10—the count varies from one analysis to another. The allocation of nouns to genders is not based on sex at all. At least one class is predominantly made up of nouns denoting human beings, another of animals, a third of trees, a fourth of abstractions, and so on. Some Niger-Kordofanian languages have no noun classes at all, e.g. the Mande and most of the Kwa subgroups. The most plausible explanation is that the classes have been lost.

Despite the differing principles these various genders involve, the agreement rules for all systems seem basically the same. In fact a single formula using a transformationalist representation is possible to account for agreement between noun and adjective, verb, etc. In simplest terms, the rule says that certain features of a noun (or noun phrase) such as gender and number must be rewritten onto the modifying word:

Noun [Features] + X → Noun [Features] + X [Features]

where X represents any adjective, demonstrative, verb, etc. A rule such as this accounts for items as diverse as English *John goes* and Swahili **kitabu kikubwa** *big* (**-kubwa**) *book*.

e.g. *John* [3rd person singular] + *go* ⟶
  John [3rd person singular] + *go* [3rd person singular]

(where the *go* plus features is ultimately realized as *goes*)

  kitabu [ki-class] **-kubwa** →
  kitabu [ki-class] **-kubwa** [ki-class]

(where the adjective plus features is ultimately realized as **kikubwa**).

In Bantu languages, the rule would seem to be most often: rewrite the prefix of the noun onto the modifying words, but several exceptions to this formulation exist.[6] For example, there is sometimes more than one feature, and in some instances one is realized and in others, the others. In Swahili nouns of class 5 (normally with zero-prefix) denoting people sometimes take class 5 agreements and sometimes animate agreements; e.g.

baba y-angu	*my* (-angu)	*father* (baba)
	with class 5 agreement (y-)	
BUT baba wa taifa	*father of* (-a)	*the country* (taifa)
	with animate agreement (w-).	

The actual morphophonemic realization of agreement may be quite complicated but the underlying rule for distributing the agreements seems, as we have suggested, to be basically quite straightforward.

Notes and References

An important source for the distribution of various grammatical features is the *Handbook of African Languages*, particularly A. N. Tucker and M.A. Bryan, 1966, *Linguistic analyses: The non-Bantu languages of North-Eastern Africa*, Oxford.

A world-wide sample of correlations between basic word order patterns and other grammatical features has been undertaken by Joseph H. Greenberg in his article, Some universals of grammar with particular reference to the order of meaningful elements, in *Universals of language*, ed. by Joseph H. Greenberg (1963), Cambridge, pp. 58−90.

1) This was drawn to my attention by Joseph H. Greenberg.
2) Taken from Kay Williamson, 1965, *A grammar of the Kolokuma dialect of Ijo,* West African Language Monograph Series 2, London.
3) Taken from A.O. Awobuluyi, *Studies in the syntax of the standard Yoruba verb*, (unpublished Ph.D dissertation, Colombia University).
4) There are a number of problems with this formulation. See Herbert Stalke, 1970, Serial verbs, *Studies in African Linguistics*, 1.2:60−99, and Edward H. Bendix, Serial verbs in Creole and West African [*sic*], unpublished paper read at the annual meeting of the American Anthropological Association held in San Diego, November 1970.
5) William E. Welmers, 1964, The syntax of emphasis in Kpelle, *Journal of West African Languages* 11:13−26.
6) See Edgar A. Gregersen, 1967, *Prefix and pronoun in Bantu*, Bloomington.

CHAPTER VI

Morphology

In morphological analysis it is useful to distinguish between a STEM, which functions as the core of a word and bears the "basic meaning" of it; and AFFIX, which modifies the meaning of a stem in some way. Thus in English, *bake* would be the stem in *bakes* and the *-s* an affix.

Several kinds of affix occur. Affixes that precede a stem are PREFIXES; those that follow, SUFFIXES. They should be familiar enough from English (*un-* in *undo*, a prefix; *-ness* in *goodness*, a suffix). Quite commonly, a prefix in one language will correspond to a suffix in another related language—suggesting for the most part that these affixes were at one point free forms or independent words, not bound as at present. The situation may be compared to the correspondence in some instances between prepositions and postpositions, mentioned in the last chapter. The most spectacular example of affix variation is found in the noun class system of Niger-Kordofanian. The noun class of a noun is usually marked by an affix, but this may appear as a prefix in one language, as a suffix in another, as an optional prefix or suffix in a third, and in a fourth found as both simultaneously (sometimes referred to then as a CIRCUMFIX).

	o *human*	ma *liquid*	li *thing*	ki *thing/body part*
Bulom	o-/u-	m-	li-/de-	ku-
Tem	-o	-m	-re	-ka
Gurma	o- -o	m- -ma	li- -li	ki- -ga
Gola	(o-) (-ɔ)	(ma-) (-ma)	(e-) (-lɛ)	(ke-) (-ɛ)
Proto-Bantu[1]	*m-o-	*ma-	*de-	*ke-

In the Gola example, the affixes are almost independent forms. In the singular an indefinite noun has neither prefix nor suffix; a definite noun may have either or both so that the affixes are almost like the English article *the*: ɲun (*a*) *person*; o-ɲun or ɲun-ɔ or o-ɲun-ɔ *the person*. And when an adjective modifies a noun in Gola, the suffix, otherwise placed after the noun, is placed after the adjective; e.g. sĩa *good*: o-ɲun sĩa-ɔ *the good person*.

A good example of an unambiguous circumfix is given by Westermann and Bryan for the West African language Tobote: ké-jì-ké *knife* (stem jì), pl. ń-jì-ḿ, where ké- -ké and ń- -ḿ are circumfixes.[2]

56

Tones very frequently count as morphemes in their own right and when used as affixes form a subclass known as SUPRAFIXES. In Gã for example various verbal forms differ merely in tone; e.g. **o** + **bi** *you* + *ask* have the following meanings when accompanied by various tonal patterns: **ò bí** *you asked*, **ó bì** *you have asked*, **ó bí** *may you ask*. In Hausa, we find another kind of difference in addition to this, so that **ƙarfafaa** (related to the noun **ƙarfii** *strength*) means *to strengthen* with the suprafix $\{\prime\ \vee\prime\}$ (**ƙárfàfáa**), *to be(come) strong* with $\{\vee\prime\prime\}$ (**ƙàrfáfàa**).

An affix may be directly inserted into a stem; such an affix is an INFIX. An example of an infix is the **-om-** in the Malagasy word **t-om-aɲy** *to rain* (cf **taɲy** *rain*). In Niger-Kordofanian languages, infixation rarely occurs but a curiously unsymmetrical use of it has been reported from Mba. In this language, the numbers up to *three* show agreement with a noun they modify. *One* and *three* do this by prefixes, but *two* infixes the gender maker with inanimate nouns but not with animate ones; thus **-íma** *one*: **là-lɛ̀ l-íma** *one eye*; **ɓìnè** *two*: **jwîɓé-ɓìnè** *two women*; BUT, with infixation **la-sɛ́ ɓi-sì-nè** *two eyes*.

The phonemes that make up a morpheme may all be uninterrupted or they may be discontinuous, that is, (part of) another morpheme may intervene. By definition, all circumfixes are discontinuous. In Afro-Asiatic languages, other kinds of discontinuous morphemes are quite common. In Arabic, for example, words are normally built up of a consonantal stem, generally composed of three consonants. The affixes are partially (discontinuous) vowel infixes, in addition to prefixes and suffixes of various shapes. Thus, the consonant stem **ktb** has something to do with the concept of writing. Compare the following words, where the stem is indicated with capitals.

KiTaaB	*book*	KuTuB	*books*
KaTaB	*he wrote*	yi-KTiB	*he writes*
KaaTiB	*writing*	ma-KTuuB	*written*

Sometimes, a more abstract kind of morpheme has to be posited involving the process of replacement. In English the plural of *man,* viz. *men,* has been described in a number of ways, many of them awkward, but it is clear that the *a* has been replaced by *e*, and that this replacement is itself the mark of the plural. In English such formations are rare, but they are quite common, for example, in Nilotic languages; e.g. the Luo forms **kɔŋɔ** pl. **kɔ̃ɔŋ** *beer,* **kwac-kwec** *leopard,* **ɖiaŋ-ɖok** *cow,* **mɔ-moɖi** *oil,* **ɔt-udi** *compound,* **dagɔ-degini** *šwamp,* etc.

As the examples have demonstrated, affixes can be used to form new words from stems and other words, thus *bake- baker,* where *-er* has made a noun out of a verb. Such a use is DERIVATION. Or else affixes show dimensions such as number, tense, agreement. This is called INFLECTION. Examples from English include *bake-bakes-baked*, or *baker-bakers.* In the rest of this chapter some of the high-

lights of these two uses, particularly inflection, as found in African languages are
presented.

First, however, let us consider a kind of morphological device used for both
inflection and derivation that has been particularly associated with African languages: REDUPLICATION. In European languages, it is frequently associated with
nursery words and informal items on the order of *papa, mama, bow-bow*, in
French with pet names (*Nana, Zaza, Loulou, Dodo, Clouclou*), and in English with
miscellaneous items (usually showing only partial reduplication) such as *razzle-
dazzle, harum-scarum, jingle-jangle*. Because of the peripheral nature of reduplication in European languages—and especially because of the baby talk connotations—reduplication has been branded by some as a primitive characteristic. It is
hard to see on what grounds such a judgment could validly be made apart from
ethnocentricity (here, I suppose, glottocentricity might be a more appropriate
term).

The role played by reduplication in many African languages is indeed great.
Gilbert Ansre reports that "on the average, eight of every hundred words [in a
random count from various texts] in Ewe are reduplicated forms".[3] So high a
percentage probably does not hold for most other African languages, but it is
perhaps suggestive of the importance of reduplication. Let us consider some of
its uses and forms in Hausa and Swahili.

In Hausa, reduplication is the favorite morphological process in the language.
Noun, less commonly adjective, plurals nearly always involve some sort of reduplication. The exact pattern varies. The doubling may be of a whole word as
in **nâs** *nurse* pl. **nâs-nâs'**, **írìi** *kind, type*—**írì-írìi**, **dàbám** *different*—
dàbám-dàbám; or of syllable (sometimes obscured by sound changes of various
sorts) as in **màgánàa** *matter, affair, utterance*— **màgàngàn-úu**, **líttáafìi** book—
lìttàttàafáy (presumably from **lìt-tàaf-tàaf-áy*); or of a single consonant as in
shúuɗii *blue* **shûɗɗíi**, most frequently with an intervening element: **wáaƙàa** *song*—
wáaƙóoƙíi, etc.

Intensive verbs, which indicate that an act is performed more than once by
many subjects or on different occasions or on different objects, etc., are formed
by reduplicating the initial syllable of the verb, usually with sound changes; e.g.
tàmbáyàa *ask*—**tàn-tàmbáyàa**, **káawóo** *bring*—**kákkáawóo**, **cí** *eat*—**cíccí**. Occasionally, there are (internally) reduplicated verbs without a corresponding unre-
duplicated form, at least in the modern language, e.g. **gírgìzáa** (from
*gíz-gìz-áa) *to shake*.

Verbal adjectives or adjectives always require partial reduplication: **sánìi**
know—**sànánnée** *known*, **hàrbá** *kick, shoot*—**hàrbábbée** *kicked, shot*. Intensive
adjectives related to abstract nouns show two kinds of reduplication: that of the
initial syllable in the singular, final syllable in the plural, e.g. **fáaɗíi** *breadth*,
stem **fáaɗ-**, **fáf-fàaɗ-áa** *very broad* singular, **fáa-ɗàa-ɗáa** plural. Similarly, re-

lated verbs have final syllable reduplication, e.g. **faá-ɗà-ɗáa** *broaden*, **fàa-ɗá-ɗaà** *be(come) broad*.

Inherent reduplication is fairly common for adjectives and nouns. A very large number of adjectives with a reduplicated final syllable such as **kúntúmée-mèe**, **dánƙwáléelèe**, and so on, generally have the meaning of *huge, big* (and very frequently refer to round objects); the normal plurals for such forms shows reduplication of the stem: **kúntún-kùntùn**, **dánƙwál-dànƙwàl** respectively. The few internally reduplicated adjectives have the meaning *small, short* (and usually *broad*), e.g. **dìgírgìríi**.

Internally reduplicated nouns often denote insects, spiders, millipedes, and the like: **gízó-gízòo** *spider*, **táwtàw** *kind of spider*, **shànshàaníi** *centipede*, **kùríkùrí** *kind of beetle*, **kyànkyásòo** *cockroach*, **ƙà-dándóonìyáa** (from **ƙá-

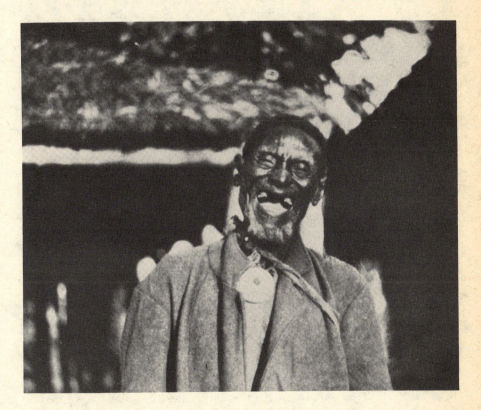

Figure 6   SHONA SPEAKER WITH FRONT TEETH EXTRACTED

A Tonga headman displaying the traditional fashion that required evultion of the four upper front teeth.

dóon-dóon-ìyáa) *millipede*, **kàa-zún-zùm-íi** *bed-bug*, etc. Such a pattern rarely occurs for higher animals.

In Swahili, reduplication is rarely used for inflection. Indeed, when two identical syllables of inflection come together, in at least one instance one of these syllables can be dropped—a phenomenon known as HAPOLOGY (itself an example of the phenomenon; the etymologically expected form is *haplo-lo-logy*), e.g. **nunuliliwa** *to be bought for* often reduces to **nunuliwa**. Verbs may be reduplicated to imply continued action: **vaa** *dress*—**vaavaa** *keep on dressing*, **tanga** *stroll*—**tangatanga** *keep on strolling*. Sometimes, however, reduplication of verbs and generally so of adjectives indicates a lessening of degree or intensity: **jaribujaribu** *try (but not very hard)*. **mponjwamponjwa** *rather sick*, **maji-maji** *somewhat wet*.

Both Swahili and Hausa use full reduplication to indicate distributiveness: Hausa **úkù-úkù** *three each, three by three;* Swahili **tano tano** *five each, in fives, five by five*, **shilingi shilingi** *a shilling a piece*, and similarly **namna namna** *various kinds*, etc.

Inherent reduplication is quite common in Swahili. With nouns it often occurs in words denoting lower animals, as in Hausa, but not so often insects: **m-dudu** *insect*, **sungusungu** *black ant*, **yavuyavu** *jellyfish*, **yungayunga** *worm*, **koikoi** *heron, stork*, **yangeyange** *egret*. With verbs, only the first syllable can be inherently reduplicated. Such verbs normally indicate that the activity implied in the verb stem is made up of a number of acts: **babata** *tap*, **pepeta** *sift, winnow*, **tetema** *tremble*, **gogota** *knock at*, etc. (cf. Hausa **fiffitaa** *fan*).

One of the commonest connotations for inherently reduplicated nouns and verbs in Swahili is that of confusion, unstableness, giddiness of mind, or other uncertain behavior: **daghadagha, dungudungu**, etc. *perplexity*, **zulizuli** *giddiness*, **ki-mkumku** *madness*, **tingetinge** *shaky bridge;* **zongazonga** *confuse*, **lega-lega** *waver, totter*, **yugayuga** *stagger*, **garagara** *roll from side to side* (cf. Hausa **dàlò-daloo** *useless going about from place to place*). Adjectives of this sort often denote feebleness or lack of vigor: **dabwadabwa** *flabby, soft*, **kejekeje** *slack*, **-kuukuu** *old, worn out*, **goigoi** *lazy, weak, useless*.

Most of these examples could be reproduced for a great many other African languages. The important thing is that reduplication does not differ in effectiveness, efficiency, or subtlety from other morphological devices.

Certain categories of inflection, such as number, are linguistic universals—or near universals. There may be no overt form in nouns for showing the distinction between one and many, but in pronouns the dimension always exists. A number of African languages reportedly have no inflection to indicate the plural of nouns; these languages include Berta, Malagasy, Uduk, Koma, and some Mande and Kwa languages such as Yoruba. In Yoruba, however, the plural can be indicated by using the word for *they* before the noun; this might be considered an inflection. Similarly in Ewe, the plural affix is really a suffixed *they*. As a matter of fact many other languages throughout the continent seem to have a plural marker derived from the pronoun form for *they,* or at least related to it.

Very rarely does a distinction between singular, dual (two), and plural (more than two) numbers occur in African languages. In the Ancient Egyptian of the Old Kingdom and in Classical Arabic such a three-fold set-up existed for nouns, adjectives, and pronouns, and this may represent the original Afro-Asiatic pattern. By the Middle Kingdom, dual pronouns (*we two, you two, they two*) had become archaic in Egyptian, resulting in the unusual situation where nouns have more overt number distinctions than pronouns (more frequently it is the other way round). In modern Arabic, the dual has been dropped entirely, except in

Figure 7   SHONA WITH SUNKEN UPPER LIP

Chief Sikalenge, a Tonga speaker of Shona from Zambia, with a jut-jawed appearance caused by the extraction of the upper front teeth.

certain set phrases. In Kunama, a Nilo-Saharan language spoken in the Sudan Republic near the Afro-Asiatic languages just mentioned, pronouns have singular, dual, and plural, but the noun has only singular and plural forms. In other Nilo-Saharan languages, such a three-way pattern does not seem to occur. Nor does it occur in any of the Niger-Kordofanian languages where, as P.W. Schmidt suggests, the frequent presence of rather numerous gender classes would have produced a fairly involved and complicated morphology if more than a singular-plural dimension existed. Only in members of the Khoisan phylum do we find at present a consistent three-way number set-up for nouns and pronouns in African languages, as is true of Nama Hottentot and Naron Bushman. As a matter of fact, a four-fold division has been reported for some varieties of Bushman; singular-dual-trial (three)—plural (more than three): apparently a unique instance of a trial anywhere in Africa. The trial is rare everywhere in the world except in Melanesia and Polynesia. The most complicated number system with a five-fold division, including a quadrual (four), is reported for Marshalese in the Pacific but does not occur at all in Africa.

We have already discussed in part the feature of gender in African languages. As a rule, gender distinctions are overtly marked in pronouns only in the third person, i.e. in pronouns corresponding to English *he, she, it, they.* Sometimes nouns are not overtly marked for gender, but pronouns are, as in Sandawe, where special masculine and feminine pronouns exist in both singular and plural, but the nouns have no special gender affixes. Only in languages with a masculine-feminine distinction do non-third person pronouns show gender, but not all in the same way. In Afro-Asiatic there is normally a *you masculine* and *you feminine*, but only in the singular. In various Khoisan languages, the distinction occurs also in the plural. Gender in the first person is exceedingly rare in worldwide distribution. In Nama Hottentot, it occurs in the dual and plural only, so that we find forms that can be glossed as *I, we two masculine, we two feminine, we plural masculine, we plural feminine*—five pronouns for English two. The only language in Africa to my knowledge with *I masculine* and *I feminine* is Tuareg, which is Afro-Asiatic.

In a great many African languages, a distinction is made between a form of *we* that includes the person spoken to (the INCLUSIVE), as opposed to an EXCLUSIVE *we* that omits the person spoken to. The distinction is found in all the major language groupings in Africa, e.g. in Lendu, Fulani, Shilluk, Somali, Hottentot. In form, the two pronouns may be totally unrelated; e.g. Ndogo *ze* exclusive, **ndɔ** inclusive.

A third dimension of inflection is case. All languages work in terms of relationships such as subject, object, possessor; but the way these relationships are realized entails considerable variation. Mere position in a sentence may be enough, as in most instances in Bantu and many Western Sudanic languages; or else prepositions or postpositions may be employed. For the present discussion, the term "case" will apply only if there is some overt mark in the noun or pronoun, by means of affixes or internal changes.

The major groups of African languages where case systems occur are the Kushitic, Semitic, Kanuric, and a few Eastern Sudanic languages. Case systems in African languages appear to be either of the accusative type—where one case is used for the subject of any sort of verb, while a second is used for the object of a transitive verb (as in Latin or German)—, or the nominative type—where a single case appears in both positions but other cases also exist. Ergative systems reported for Eskimo and Georgian, where one form is used as the subject of an intransitive verb and the object of a transitive verb, while another form is used for the subject of a transitive verb, have not been reported for any African language to my knowledge.

In Nuer (Eastern Sudanic) three, possibly four, noun cases are reported, but there seems to be no true parallel for the pronouns. The cases are generally marked by internal change; e.g. lêp *tongue* (nominative), lɛ̀àb (genitive), lɛ̀b (locative). Some nouns have a distinctive accusative form as well, but usually this is identical with the nominative. Formation would seem to be quite complicated from published accounts and although certain patterns are discernable, they are not readily predictable.

In most of the so-called Nilo-Hamitic languages, there are two cases usually marked by tonal differences only: nominative and accusative. Maasai examples include the following.[4]

	NOMINATIVE	ACCUSATIVE
woman	enkítòk	enkitók
girl	entíto	entitó
horse	ɛmbartá	ɛmbártá
giraffe	ɔlmɛ́ɷt	ɔlmɛɷ́t
ɛ́dɔ́l enkítòk	*the woman sees (him)*	
ɛ́dɔ́l enkitók	*he sees the woman*	

Some nouns also distinguish a special locative form. As a matter of fact, in several languages with no other cases, special locative forms are sometimes found. This holds true of Hausa, where one can hardly speak of a locative case because of the haphazard formation and rarity of such forms. The "locative" of cíkìi *belly* is cíkí; of ɗáakìi *room*, ɗákà; of kây *head*, káa.

In Kushitic, a three-case system (nominative, genitive, accusative) is common, but for Bilin and Awiya seven cases are reported, labeled: nominative, genitive, dative, accusative, ablative, comitative, directive.

In the Kanuric languages a problem of interpretation exists. The borderline there between case suffixes and independent postpositions appears hazy and authorities differ in interpretation. One difficulty is the fact that the "suffixes" can be used at the end of phrases rather than nouns. In a possessive phrase, which has a possessed-possessor order, the case ending that would otherwise have been suffixed to the noun denoting the possessor is tacked on to the end of the whole phrase, after the genitive suffix of the possessor; e.g. **tátà kámú-bègá rúskɔ̀nà** *I saw* (**rúskɔ̀na**) *the son* (**tátà**) *of the woman* (**kámú**)—rather than ***tátà-gà kámú-bè.** . . The problem is, of course, fairly trivial, but points up the arbitrariness of the classification attempted. Similar constructions are reported from Nubian and some other African languages, not to speak of English where we find *the king of England's crown* rather then ******the king's of England crown* (earlier usage required *the king's crown of England*).

In point of fact, possessive phrases with the possessed-possessor order often pose a number of problems of interpretation. Quite frequently, the first item has a different form from its corresponding citation (or absolute) form. In Luo, for example, the word **lɛ́·p** *tongue* (cf. Nuer **lɛ̀b**, above) has the form **lɛ́w** when functioning as the possessed or APPERTENTIVE noun: **lɛ́w dà·nɔ̀** *tongue-of person*. The form **lɛ́w** never occurs in isolation. In classical Arabic a similar situation obtains: a noun in isolation is either definite and preceded by the article **ʔal** *the*, or indefinite and followed by **-n**; e.g. **ʔal-baytu** *the house*, **baytu-n** *a house*. As the appertentive noun, both are dropped: **baytu Muħammadin** *Mohammed's house*. In both Luo and Arabic constructions no additional word (for example, an adjective) can intervene between the possessed and possessor, and this suggests that we may really be dealing with compound nouns with morphophonemic alternations rather than inflection for case. The situation is, however, somewhat more complicated than described here and open to a number of interpretations.

Some languages with the same ordering within the possessive phrase have solved the problem of how to modify an appertentive noun. In Arabic, the construction just mentioned could not be used at all if we wanted to say *Mohammed's* BIG *house*; another way of saying it would have to be found. In Luo, a certain ambiguity would arise since the corresponding phrase could mean either *Mohammed's big house* or *big Mohammed's house*. In Chadic and Bantu the solution is to use some sort of recapitulatory element, or pleonastic pronoun, to stand for the appertentive noun. The phrase would then literally be *house (big) it-of Mohammed*. This sort of construction is the mirror image of an earlier English construction found in prayers: *for Jesus Christ HIS sake,* and still common in colloquial Dutch (e.g. **de jongen ·z'n mes** the boy's knife) and west-country Norwegian (**gutten sin kniv**). In Swahili, the comparable example would be **kisu ki-a** (written **cha**) **kijana** (kisu *knife*, kijana *boy*). Here the **ki-a** involves a pronominal stem plus the appertentive marker **-a**. In an influential model of

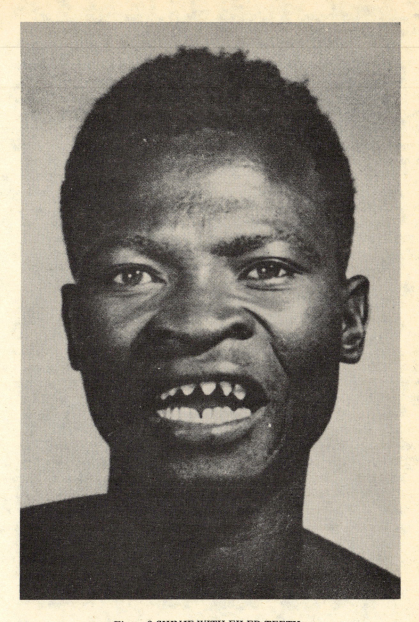

Figure 8 SHINJE WITH FILED TEETH

A man from Angola with one of many possible styles of filed teeth popular among Central Bantu-speaking peoples.

Bantu grammar proposed by C.M. Doke,[5] the **ki-a** is considered as an inflection of **kijana** and would be written solid with it, even though other words can intervene.

One characteristic of nouns (and occasionally of verbs as well) among certain West Atlantic languages of the Niger-Kordofanian group has occasioned a good deal of discussion. This is the alternation in the initial consonant of stems for no obvious phonological reason, a phenomenon known as PERMUTATION, an example of the more general sound change known as ABLAUT (like the vowel changes in *sing-sang-sung*). The consonant changes in the West Atlantic languages can be organized into certain series. Thus, in Fulani, there is a d-r-nd series, so that a particular noun or verb stem with d- in some instances will have alternates r- or nd- in others; e.g. **rawaa-ndu** *dog* (with r-), **dawaa-di** *dogs* (with d-); **dawa-ŋgel** (with d-) *small dog*, **ndawa-kon** *small dogs,* (with nd-). In Fulani other series of this type include; b-w-mb, g-w(or y)-ŋg, k-h-k, etc. Similar systems are reported for Serer, Wolof, Biafada, Kpelle, Konyagi, Pajade, Tanda, Cobiana, Cassanga, Banyun, although details differ and in some languages such alternations are only sporadic and no longer productive.

The eminent scholar Carl Meinhof thought that the permutations found in Fulani nouns actually constituted a noun class system independent of the 20 or so classes based on suffixes. According to Meinhof,[6] there was a basic personal-nonpersonal bifurcation that could be established in this way: nouns denoting persons have stops in the singular and spirants in the plural, and nouns denoting things, spirants in the singular and stops in the plural. For example, **pul-o** *a Fulani person* pl. **ful-ɓe** (p-f), but **faɗ-o** *shoe* pl. **paɗ-e** (f-p). He further posited, somewhat gratuitously, that these personal-nonpersonal classes had survived from a fairly early and similar kind of division, which later on developed into the masculine-feminine categories of languages related to Fulani—and these languages he thought were Afro-Asiatic. Meinhof seems to have been wrong on all counts—not only on linguistic affiliation (Fulani is Niger-Kordofanian, not Afro-Asiatic), but also on the nature of permutation. Klingenheben[7] later demonstrated conclusively that the particular grade (stop, spirant, prenasalized stop) of the initial consonant of a noun is predictable from the suffix; e.g. the suffix **-kon** requires the prenasalized grade. Since all the suffixes that end on -1 require the stop grade, and the **-dam** and **-kon** suffixes ending on a nasal require the prenasalized stop grade, it may well be that the present-day sufixes were once independent words or clitics that preceded the noun modified, and that the permutations were originally nothing more than straightforward morphophonemic alternations.

In those languages where adjectives do not morphologically constitute a subgroup of verbs, as in Yoruba and Kongo, they are often practically indistinguishable in form from nouns. Special comparative degrees of adjectives (e.g. *tall-*

taller-tallest) are, apart from Semitic, unknown in African languages, so that this difference with nouns does not exist. Of course, in languages where adjectives show formal agreement with nouns, the noun will possess an inherent gender and the adjective a derived one. In Bantu languages, one formal distinction is the fact that nouns may have more than one prefix, but adjectives never have. Consider the following examples from Swahili: **m-ti** *tree*, **ji-m-ti** *large tree* (augmentative), **ki-ji-m-ti** *small tree* (diminutive), **ji-ji-m-ti** *very large tree,* **ki-ji-ji-m-ti** *very small tree*. The adjective that modifies these forms will have only one prefix, and that identical with the prefix farthest to the left of the noun stem (apart from morphophonemic alternations); **m-ti m-zuri** *beautiful tree*, **ki-ji-ji-m-ti ki-zuri** *very small beautiful tree,* etc.

In languages as diverse as Chadic and southern Bantu, an adjectival phrase such as *the tall boy* boy may be construed in a way that is identical with a possessive phrase. A literal rendering of the construction as found in Karanga, Yao, and Nyanja is: *boy he-of tall* (NOT *tallness*). In Hausa, a slightly different form is assumed: *tall-of boy*, (**dóogó-n yáaròo**) in effect the reverse of the Bantu construction. To my knowledge, such an idiom is found only in Africa, but a limited European parallel may perhaps be found in French **quelque chose de merveilleux** *something (of) marvelous.*

The dimensions of the verb and characteristics of the verb phrase are somewhat less easily sketched because of considerable variation as well as divergent analysis.

In perhaps the majority of African languages the verbal phrase shows agreement with its subject and sometimes also with an object. In Nubian, subject agreement is shown by suffix: **kab-ir** *I eat*, **kab-nam** *you* (sg) *eat*, **kab-in** *he/she eats;* in Zande by prefix: **mì-na-máŋgà** *I do,* **mɔ̀-na-máŋgà** *you* (sg) *do,* etc.; in Kanuri by suffix, but by prefix in the third person in some tenses, and normally by no agreement marker at all for the singular. Zero markers in the third person singular are the rule for Malagasy and in some forms in Arabic as well as other languages.

When the subject agreement element precedes the verb stem, tense or aspect particles usually intervene; thus, in the Zande example **mì-na-máŋgà**, the -na- is an element that means "present tense", or the like. Compare the parallel form in Swahili **ni-na-fanya** (I-present-do), and in Hausa **í-nàa yîi** with the same order.

The proximity of the subject prefix and a tense or aspect morpheme has often led to a coalescence of the two. In some instances, the word boundaries are unclear and a few proposals have been made for setting up the subject marker as a separate pronoun, as in Hausa, with the result that pronouns would in effect be inflected for tense or aspect rather than the verb. In Hausa we find the following: **yáa** *he (perfective)*, **yâa** *he (potential)*, **yá** *he (consecutive)*, **yà** *he (subjunctive)*. In Mende, much the same sort of thing has been reported, and the following forms occur for *I*: ŋgá (*future*), ngí (*past*), ŋgàá (*potential*). Similarly in Luo, where, however, contraction remains optional in some cases and the tense/aspect particle precedes the subject marker; e.g. á ríŋgɔ̀ *I'm running*, à rîŋgɔ̀ *I ran*, â· rîŋgɔ̀ *I have just run*. The latter is clearly a contraction of âa à rîŋgɔ̀ ; *he has just run* is, uncontracted, âa ɔ̀ rîŋgɔ̀, contracted ɔ̂· rîŋgɔ̀. In the plural, however, contraction is blocked because the subject pronoun begins with a consonant, or did until quite recently: âa gì ríŋgɔ̀ ; *gî- ríŋgɔ̀ does not occur. Interestingly, in the speech of children the *you pl* form, which until recently was probably *wu but which become u, is often made to contract although adults reject this as a mistake.

In many African languages, verbs fall into morphological classes not unlike the conjugations of Latin or Greek. In Hausa, for example, three regular classes of transitive verb occur, which can be defined in terms of the tones of the stem. Furthermore, members of these classes take special endings depending on what kind of object follows; thus, in the perfective, the following scheme applies:

	I. HIGH–LOW	II. LOW–HIGH	III. HIGH–HIGH
No object	káɽyàa *break*	hàrbá *kick, shoot*	bíyáa *pay*
Noun object	káɽyà	hàrbí	bíyáa
Pronoun object	káɽyàa	hàrbée	bíyáa

Such a pattern is not typical for African "conjugational" languages or others: verbs are normally invariable for objects.

With regard to tenses or aspects and other similar dimensions of verb inflection, we may note as a minimum: a command form (imperative), and at least two distinctions of manner or state (aspect): completed vs. incompleted, usually termed perfective vs. imperfective (or continuous), respectively; or three distinctions of time (tense): past, present, future. In addition to these, a special form normally occurs in wishes and various dependent clauses (often called a subjunctive). The morphological resources of particular languages vary enormously. In modern Egyptian Arabic, we find basically the minimal scheme described above: imperative, perfective, imperfective, and subjunctive. On the other hand in many Bantu languages the tense-division is expanded enormously to include remote past, immediate past, habitual past, present, habitual, immediate future, remote future, habitual future—in addition to subjunctive, imperative, and sometimes other forms variously labeled as progressive, potential, etc. In addition, corresponding negative forms may require special inflection, as in the following Zulu example.[8]

	POSITIVE		NEGATIVE
Remote past	ngahamba	*I traveled*	angihambanga
Immed. past	ngihambile		
Present	ngiyahamba	*I travel*	angihambi
Immed. future	ngizokuhamba	*I shall travel*	angizukuhambi
Remote future	ngiyokuhamba		angiyukuhamba

In most African languages (except perhaps in various parts of West Africa), verb derivation is extensive and productive. A great many concepts are involved, such as motion towards the speaker, (e.g. *come, bring*), motion away from speaker, (*go, take*), causative (*teach*, i.e. cause to learn), neuter or stative (*be broken*, i.e. be in a broken state), reversive (*undo*, reversive of *do*), inceptive (*begin to do*), passive, benefactive (or applied), etc. In English, one sometimes finds traces of similar formations (e.g. *to fell* as the causative of *to fall*, meaning *to cause to fall*), but they are sporadic and nonproductive. Examples of such derivatives can, however, be found throughout the languages of the continent.

Teso:[9]

ai-ŋɛdɛ	*to cut*
aɪ-ŋɛd-ɔ̀nì	*to cut towards* (motion towards)
a-ŋɛd-àrì	*to cut away* (motion away)
a-ŋɛd-akìnì	*to cut for* (benefactive)
a-ŋɛd-ià	*to cut with* (instrumental)
a-ŋɛd-a	*to be cut* (neuter) or *to cut oneself* (reflexive)

Swahili:

ku-pig-a	*to beat*
ku-pig-w-a	*to be beaten* (passive)
ku-pig-ish-a	*to cause to beat, flap* (causative)
ku-pig-an-a	*to beat each other, fight* (reciprocal)
ku-pig-ik-a	*to be beaten* (neuter)
ku-pig-i-a	*to beat for* (benefactive)

Combinations of affixes are usually tolerated and fairly extensive; e.g. Swahili **ku-pig-an-ish-a** *to cause to fight* (causative of reciprocal), **ku-pig-an-i-w-a** *to be fought for* (passive [-w-], of reciprocal [-an-], of benefactive [-i-]).

The discussion so far has been restricted to the development of words from a single stem with the same part of speech, e.g. the creation of verbs from a verb stem. For all languages where adequate information is available, derivation can cut across word classes so that nouns and verbs can be produced from a common stem. At a minimum, languages usually have productive patterns for producing agent nouns (meaning someone who does what is implied in the stem, e.g. *baker*), verbal nouns (*baking*), and adjectival abstract nouns (*goodness*). In Bantu, derivation is extraordinarily productive, and the mechanism of it usually transparent (one of the reasons, perhaps, why the study of Bantu languages is almost invariably found to be delightful). In Swahili, for example, we find based on a stem -**chez**-: **ku-chez-a** *to play*, **m-chez-i** *player*, **m-chez-aji** *habitual or skilled player*, **chez-o** or **m-chez-o** *game, sport*; similarly from -**sahau**- **ku-sahau** *to forget*, **m-sahau** *forgetful person*, -**sahau** -**lifu** *forgetful*, **u-sahau** -**lifu** *forgetfulness*.

From examples such as these, it should be clear that African languages need leave no one tongue-tied, and that they have ample resources for creating new words appropriate to the new life styles impinging on African cultures.

Notes and References

An interesting, but by now outdated, study of the world-wide distribution of various morphological distinctions is given in P.W. Schmidt, 1926, *Die Sprachfamilien und Sprachenkreise der Erde*, Heidelberg.

1) The Proto-Bantu forms are reconstructions from comparative data. The **m-** in the o *human* column is a Bantu innovation. The examples are for the most part taken from Diedrich Westermann, 1927, *Die westlichen Sudansprachen und ihre Beziehungen zum Bantu (Mitteilungen des Seminars für orientalische Sprachen* 30), Berlin.
2) *Languages of West Africa* (1952), p. 71.
3) Reduplication in Ewe, *Journal of African Languages* (1963), p. 128.
4) The examples are taken from A.N. Tucker and J. Tompo Ole Mpaayei, 1955, *A Maasai grammar*, London.
5) This model is presented in a number of grammers of particular languages, but may perhaps most easily be seen in his *The southern Bantu languages* (1954), Oxford. See also his *Bantu linguistic terminology* (1935), London.
6) As presented in his *Die Sprachen der Hamiten* (1912), Hamburg.
7) A. Klingenheben, 1923–4, Die Präfixklassen des Ful, *Zeitschrift für Eingeborenensprachen* **14**, 189–222, 290–315.
8) Doke, 1954, p. 107.
9) The Teso examples are taken from A.N. Tucker and M.A. Bryan, 1966, *Linguistic analyses: The non-Bantu Languages of northeastern Africa*, Oxford, p. 451.

Part Three   HISTORICAL PERSPECTIVES

CHAPTER VII

Historical Linguistics and Language Classification

In every normal speech community, grandparents can speak with their grand-children and be understood without difficulty—at least in some senses! The same would undoubtedly be true of great-grandparents and their great-grand-children, and perhaps—with populations of unusual longevity or highly developed mechanical devices such as tape recorders—even more generations. Of course, these are recorded instances of peoples who have lost their own language and taken up another, as witness the Gauls in France who acquired Latin. This seems to have been the case also with the Hima of Uganda, who are presumed to have spoken a Nilotic language at one time, and given it up entirely for a Bantu one. But for the present discussion, we shall assume continuity in the speech community.

Despite the possibility of communication across generations, language clearly and ineluctably changes even over a fairly short span of time. In England, for example, a great many traditional pronunciations have recently become old fashioned or even obsolete; e.g. *clothes* was formerly always /klowz/, and now is almost always /klowðz/; *soon* and *tooth* were /sun/, /tuθ/; *toward* /tohd/ now /təˈwohd/, *vase* /vohz/ now /vahz/, etc. Almost all of these are spelling pronunciations, i.e., attempts to approximate the written form more closely in pronunciation. Changes of this sort, bound as they are to a firm written tradition, have few parallels in African languages understandably enough, but the remarkable thing is that orthographies recently introduced should have had any influence at all. Tucker notes that in Moru, the established spelling sometimes represents ky and gy by c and j, which normally stand for tsw and dzw. He goes on to say that "I have found that the spellings *kuci*, *koce*, *ji*, and *je* were actually responsible for a growing 'school-boy' pronunciation kutsʷi, kɔtsʷɛ, dzʷi, and dzʷe at the Mission, instead of the traditional pronunciation kukyi, kɔkyɛ, gyi, and gyɛ".[1]

Another kind of change has swept the English speaking world. Owing to the recent introduction of the "restored" pronunciation of Latin and Greek, a considerable number of traditional pronunciations have been lost or are competing with modern puristic and often inconsistent pronunciations; e.g. *a priori* /ey pray'ohray/, newer /ah pri'ohri/; *alumnae* /ə'lʌmniy/, newer /ə'lʌmnay/; *spontaneity* /spontə'niyiti/, *newer* /spontə'neyiti/.

In West Africa, among groups that have been Islamized for many centuries a similar phenomenon has occurred: Arabic words once borrowed from colloquial forms and subject to various changes over the years are competing with forms more nearly in accord with the classical written norm. Thus, in Hausa, we find the doublets càsà?ín (older) - tìs?ín (newer) *ninety* (Arabic tis?in); àlƙáalíi *judge* (Arabic (al)-qaaẓiy-; ƙ has now been adopted to render Arabic q); in Kanuri làvâr-havâr *news* (Arabic al-xabar; the l in the first form represented the al-, and the 1x cluster was simplified).

Much more important changes occur universally: phonemes may be realized differently; phonemic contrasts may be lost or phonemes may split; words may be dropped from the vocabulary, new words created; grammatical structures may alter, etc. All of these are attested in languages with written records. By extrapolation, we must assume that languages lacking such documentation underwent the same kinds of change. One of the goals of linguistics is the reconstruction of former stages of particular languages. Two complementary techniques have been devised for accomplishing such a task: (1) internal reconstruction, and (2) the comparative method.

Internal reconstruction assumes in part that irregular or skewed forms may be the descendants of more regular ones. In English, for example, we can account for the present day allomorphs of the plural (-ez, -s, -z as in *watches*, *books*, *dogs*) if we posit that at an earlier stage there was a single ending, say -ez, and that the -e- was dropped in all positions except after sibilants (s z ʃ ʒ), and that the remaining consonant was modified by the preceding sound. In short, we posit a single allomorph instead of three and invoke plausible sound changes to take care of the contemporary facts. The reconstruction in this instance cannot be too wrong in light of the fact that earlier written forms of English shows spellings such as *dogges* for *dogs*, presumably with an -e- that was pronounced.

Many similar examples can be drawn from African languages. Consider one from Swahili. There, as we have already seen, adjectives agree with the nouns they modify and agreement normally involves mere repetition of the noun prefix: **vi-tabu vi-zuri vy-eupe** *beautiful* (**-zuri**) *white* (**-eupe**) *books* (**vitabu**), the vi- becomes vy before a vowel. With another class of noun we find a much more complicated set up:

n-goma	*drum*	ny-eupe	*white*
		n-zuri	*beautiful*
		m-baya	*bad*
		kubwa	*big*

Other nouns of this class include: **m-boga** *vegetable*, **chupa** *bottle*, **tundu** *hole*, **kuku** *chicken*, **paa** *gazelle*. The simplest way to account for both noun and adjective prefixes is to posit an original prefix ***ni-** for all the forms. Before a stem beginning with a vowel, the i became y: **ny-eupe** (cf. **vi** and **vy**: **vyeupe**). Before a consonant, the i was dropped, thus **n-goma, n-zuri**. Before a b, the n became m: **m-boga, m-baya**. Before a voiceless consonant, the n disappeared: **chupa, tundu, kuku, paa , kubwa**.

The validity of such a reconstruction rests on the plausibility of the sound changes posited based on what we know about developments historically attested in other languages. Furthermore, languages that are related to Swahili but did not undergo the same changes (although they underwent others) also tend to support such reconstructions; in Ganda the word related to Swahili **kuku** is **(e-)nkókó**, in Kikuyu **ngókó**, in Shambala **ngúkú**—all with the anticipated n.

Another example of internal reconstruction, again from Swahili, is somewhat different. The stem of the verb **pika** *cook* is **-pik-**. In the present negative we find **ha-pik-i** *he doesn't cook*, with the k of the stem maintained before final -i. But in the corresponding agent noun, the k changes to ʃ (sh) before an i: **m-pish-i** (*a*) *cook*. An examination of negative and agent nouns in general shows an underlying rule: k before negative -i remains unchanged, but before agent -i becomes ʃ. The simplest reconstruction seems to be that there were originally two i's, which we can call i_1 and i_2, one that modified preceding k's and one that left them unchanged. Again information from related languages supports this particular reconstruction. Swahili has five vowels (i e a o u); the related Kikuya has seven (i e ɛ a ɔ o u). Normally, wherever we set up i_1 for Swahili, we discover that Kikuyu has i, but for i_2 Kikuyu shows e (by the same token there are two u's in Swahili). We must conclude that originally Swahili also had a seven vowel system like the Kikuyu one, and that in modern Swahili, the high vowels have coalesced:

$$
\left.\begin{array}{cc} \text{i} & \text{u} \\ \text{e} & \text{o} \\ \varepsilon & \mathirm{ɔ} \end{array}\right\} \longrightarrow \begin{array}{cc} \text{i} & \text{u} \\ \\ \text{e} & \text{o} \end{array}
$$

$$ \text{a} \qquad\qquad\qquad \text{a} $$

Proto - Swahili   Contemporary Swahili

In neither of these reconstructions were written records available to corroborate hypotheses. Indeed, even for languages with written records of considerable antiquity such as Egyptian, Nubian, and Semitic, fairly few reconstructed changes can be attested because the records are simply not old enough. For example, in Kongo and neighboring languages, an l changed to n when preceded by another n or m (cf. **teka** *to sell,* **tek-ele** *sold*, but **lêma** *to burn*, **lêm-ene** *burnt* for presumably earlier ***lem-ele**). On the face of it the change seems quite a low-level one and probably recent. Nevertheless our earliest records of Kongo (from the sixteenth century) show that the change had been completed by that time.

Throughout our discussion so far we have referred to corroborative evidence from "related" languages, without defining the term "related". By definition, languages are related if they are the divergent continuations of a single language spoken at an earlier time. We are all familiar with the statement that French, Italian, Spanish, Roumanian,—and Ladin (spoken in Switzerland)—are related and are really descended from Latin. This implies that if we were to trace each language back in time, we would find increasing similarities until finally we would be dealing with a single language.

When languages are known to have developed out of a common ancestral language they are said to be GENETICALLY related. The ancestral language is usually referred to as the PROTO-language (by some, Ur- is used instead of proto-; thus, Urbantu instead of Proto-Bantu). The languages derived from this are said to be its daughter languages, and the degrees of interrelatedness are often described by using the metaphor of a family tree (*Stammbaum*). Such kinship allusions are misleading, however; instead of a parent-child relationship, the situation can more accurately be likened to the life history of an amoeba experiencing fission (and extinction) at various times.

Even today, because of the enormous store of shared elements and constructions that constitute an inheritance from their common source, related languages display a great many unique and systematic correspondences setting them off as a natural group distinct from all the other languages of the world. Compare the following forms (given in phonemic transcription rather than in the official orthography).

	Italian	Spanish	Roumanian	Ladin	French
nose	'naso	'naso	nas	nas	ne(z)
head	'kapo	'kabo	kap	caf	ʃef
goat	'kapra	'kabra	'kabrə	'cavra	ʃevr

Resemblances of this sort can hardly be due to chance. Borrowing from one language to another must probably also be ruled out because the words (particularly the first two) are so basic and learnt so early in life by a native speaker that a reason for borrowing would have to be quite unusual. The forms of the ancestral language are actually known in this instance (viz. Latin **naasum, kaput, kapram**—although our reconstruction would provide only *naso, *kapo, *kapra from the data available in the example—the asterisk indicating a hypothetical form), as well as intermediate forms, so that the plausibility of our reconstructions and arguments for reconstruction can be tested.

The obvious resemblances in forms such as these can be pinpointed more precisely by setting up sound correspondences. Thus, Italian k corresponds to

French ʃ in the examples; numerous other words can be found showing the same correspondence, e.g., Italian **'karo**—French ʃer (*cher*) *dear*, **kan'tare**—ʃāte (*chanter*) *sing*, **'kamera**—ʃābr (*chambre*) *room*. With details of this sort we can establish a technique for showing the relatedness of languages even in the absence of written records. This technique is the COMPARATIVE METHOD. It requires that regular sound correspondences (by tradition, in at least three items for every sound) be set up in the vocabulary that was probably shared by the putative ancestral language (this rules out culture-specific vocabulary items such as *television* and *cocktail*, and in some areas even *cow* and *table*).

In closely related languages—that is, languages that have recently diverged from the common ancestral language—correspondences are often transparent. Consider the following examples from Bantu languages.

	Swahili	Zulu	Duala	Pedi
send	tuma	t^{h}uma	loma	roma
three	tatu	t^{h}at^{h}u	lalo	raro
cheek	tama	t^{h}ama	lama	rama

Reconstruction of putative ancestral forms involves nothing more, really, than stringing together formulas of correspondence. In the Bantu example chosen there are a number of obvious correspondences.

1.	t	t^h	l	r
2.	u	u	o	o
3.	m	m	m	m
4.	a	a	a	a

In formulas of correspondence, symbols are used that suggest the actual phonemes of the daughter languages; thus, series 3 and 4 of the example would undoubtedly be shown as *m and *a by all linguists since no other values occur. For series 1 and 2, however, the answer is not so clear even from the restricted data. If only this information were in fact available, any symbol chosen from each series would do; series 2 could be either *u or *o. But in the total context, the choices may be much more restricted. For 2, for example, we must take into consideration the fact that Pedi has 7 vowels and Swahili 5, but that in Swahili—as internal reconstruction has already indicated—u represents two originally different vowels. Indeed, the Swahili-Pedi correspondence u-o given here must be contrasted with another series u-u as in Swahili **fumo**-Pedi **(le-)rumɔ** *spear*; Swahili **fuma** *sew*—Pedi **ruma** *hem*. Hence, an appropriate symbol for 2 would be *o, not *u.

Of course, the data can be enormously complicated. Even the introduction of *spear* and *sew/hem* into our minuscule corpus introduces an f-r correspondence that at first sight contrasts with the t-r correspondence set up before. An examination of the total data reveals that t never occurs in Swahili before an u corresponding to Pedi u, but t does occur before an o corresponding to Pedi o: Proto-Bantu *to became tu in Swahili, but *tu developed into fu — most likely with an intermediate stage *θu (cf. Cockney *fing* for *thing*/θiŋ/). Consequently, f-r and t-r do not contrast but represent a splitting of a single original phoneme *t. A phonemic reanalysis of reconstructed elements should theoretically catch and solve problems of this sort.

In technical jargon, the realizations in a daughter language of a phoneme in the protolanguage are the REFLEXES of that phoneme: Swahili t and f are both reflexes of Proto-Bantu *t; in Pedi, the main reflex is r. It should be clear enough that a considerable range of change is possible for a phoneme so that its reflexes may be quite different, and related words (technically, COGNATES) may not look alike at all. Thus, Hausa **súunáa** and Tera **ɓəm** *name* are almost certainly cognates, as are **sáywaa** and **ɓər** *root* from the same languages.[2] Nor are examples such as these extreme if we compare them to a correspondence accepted as legitimate by all knowledgeable scholars in the Indo-European field, viz., Armenian erk—and Greek dw—as in Armenian **erkar**, Greek **d(w)aar-ón** *long* etc. Clearly, systematic correspondence, not occasional identity of elements, is the crucial point here. The fact that in Nile Nubian the pronunciation of the word for *I* is virtually the same as in English (**ay**) proves nothing with regard to the relationship of English and Nubian.

Although an enormous range of change is possible, some changes are more likely than others and have occurred time and time again in various languages throughout the world. Thus, either t d or k g may become c j respectively before vowels like i or e—sometimes one, sometimes the other. In Kanuri (as well as Latin), it was k g that changed. In Hausa, spoken by a neighboring people, it was t d. In yet another neighboring language, Songhai, both t d and k g have changed (but whether the pairs have actually coalesced to a single pair c j is not clear from published accounts). In general, sounds tend to become similar to or even identical with adjacent sounds. The combination mb for example, so common in African languages, may have developed from n + (vowel) + b, as in the Swahili form **mbaya** quoted before (presumably from *nibaya , with loss of i): here, an alveolar-labial combination has been changed to a labial-labial one. Sequences of sounds tend to be reduced or simplified. In many languages we find diphthongs of the type ai changed to e, as in colloquial Arabic, Swahili, Hausa, and Italian. Double stops and the like seem generally to represent the reduction of a syllable type CVC (cf. frequent pronunciations in English of *believe* or *police* with bl-, pl-). This seems to be true for Margi, as substantiated by comparative evidence: Margi **bɓə**—Tera **bəɓə** *forge*, Margi **p̂cu**—Ga'anda **fice**. Since the intervening vowel may vary unpredictably in the non-Margi forms, it is easier to reconstruct a protoform with a vowel and posit the loss of it rather than the other way round. Incidentally, in "careless" Margi, the double consonants are themselves reduced: p̂tal *chief* is frequently pronounced as **tal** (cf. Ga'anda **kutira**; the expected *k̂t apparantly having merged with p̂t).[3] The general effect of all these sound changes is towards a simplification of the movements that make up the utterance of any given linguistic form. Some linguists have tried to account for most instances of sound change in terms of a principle of least effort, and Martinet has suggested that language communities undergo periods with varying degrees of laxity of pronunciation. Of course, some sound changes seem not to fit into this pattern; e.g., when the position of phonemes are reversed in a word (in META-THESIS), as Swahili **paka**—Ganda **kkapa** *cat* or the use of a form **mel**, etc., in various West Atlantic languages, whereas elsewhere in Niger-Kordofanian we find **lem** or similar forms for *tongue*. Whatever the cause, it is clear that a variety of phonological changes is unavoidable in the long run.

Principles similar to the comparative method for phonology can be applied to morphology and syntax. But fairly little reconstruction of African languages has so far been attempted on any level. In the main, Africanists have hitherto forgone reconstruction to establish first of all the facts of relationship between languages.

All languages can be classified unambiguously and nonarbitrarily in terms of genetic relationship. Of course, they can be classified by any number of other criteria, and we have already had occasion to do so when we spoke of tone languages, languages with seven vowel systems, gender languages, languages with a basic word order SOV, etc. The number of criteria could be enlarged and an exhaustive classification developed. But such a classification would be arbitrary in the sense that any criterion or combination of criteria might be used with consistent, but not equivalent results. Classifications of this kind are typological. A crucial point to bear in mind is that *typological classifications have no necessary historical implications*. As evidence for this assertion consider the following. English which is nontonal, is genetically related to Swedish, Lithuanian, and ancient Greek, which are tonal (in some sense). Conversely, Swahili, Lunyoro, and Nyakyusa are nontonal but genetically Bantu, most other members of which are tonal. Some dialects of English reportedly have only six phonemic vowels (i e a o u ə); others, at least nine (i e æ a ɔ o u i ə). Similarly, Dinka has something on the order of 15 vowels, the genetically related Luo only 9. English has no overt gender or case system for nouns, but German, which is genetically related, has both. The conclusion is inescapable: genetic and typological classifications deal with different orders of fact and must not be confused. It is somewhat surprising, therefore, to find prominent Africanists trying to "define" presumably genetic groupings by typological criteria. Malcolm Guthrie, one of the most prominent Bantuists of our time, has set up the following criteria for considering a language as Bantu (they are somewhat abbreviated here):

1) the presence of grammatical gender and concord indicated by prefixes

2) a vocabulary, part of which can be related by fixed rules to a set of hypothetical common roots

3) invariable stems from which words are built up by affixes

4) a 5 or 7 vowel system.[4]

Languages that meet some but not all of these criteria are considered as being incompletely Bantu. Languages that seem to meet criterion 1 but not 2, such as Batut spoken in Cameroun, are called Bantoid (it is not clear whether certain American Indian languages could not fit the definition of Bantoid). Languages that meet at least criterion 2, but not 1, such as Bira and Maŋgala, are called Sub-Bantu—of course, no value judgments are necessarily implied in these labels. Guthrie has chosen these criteria in part to accommodate a pan-Bantu grammatical model he has constructed. But his "Bantu" is an ad hoc grouping to start with, only partially genetic, and not consistently typological. A Bantu language in the genetic sense is one that can be shown to have developed from Proto-Bantu. To return to a more familiar situation: English is a Germanic language because it can be shown to have developed from Proto-Germanic. That English no longer has a noun case and gender system does not make it any less Germanic than German; it merely means that it is a Germanic language lacking these features. Quite frequently an imposing and significant list of characteristics shared by many genetically related languages can be drawn up, as Guthrie has partially done, but that is doing something quite different from DEFINING a genetic group in typological terms.

Such a mixture of methods has led to an issue that has received considerable attention in the Africanist field, but rarely elsewhere, namely the notion of a *Mischsprache* (literally, *mix[ed] language*). A controversy has developed focussing on the affiliation of the socalled Nilo-Hamitic languages: Maasai, Turkana, Teso, Bari, Lotuho, Kalenjin (Nandi and Kipsigi), and Päkot (Suk). According to the advocates of the Mischsprache theory, a language may be the lineal descendant of two proto-languages—in this particular instance, the daughter languages are in some sense both Nilotic and Hamitic (an older term designating Kushitic and usually also Ancient Egyptian and Berber). Since these in turn are subdivisions of two larger subgroupings, Nilo-Saharan and Afro-Asiatic, the ramifications of the Mischsprache hypothesis are indeed formidable here. To be sure, the term Nilo-Hamitic need not imply dual ancestry in the strict sense, some linguists arguing that they are basically "Hamitic" languages spoken near the Nile (as did Meinhof); others, that they are basically Nilotic but strongly Hamiticized (this seems to have been Westermann's view). A third position, long associated with A. N. Tucker and G. W. B. Huntingford, is that they really have mixed ancestry, otherwise it would be difficult to explain (a) the large number of basic vocabulary items shared with Nilotic languages, and (b) the large number of Kushitic-like affixes—especially reminiscent of Somali. This last position has now generally been abandoned for a somewhat vaguer one, viz., that both Nilo-Hamitic and Kushitic languages share a common substratum provided by an unknown language (or languages), the socalled T/K substratum. The facts, however, are reasonably clear. A considerable number of basic vocabulary items are shared by Nilotic and Nilo-Hamitic such as *child, die, drink, ear, eye, fire, four, go, heart, jaw, knee, leg, meat, milk, navel, neck, sing, small, split, stone, sun, tooth, two, urine, water, who?, with*. Subject pronouns are almost identical: Maasai **a-mat** *I drink*, **i-mat** *you drink*, **e-mat** *he/she/it drinks* parallel Lango **a-mato**, **i-mato**, and **e-mato** (or **o-mato**) with the same meanings respectively. As a matter of fact, the group traditionally labeled Nilo-Hamitic seems not even to comprise a unity co-equal with Nilotic, but may rather—as Köhler has suggested[5]—represent two groups, each of which is co-ordinate with Nilotic. We find, therefore, the following divisions using revised terminology: (1) Western Nilotic (Shilluk, Dinka, Nuer, Lango, Luo, Acoli, etc.; i.e., traditional Nilotic), (2) Eastern Nilotic (Bari, Maasai, Turkana, etc.); and (3) Southern Nilotic (Kalenjin, Päkot, Tatoga)—(2) and (3) representing traditional Nilo-Hamitic.

In light of these considerations it is difficult to understand why the Nilo-Hamitic controversy should ever have arisen. The reason must be, as suggested earlier, a confusion of typological with genetic classification. For example, "Nilotic" languages normally have a SVO order, Nilo-Hamitic normally VSO, which is associated with Afro-Asiatic in general but NOT with the crucial Kushitic group, where SVO is the rule. But even the unquestionably Nilotic language Nuer has a SVO order. Since Nuer is almost mutually intelligible with Dinka with VSO, this sort of argument falls short of being compelling. The most important reason for singling out a separate Nilo-Hamitic group is the presence there of masculine and feminine genders. Because of the relative rarity of such a dimension in African languages, and the occurrence of much the same features in neighboring Kushitic, this has been a major line of defense in the Mischsprache position. But even here the argument evaporates. In Nilo-Hamitic gender is not indicated in pronouns, but is in Kushitic. Maasai has a locative gender totally lacking in Kushitic. As for the affixes, the supposed similarities are tenuous at best. Never has an attempt been made to establish sound correspondences between Nilo-Hamitic and Kushitic in the affix system, let alone basic vocabulary, and the attempt does not look possible. In short the case for dual ancestry is pretty dismal.[6]

To my knowledge, only one language in the world even barely approaches a situation where core elements of a language (basic vocabulary and mor-phological elements) can be traced equally to two distinct protolanguages. This is Mbugu (Maʔa), spoken in south central Tanzania, which has been said to be both

Kushitic and Bantu. Greenberg classifies it as Southern Kushitic, along with Iraqw, Sanye, Mbulunge, and Mogogodo.[7] The classification is contested by others,[8] but these languages are clearly not Bantu whatever else they might be. In Mbugu we find a basically non-Bantu vocabulary, probably Kushitic, but also an obviously Bantu noun class and concord system. Thus, the word for *person* is **mu-hɛ**, plural **βa-hɛ**; for *tree*, **mu-xatu**. The stems are almost unquestionably related to Iraqw **hɛɛ** and **xaʔasno**, respectively, but the prefixes as well as the pronoun concords **a - βa**, and **u - i**, are clearly Bantu. But precisely how one should account for the Mbugu situation remains doubtful at present.[9]

No matter how arbitrary, typologies can prove useful and enlightening even if they have no genetic significance. The whole question of convergent development, for example, whereby genetically unrelated languages develop the same sort of structure (say gender systems) is a fascinating one and involves typological classification in the most legitimate way. Several comprehensive typological classifications exist but even the most prominent method, outlined below, has fallen into disuse in most contemporary linguistic work but still figures prominently in much Africanistic materials. In this system, first proposed by Friedrich von Schlegel and his brother A. W. Schlegel in the early nineteenth century, a tripartite typology is set up, each type defined by the usual relation in any given language of stem and affix. Languages with monosyllabic words and no affixes (this was the traditional description of Chinese) are ISOLATING. West African languages such as Ewe have usually, but erroneously, been put into this category. Languages where the boundaries between stems and affixes are clear-cut are AGGLUTINATING. Turkish and Swahili are cited as classic examples. Languages where the boundaries between the stem and affix merge or are hazy or where infixes and other internal changes of the stem occur are INFLECTIONAL. Latin and Greek are the usual examples, to which may certainly be added Amharic, Hausa, Nuer. The validity of such a scheme has encountered serious challenges. The isolating group, for example, may be just a fiction based on inaccurate word boundaries. As for the distinction between agglutinative and inflectional, a simple sound change could transform the first into the second. From the point of view of rigor, these categories fall flat, but as thumb-nail sketches of a total grammar, they are occasionally provocative. And they can suggest problem areas for the linguist.

For example, the recognition of genetic relationship among European languages was aided by the detailed similarities in the inflection of Latin, Greek, and Sanskrit. All three have a masculine-neuter genitive in -s and an accusative in -m or -n, etc.; this, in addition to obvious vocabulary resemblances involving fairly long words, validated setting up a language family despite the fact that sound correspondences had not fully been worked out. With "isolating" or nearly isolating languages such as Ewe and other West African examples, the establishment of sound correspondence is considerably rougher going.

Greenberg's use of mass comparison tries to overcome the problem of working with rigorous sound correspondences from the start, and is largely a formalization of a practical approach used in the very earliest attempts at classification. In essence, the method requires one to compare as many languages at a time as is feasible. For example, if we considered forms such as Dinka **yaŋ** and Maasai **ɛŋkitɛŋ** *cow* in isolation, we would probably be less willing to grant a possible relationship than if we were aware of forms in other relevant languages, such as **dyaŋ**, **kitɛŋ**, **nɛtɛŋ**, etc., whereby the Maasai **ɛŋ**-**ki**-elements prove to be affixes. Furthermore, use of mass comparison cuts down on setting up unwarranted cognates based on superficial resemblances. Thus, Nubian **ay** and English **ay** *I* become less plausible when further comparisons with other languages clearly related to English are considered: German **ix** (*ich*), Dutch **ik**, Swedish **yaag** (*jag*), etc. F. W. Parsons, in attempting to demonstrate the difficulties inherent in vocabulary comparison without rigorous sound correspondences, succeeded in compiling a list of superficial lexical resemblances between English (with the occasional aid of German) and Hausa; e.g., **hand-hannuu**, **lip-leeɓèe**, **kraft** (*strength*)-**karfii**.[10] But any relationship between English and Hausa would have to be a remote one, transcending Afro-Asiatic and Indo-European. And so, Hausa would have to show a more or less equal degree of similarity to other Indo-European languages as it does to English; and English in turn would have to show similar correspondences with Afro-Asiatic languages. But they don't.

In Greenberg's presentation of his classification of African languages, he merely presented a portion of the more plausible cognates culled from mass comparisons without spelling out the sound correspondences in most instances. He has been vigorously attacked for not doing so. It must be done some day but the kind of comparisons given are usually of such high quality that specification of sound correspondences will likely do little more than verify in all essentials Greenberg's classifications.

Degrees of genetic relationship exist. English is obviously closer to German than to Russian or Hindi, but all are Indo-European. Quite often it is easier to specify the fact of relationship without being able to pinpoint degree. This is not infrequently the case in Greenberg's present classification: The relationship between two subgroups within Niger-Kordofanian (Kwa and Benue-Kongo) has recently been questioned without questioning the validity of Niger-Kordofanian in the first place.

The criteria used in subgrouping are fairly straightforward, however. Obviously languages that share a greater number of cognates are genetically closer than those that share a lesser number. Furthermore, languages that share an innovation of any kind are closer than those that do not. A fairly telling example has been given by Greenberg in defense of his subgrouping of Bantu within

Niger-Kongo. As a general rule, within Niger-Kongo, the class affix of nouns denoting human beings is u or o, and the pronominal concord is generally the same. The pronoun form in Bantu follows suit, but the noun prefix itself has an initial m-. Since as a general rule, the pronoun is identical with the noun prefix in Bantu, the m-less forms are clearly earlier (a common Niger-Kongo retention), whereas the m-forms are innovations. Hence, Bantu cannot be co-ordinate with Western Sudanic languages as Westermann had supposed, but must be a subgroup of it.

Terminology in subgrouping is not completely standardized. A lower-level grouping is usually called a language FAMILY. The highest level grouping is called a PHYLUM, SUPERSTOCK, or even FAMILY. In the usual jargon, Zulu would be described as a language of the Bantu subdivision of the Benue-Kongo family, which is a subgroup of the Niger-Kongo branch of the Niger-Kordofanian super-stock or phylum.

Notes and References

The interested reader is referred to the following works dealing with the topics covered in this chapter.

Joseph H. Greenberg, 1963, The methodology of language classification, chapter 1 in his *The languages of Africa*, Blomington.
Henry M. Hoeningswald, 1960, *Language change and language reconstruction*, Chicago.
Henry M. Hoeningswald, 1963, Are there universals of linguistic change?, in Joseph H. Greenberg, ed., *Universals of language*, Cambridge, Mass., 23–39.

1) A. N. Tucker, 1940, *The Eastern Sudanic languages*, Vol. 1, p. 318 fn.
2) See Paul Newman and Roxana Ma, 1966, Comparative Chadic: phonology and lexicon, *Journal of African Languages*, S.3.218–259.
3) Carl Hoffman, 1963, *A grammer of the Margi language*, p. 43, The development of kt to pt is particularly interesting in light of Jakobsonian distictive feature theory. See Roman Jakobson and Morris Halle, 1956, *Fundamentals of language,*'s Gravenhage.
4) Malcolm Guthrie, 1948, *The classification of the Bantu languages*, London.
5) Oswin Köhler, 1955, *Geschichte der Erforschung der nilotischen Sprachen*, (*Afrika und Übersee*, Beiheft 28).
6) A fairly extensive literature on the subject exists. See in particular: Joseph H. Greenberg, 1957, Nilotic, "Nilo-Hamitic", and Hamito-Semitic, *Africa*, 27.364–378, and M. A. Bryan, 1959, The T/K Languages, a new substratum, *Africa*, 29.1–21.
7) Harold Flemming extends this list to include Asa and Aramanik. See his Asa and Aramanik: Cushitic hunters in Masai-Land (to appear). Also Christopher Ehret, n.d., Southern Cushitic and Eastern Bantu: a significant contact (paper given at Mount College in April 1968).
8) See A. N. Tucker, 1967, Fringe Cushitic: an experiment in typological comparison, *Bulletin of the School of Oriental and African Studies,* 30.3 655–680.
9) See Morris Goodman, 1971, The strange case of Mbugu (Tanzania), in Dell Hymes, ed., *Pidginization and Creolization of Languages*, London: 243–254. A similar situation has been reported by M.B. Emmeneau for Brahui, a Dravidian language spoken in Baluchistan, Pakistan, which has borrowed extensively from neighboring languages such as Sindhi, Balochi, and Persian.
10) As quoted in A. N. Tucker, 1957, Philology and Africa, *Bulletin of the School of Oriental and African Studies*, 20.541–554.

CHAPTER VIII

History of Work on African Languages

No truly scholarly work seems to have been attempted on any African language, except Arabic, until the seventeenth century. In point of fact, apart from the Arabs, Africans failed to develop an independent tradition of linguistic analysis, written or oral, and nearly all work in this field—with a few notable exceptions —has been done by non-Africans. Since the seventeenth century, however, a considerable literature has appeared, some of it first rate.

ANTIQUITY

The ancients have told us almost nothing about the African languages of their time.

The Egyptians seem to have produced no study or analysis even of their own language. Although as early as the seventh century BC their contemporaries the Assyrians and Babylonians developed dictionaries of a sort to explain archaic or unusual word signs used in writing, there is no evidence that the Egyptians ever produced anything comparable despite the fact that their own writing was fraught with similar problems. The only extant work on Egyptian by an ancient Egyptian is a treatise on hieroglyphs from the fifth century AD, *Hieroglyphika* by Horapollo—probably originally written in Koptic, but surviving only in a Greek translation. The treatise provides correct glosses for a number of signs (which had a few years previously gone out of use, the last hieroglyphic inscriptions dating from c. AD 390) but couched in fantastic explanations of their origin.

The Greeks and the Romans both produced grammars and dictionaries of their own language, but nothing on others. African languages were not singled out with some particular slight in mind in these matters since no classical description exists even of European languages spoken by neighbors of the Romans such as the Etruscans or Ombrians. Even Juba II, a king of Libya and a native speaker of Berber, apparently ignored his mother tongue in favor of Greek in his no longer extant essay on grammer, *Perì phthorâs lekséôs* (*On the corruption of speech*). It is particularly remarkable, however, that the Egyptian city of Alexandria should have produced some of the greatest names of Greek lexicography, but apparently not a single African word list of even the smallest proportions—including Egyptian. The geographer Strabo records the only reference to a vocabulary, now lost, of an African language compiled in antiquity. He tells of a Eudoxus of Cyzicus (c. 120 BC) who while on a journey to India through the Red Sea was forced to land in Ethiopia (the general term used in antiquity for Africa south of Egypt), became friendly with the people, and wrote down several words of their language.[1] Strabo thinks the story may be apocryphal because Eudoxus is said to have been taken a trip down the West African coast later on and met people speaking the same language. Strabo found this unlikely. We must probably agree.

A few remarks about African languages are scattered through the works of classical geographers and others, but these comments are frequently so grotesque and fanciful that they can hardly be taken seriously, although some element of truth may be hidden in them. For example, Herodotus mentions that a group he calls the Troglodytes "speak a language unlike any other, shriek like bats".[2] Pliny, apparently speaking of the same group, enlarges on this: "they have no articulate voice, but only a kind of squeaking noise, and thus are they utterly destitute of all means of communication by language".[3] Perhaps some sort of "whistle language" provides the basis of such descriptions; it is difficult to say. The same author describes another group, the Atlantes, as strange in neither being "visited by dreams like the rest of mortals" nor having a "mode of distinguishing each other by names".[4] Here perhaps a reference to secret names (a fairly common practise in West African societies) may be inferred, since naming is otherwise a cultural universal.

Occasionally hints are given about the boundaries of language communities. Thus, Herodotus says that certain Nasamonians from Cyrenaica traveled south, crossed a desert (the Sahara?) and encountered little men (*pygmoi*) living near a great river (the Niger?). He adds that "the Nasamonians could not understand a word of their language, nor had they any acquaintance with the language of the Nasamonians".[5] In the same vein, Herodotus says of the Ammonians, who lived in the oasis of Ammon, that they spoke a mixture of Egyptian and Ethiopian[6] — surely the first mention of a *Mischsprache*! But information of this kind, even when accurate, has more relevance for the culture historian than the linguist.

Some attempt has been made to identify specific African words that seem to be quoted in the classical literature. The results are as a rule quite tenuous. For example, Herodotus mentions in his account of the Nasamonians, certain altars of the *philainoi*, which Meek[7] has suggested as perhaps associated with the modern Fulani. Since the ancestors of the modern Fulani were undoubtedly nowhere near North Africa in the time of Herodotus, moving away as they did from the general Senegal area only after the tenth century AD, Meek's suggestion must probably be rejected. A much sounder example has been taken by Delafosse[8] from the *Períplous* of Hanno, a Carthaginian admiral of the fifth century BC. Hanno writes that the traveled down the west coast of Africa, "past the Ethiopians" (and presumably past the Senegal River), and came to an island "full of savage men ... They had hairy bodies, and the interpreters called them **gorillae** ... We killed them and flayed them, and brought their skins back to Carthage".[9] Whether or not these beings were in fact men or gorillas as some authorities maintain is irrelevant here. The important thing is that the word **gorillae** itself apparently contains a stem **gor-** related to words for *man* in certain Western Sudanic languages such as Wolof: **goor**, etc. As a matter of fact, this may well represent the first record of a Niger-Kongo word, which curiously enough has spread throughout the world.

An Ancient Egyptian word **pwn.t** (usually anglicized as *Punt*) has occasioned considerable interest. It is the name of a country to the south of Egypt, perhaps present-day Eritrea or French Somaliland, and was mentioned as early as King Sahure of the Fifth Dynasty (c. 2750 BC). Several eminent scholars have tried to identify the name as a Bantu word. These attempts warrant some examination because they are totally disastrous and are a model for how not to do reconstruction. C. M. Doke[9] has suggested, for example, that Punt is really an old Bantu word **bunt(u)**. Doke believed that Egyptian writing did not clearly distinguish **b** and **p**; that the stem of the word was **-ntu**, which he identifies as the same as that in Proto-Bantu **mu-ntu** *person* (as in **Ba-ntu**, literally *people*); and that the **bu-** was a locative prefix and the word itself could be correctly glossed as *place of people*. He concluded that Punt referred to the ancestral home of the Proto-Bantu speakers. Both reconstruction and conclusion are most unlikely. In the first place, Ancient Egyptian writing could distinguish between **p** and **b** (by the symbols □ and 𐧉 respectively). In the second, various lines of evidence suggest that **pwn.t** was probably vocalized as **pwaane(t)**—the **-t** is a feminine suffix that was early dropped in pronunciation. Finally, the ancestral home of the Bantu was nowhere near the probable location of Punt, but was to be found in West rather than East Africa. The generally accepted modern theory holds that Bantu speakers arrived on the east coast only about the tenth century AD, about three millenia too late.

Another etymology of the word has been offered by Carl Meinhof, the leading Bantuist of his time, and followed by Zylharz and Krumm.[11] Meinhof proceeded from the vocalized form pwaane and suggested as the source the Swahili word **pwani** *shore*, where the **-ni** (now petrified as part of the stem) was originally a locative suffix meaning variously *to*, *at*, *in*. Again, the historical facts are against such an hypothesis. So are the linguistic facts. Meinhof does not account for the original **-t**, but he also forgot, although he was perhaps the first to point it out, that in Proto-Bantu there was no locative suffix, but rather that there were locative prefixes **ku**, **pa**, **mu**, which only recently coalesced in some Eastern Bantu languages to **-ni** (presumably at first a positional variant of **mu**).

We must conclude that the ancient Egyptians could hardly have borrowed a form from Proto-Bantu that did not exist in Proto-Bantu.

THE MIDDLE AGES

Our information for this period is somewhat better. Several African words were recorded by Arab traders, and Christian groups in the northeastern part of the continent have left a number of written records.

The spread of Christianity—so important in modern times for the study of African languages—proved almost negligible in this early period. Of course, the conquest of North Africa by Muslim Arabs in the seventh century effectively cut off Christian proselytizing. But even before that, the liturgical languages used by Christians were Greek in Egypt and other areas under the patriarch of Alexandria, and Latin in the west. This tradition never had the opportunity to change in the west; the result is that Christian documents in Punic, not to speak of Berber, seem never to have existed. An important change did occur in Egypt. There, after the oecumenical council of Chalcedon in 451, the church split into an heretical nationalistic group, the Monophysites, and the orthodox group, the Melchites, supported by the government in Constantinople but with far fewer adherents. The Monophysites generally abandoned the use of Greek and substituted Koptic. This development proved to be of considerable importance not only in Egypt, but also in the Sudan and Ethiopia, areas converted by the Egyptians. [12] Thus, Ge'ez from the start was used as the liturgical language of Ethiopia and parts of the Bible were translated into it as early as the fifth century. And from Nubia come the earliest written records from Black Africa.

Arab conquest of North Africa brought with it Islamization of the area and Arabic as the language not only of religion, but also of administration and culture. The Arabs early developed an independent tradition of linguistic description to insure the purity of religious texts and the accuracy of their interpretation. The grammatical model developed for classical Arabic was later borrowed, probably as early as the ninth century, by Jews in Spain for Hebrew, and elsewhere for Persian. But the analysis was apparently never applied to any African language. There seem to be three reasons for this: (1) a general contempt for non-Islamic cultures; (2) the belief that Koranic Arabic was the language of the angels and the only language worthy of study; (3) a tradition, unlike the Christian one, that the Koran should not be translated. Thus, throughout the long period of Islamization that has taken place in Africa no translations of the Koran have appeared in native languages except for a few sporadic and usually incomplete attempts in the present century by a fringe sect, the Ahmadiyyists (e.g.

in Swahili, Hausa, and Yoruba)—much to the distress, even now, of conservative Muslims.

Despite such ethnocentricity, a few details about African languages can be culled from the writings of Arab travelers and geographers. As mentioned above, some 30 or so words of African origin have been identified in the literature before the coming of Portuguese explorers in the fifteenth century. Although this represents an enormous improvement over previous periods, the amount of information conveyed is really negligible. [13]

One of the difficulties in evaluating such data is the fact that they were written in Arabic script, inadequate for linguistic transcription unless seriously modified. The necessary modifications were unfortunately not provided by the early travelers. Vowels were normally not indicated although occasionally the **y** symbol was used to represent an **i** or **e**; a **w**, an **u** or **o**; and an alif (here shown as **H**), an **a**. Consonant clusters not found in Arabic were simplified, thus an **mb** would probably be represented as **b**. Sounds foreign to Arabic were represented by other sounds: **p** and **v**, for example, are not found in native Arabic words and would probably both be represented by **b**. Hence, a single symbol **b** could have an enormous range of reference in such transcriptions: **b**, **mb**, **p**, **mp**, **v**, **mv**. And of course, the African words may not have been understood or accurately transcribed even within these resources. A case in point is a form from East Africa quoted by Mas'uudii in 956 in his book *Muruuj al-dhahab (The meadows of gold)*: **wqlymy**, meaning *king* or *son of the great lord*. Meinhof has tentatively associated it with the Swahili **mfalme** *king*. [13] Actually the item probably represents only part of a phrase such as **wa m(u)falme** *of the king*, hence the initial **w**. Since in Arabic script **q** and **f** are ق and ڧ, respectively, a scribal error is not unlikely. The omission of an **m** may have been either a mistake or an attempt to simplify a cluster. This example is not a particularly complicated one, and the value of such forms for linguistic work obviously cannot be said to be great, although they are not without interest.

The only writers in which actual words are quoted are al-Hamadhaannii (AD 902), Mas'uudii (AD 956)—both for East Africa—; al-Bakri (11th century), Ibn Khalduun (14th century) and Ibn Baṭuuṭa (14th century)—all for West Africa. Other writers who recorded place names include a Christianized Arab usually known as Leo Africanus (15th century).

A few other examples of such items include the following.

(1) **lmklwɣlw** *god* (al-Hamadhaanii) and **mklnɣlw** *great lord* (Mas'uudii): apparently the oldest recorded Bantu word; interpreted by Meinhof as **mukulugulu** and compared with Zulu **unkulunkulu** *god*.

(2) **tunkH** *royal title of rulers of Ghana* (al-Bakri); cf Soninke **tunka** *king*.

(3) **bnby** *elevated throne* (Ibn Baṭuuṭa); cf. Mende **bembe** *platform, dais*.

FROM THE COMING OF THE PORTUGUESE UNTIL 1775

Although the seventeenth century represents the beginning of significant work on African languages, there were a few sporadic attempts at dealing with African languages almost as soon as the Portuguese had crossed the equator while proceeding down the west coast of Africa in 1471.

The earliest known European source from these explorations is a word list collected in 1479 or 1480 by a Flemnish traveler Eustache de la Fosse [14] in the area of what is now Guinea. Seven words are given, including **manse** *king* (cf. the item **mnsH** cited by Ibn Baṭuuta as a title used before the names of Ghanaian rulers; Mende **mansa** *king*). Nearly all seem to have identifiable modern correspondences, e.g. **dede** *good*—Twi **dede** *pleasant*, **enchou** *water*—Twi **nsu**.

Similar lists exist for various other areas. But not until 1562 was a complete sentence recorded from a Bantu language, and that a fairly criptic line from a song. The sentence, recorded in a letter by the Reverend Father André Fernandez, has been identified as early Inhambani (spoken in modern Mozambique): **gombe zuco virato ambuze capana virato** *the cow has leather for shoes, and the goat has no leather for shoes*. [15] In 1591, Pigafetta, an Italian mathematician visiting the Kongo. did quote a considerable number of words in Kongo; Doke has called his work "the first serious record from the western Coast". [16] However, no large scale dictionaries or grammars were begun until the seventeenth century.

It is interesting to compare the relatively insignificant work done on African languages up to the seventeenth century with what had been done on languages elsewhere. The comparison is perhaps startling. Apart from the classical languages, almost nothing had been done for European languages. Aelfric's Latin-Old English dictionary from the tenth century and an anonymous grammatical treatise on Old Norse from the twelfth century are interesting but exceptional. Even with regard to Arabic studies, of considerable importance one should think to Christian apologists and statesmen alike, progress was slow. The oldest grammar of Arabic by a European was published only in 1505. [17] Remarkably enough, in the same century (the sixteenth), the first concerted effort to describe foreign nonclassical and nonliturgical languages was made by Spanish missionaries in the newly explored Western Hemisphere. Most of the work done was not published, however, and probably exerted very little influence on intellectual developments. But the question remains why America and not Africa should have provided the scene for such linguistic activity. The reason must be that although European contact with Africa was earlier, no long term plans for settlement there were originally envisaged and India, not Africa, was the goal of the travelers who came in contact with the continent.

Nevertheless, a stab at linguistic classification in Africa comes from the sixteenth century. Depending on how much one reads into the statement, it may be one of the earliest attempts for any area for setting up a language family. The statement was made by Andrea Corsali in a letter written in 1515 from India to the Medici in Italy. He says

The terra firma is inhabited by a savage race of people, as is the whole coast from the straits of the Red Sea, as far as the Cape of Good Hope, and they are all of the same language; and from the Cape of Good Hope as far as the Cape de Verde Islands, they speak a different language. [18]

Doke's suggestion that Corsali was really contrasting East Africa with the Guinea Coast in the absence of evidence that he visited the Kongo or Angola seems to account for some of the factual inaccuracy of his statement. But use of the term "language" makes sense only if taken to mean "language family". At the time, terminology for talking about language and language groupings had not yet been developed; so for want of a better word, Corsali may have had to resort to existing but inaccurate terminology.

As has already been indicated, the seventeenth century saw the beginning of significant work on African languages, not eclipsed until modern times. The major impetus for the work seems in most instances to have been the desire of missionaries to spread the gospel. But other reasons existed of course, including a humanistic curiosity kindled in the Renaissance. By the end of the century, significant work had been done on members from all the major linguistic phyla.

The earliest extant texts of the period in languages without a native tradition of writing were catechisms: in Kongo (1624), Ndongo (1643) and Gɛ (1658). [19]

Several important and extensive dictionaries were produced in this period. A Koptic-Arabic dictionary, which may have been compiled in the sixteenth century, was translated into Latin by the Jesuit Athanasius Kircher in 1636. This book revived interest in ancient Egypt and probably also in Africa as a whole; later it proved to be invaluable in the decipherment of hieroglyphs. A more than 7000 word dictionary of Nubian was compiled by an Italian Franciscan, Arcangelo Carradori, in 1638; a single copy in the author's own hand survives from 1650. A dictionary of Kongo of about the same size dates from 1652. It is attributed to a Belgian Capuchin Georges de Gheel (or Joris van Gheel) but may actually represent the work of a Spaniard referred to in the dictionary as Roboredo. Lexicography on Ethiopian languages began quite early with Wemmer's dictionary of Ge'ez from 1638; a more important and still significant work was Job Ludolf's published in 1661. He also wrote a dictionary of Amharic (1698). A quadrilingual dictionary of Kongo (with explanations in Portuguese, Latin, and Italian) dated 1650 has been attributed to an Italian Capuchin Giacinto Brusciotto, famous for his other work on Kongo, but the dictionary has apparently been lost.

A more impressive development was the writing of grammars. Working essentially within the Arabic tradition of analysis, Ludolf produced a highly succesful and accurate grammar of Ge'ez (1661) as well as of Amharic (1698). A number of other grammatical works in the field had already been produced, including a comparative study of Semitic paradigms by Petrus Victorius Palma from 1596 and *A general grammar for the ready attaining of the Ebrew, Samaritan, Calde, Syriac, Arabic and the Ethiopic languages* by Christian Raue (1650). Ludolf thus had previous works of scholarship to fall back on, as well as a thorough knowledge of Hebrew and Arabic, along with their traditional grammatical analyses.

In 1659, using a Latin basis in his treatment but nonetheless showing remarkable originality, Brusciotto produced the first grammar of Kongo, or for that matter, of any Bantu language: *Regulae quaedam pro difficillimi Congensium idiomatis faciliori captu ad grammaticae normam redactae* (*Some rules for the more easy understanding of the most difficult idiom of the people of the Congo, brought into the form of a grammar*). [20] Brusciotto accurately analyzed the noun class system of Kongo and paired off singular and plural prefixes correctly. Although he gives no clear explanation of agreement, in at least one of the several extant copies of the work there is a table of concords indicating that he understood the concordial system. He correctly described certain aspects of verb derivation, most notably the socalled applied or prepositional form, which has no direct Latin analog. Brusciotto's grammar is sometimes contrasted, by way of tribute, which the analyses of much later grammarians such as Cannecattim who failed to untangle the noun class system of Mbundu as late as 1805, and Richard Burton, the famous explorer, who as late as 1860 labeled plural formation in Swahili as "artful", "intricated", and "irregular". [21]

Two other, smaller Bantu grammars from the seventeenth century exist: an anonymous one in Portuguese, *Arte de lingua Cafre*, perhaps from 1680 (mostly a set of tables of verb inflections), and a grammar of Angola by the Jesuit Pedro Dias in 1697, where the noun class and concordial system are presented fairly well.

Pronunciation in nearly all these works and in most others written until quite recently was indicated in a rough and ready way. Ludolf was lucky enough to work with languages having a native writing system that was basically phonemic to begin with. Elsewhere, of course, for languages without an existing orthography, investigators had to produce a suitable writing system on their own. Some analyses were more succesful than others but few were even adequate. Tone for one thing was consistently ignored until as late as the 1870's. A minimal discussion of tonal differences (called "accent") was exceptionally made by Antonio Mario in his 1661 revision of a catechism in Angola; he even provides contrasts: mùcua *a fruit* - mucuà *native of*. On the other hand, interestingly enough, in perhaps the earliest attempt at describing Hottentot (by a British writer, Herbert) a number of click phonemes were consistently distinguished as early as 1643. [22]

The accomplishments of the seventeenth century were not matched during the greater part of the eighteenth. Armstrong [23] has argued that the racism and ethnocentricism of Europeans of the period was to blame for a decline in the study of African languages. And this may well be the case.

FROM 1775 UNTIL 1945

This period was characterized by an increasing professionalism in linguistic studies and the development of fulltime African linguistics. German-speaking scholars effectively dominated the activities of the period.

Africanists tended to be somewhat isolated from the main stream of linguistic thought, but the same basic problems faced linguists everywhere and solutions in one area often paralleled or even influenced those in another.

Towards the end of the eighteenth century the fashion arose of gathering comparative word-lists on a huge scale. In 1787 appeared the first significant compendium, *Glossarium comparativum linguarum totius orbis*, a glossary of 285 words in 200 European and Asiatic languages, edited by P. S. Pallas and sponsored by Catherine the Great of Russia. The revised editions from 1790 and 1791 included information from 30 African languages. About two decades later, *Mithridates oder allgemeine Sprachenkunde* by J. C. Adelung and J. S. Vater, which appeared in four volumes in the years 1806 to 1817, devoted a whole volume to languages from Black Africa and covered Semitic African languages (Ge'ez, Amharic, etc) and Berber in other volumes. Africanists subsequently started producing their own compendia. One of the first of these was John Clark's *Specimens of dialects* (1848), in which he presented 10 words in 294 languages and dialects from West Africa, chiefly compiled from previous sources but also including original data for scores of hitherto unrecorded languages.

Probably the most important Africanist list gatherer is S.W. Koelle, a German missionary whose *Polyglotta africana* of 1854 is rightly hailed as a landmark. All the material on the 156 languages contained in it is based on first hand observation, mostly with expatriate slaves in Freetown, and each language is represented by the same 283 words in a uniform transcription. Despite the standardized phonetic script—the first important one in the history of linguistics, by the way, devised by the Egyptologist R. Lepsius [24]—the accuracy of Koelle's transcriptions was not thereby insured; owing to his German background he persistently confused s and z, tʃ and dʒ, for example. But his data were good enough to permit tenable groupings of languages according to vocabulary resemblances.

Many other similar compendia have followed, notably Maurice Delafosse's *Vocabulaires comparatifs de plus de 60 langues et dialectes parlés à la Côte d'Ivoire et dans les regions limitrophes* (1904) and the 2-volume *Bantu and*

Semi-Bantu languages by Sir Harry Johnston (1919).

The increase in volume of data was paralleled by a gradual increase in the accuracy of the data. Treatment of tone, effectively nonexistant until the middle of the nineteenth century, was put on a systematic basis in J. G. Christaller's study of Twi. Since most of the languages of Africa are tonal, the importance of including such a dimension in a linguistic analysis cannot be underestimated. Important work on tone was also done by Bishop Samuel Crowther, himself a Yoruba who had investigated several West African languages. After the turn of the century, tone became the subject of several monographs including those by K. E. Laman on Kongo (1922); Daniel Jones on Tswana (1928); Ida C. Ward on Efik (1933), Igbo (1936), Yoruba (1938), Twi (1939); and L. E. Armstrong on Kikuyu (1941).

Accuracy with regard to other parts of phonology also improved and many studies even attempted to work with phonemic theory being developed in Europe and America. In 1926 the International Institute of African Languages and Cultures was formed and it early adopted and encouraged the spread of its own phonetic alphabet, a slightly modified form of the alphabet of the International Phonetic Association. Directions for the use of the Africa alphabet such as those given by Diedrich Westermann (first director of the Institute) and Ida C. Ward in their handbook *Practical phonetics for students of African languages* (1933) were normally couched in a phonemic orientation. But many scholars, such as Doke, preferred a phonetic treatment as somehow more precise or even more scientific; cf. his books *The phonetics of the Zulu language* (1926) and *A comparative study in Shona phonetics* (1931). Other important works in phonology from this period include A. N. Tucker's study of Sotho-Tswana (1929) and D. M. Beach's study of Hottentot (1938).

The availability of extensive and fairly reliable comparative data eventually suggested the desirability of a linguistic classification of some sort. But until the latter part of the eighteenth century no satisfactory model for linguistic relationship had been produced. As early as 1599 Joseph Justus Scaliger grouped the languages of Europe according to their word for *god*, but the decision to do so was arbitrary, albeit pious. The notion of genetic relationship between languages did not exist and in large part the Christian belief of the time that Hebrew was the original human language and all the others were created ex novo because of the Tower of Babel, precluded such a model. Informal statements about similarities between languages can be found before the eighteenth century, but even they are rare.

A remarkably clear statement of linguistic affinity between African languages appeared in 1776 and was written by the Abbé Lievin Bonaventure Proyart in his *Histoire de Loango, Kakongo, et autres royaumes d'Afrique*. He says that although Kakongo and Laongo differ in may respects from Kikongo, never-theless

Several similar articles [presumably prefixes], and a great number of common roots, seem, however, to indicate that these languages had a common origin. [25]

His conclusion has been upheld and his reasoning proved sound. The only untenable part of his statement was that the ancestral language was still spoken: "it is not known which of the languages is the mother language [*langue mère*]". But even his kinship metaphor foreshadows the genealogical terminology of a later school. However, his ideas apparently produced no new thinking by other scholars on the matter of linguistic relationships.

A crucial moment in the development of diachronic linguistics is usually taken to be Sir William Jones's statement in 1786 on the affinity of Latin, Greek, and Sanskrit. He found such detailed resemblances in roots and inflections that chance had to be ruled out; he concluded that

no philologer could examine them all three without believing them to have sprung from some common source, which, perhaps, no longer exists.

This famous declaration, said to have initiated the discipline of comparative grammar and to have set up the Indo-European language family for the first time, is to my mind no clearer than Proyart's. From the point of view of theory, the only superiority Jones's statement has lies in its suggestion that the ancestral language may not actually exist.

Remarkably enough, the existence of a Bantu language family was asserted by at least three writers working independently of each other and also of Proyart and Jones: Heinrich Lichtenstein, William Marsden, and John Philip. Lichten-stein is usually given credit for being the first to announce his view about Bantu—in 1808 in an article *Bemerkungen über die Sprachen der Südafrika-nischen wilden Völkerstämme*. He divided the languages in southern Africa (i.e. at least south of northern Mozambique on the east coast) into two groups: "Kaffirs" (Bantu-speaking) and Hottentot. These two types are set up as "lan-guages" in Lichtenstein's discussion and he maintains that all the speech types to be found in the area are merely dialects of these two languages—a position reminiscent of Corsali. Much the same view was held by John Philip who wrote in 1824 that the "Caffres" of East Africa, "Bootsuannas", inhabitants of the Comoro Islands, and probably also those of the Congo spoke "different dialects only of the same language". Adelung and Vater incorporated Lichtenstein's position in *Mithridates* in 1812.

Of the three workers on Bantu, Marsden is particularly interesting. His inter-ests ranged over a wide field and it seems to be only by chance that his attention was drawn to the question of Bantu. He specialized in Indonesian languages and was the first to recognize the existence of the Austronesian (or Malayo-Polynesian) language family. [26] The reasons given for his position have been described by Greenberg as "superior in clarity to Jones's more celebrated pronouncement" [27] and are some 8 years earlier.

Marsden stated his views on Bantu most fully in a letter written in 1816 concerning some Congolese vocabularies compiled by a Captain J. K. Tuckey; in it he showed acquaintance with numerous other Africanist materials, including Brusciotto's work. He concluded that most of the Congolese "languages" were probably mutually intelligible and that

Between the Congo language and that of the tribes of the eastern side [i.e. the east coast of Africa], the affinity although radical is much less striking, and the people themselves must consider them as quite distinct; but the following instances of resemblance, in words expressing the simplest ideas, may be thought sufficient to warrant the belief, that the nations by whom they are employed, at a remote period, have been more intimately connected. [28]

When Marsden first formulated his hypotheses is difficult to say. It may have been as early as 1778 (this date is suggested by Greenberg [29]), at the age of 24, when he collected a vocabulary from an African servant originally from Mozambique who spoke Makua, whom Marsden engaged while in Sumatra. If he had in fact read Brusciotto or indeed any other relevant source he could possibly have made a fair judgment then. But in his 1816 letter he lists very few sources and the only book mentioned was one by Sparrman, *Resa til Goda-Hopps-Udden* (*Voyage to the Cape of Good Hope*) with word lists of "Kafir", published in 1783. Marsden's hypothesis may have been formulated several years before Jones's, and as many as three decades before the publication of Lichtenstein's view. But the facts are not clear.

By the early part of the nineteenth century, a number of language groupings were fairly well defined in the Africanist field: Bantu and Hottentot in southern Africa, Austronesian in Madagascar. In 1781, Ludwig von Schlözer first proposed a Semitic group of languages following the Biblical story of the children of Noah and their descendents. [30] In the following century a parallel Hamitic family was proposed including Ancient Egyptian, Berber, and Kushitic. As early as 1826 Adrien Balbi in his *Atlas ethnographique du globe ou classification des peuples anciens et modernes d'après leurs langues* presented a general linguistic classification for all of Africa. This was soon superseded by classifications that have proved influential up to the most recent times, viz. those of R. Lepsius and F. Müller (especially as adapted and popularized by R. N. Cust, an Englishman), and Westermann and Meinhof. These classifications showed a certain modicum of agreement. All recognized Bantu, Semitic, and Bushman as independent and unrelated; most set up a larger Hamito-Semitic grouping as well. Languages outside these families and some others occasioned a good deal of controversy, such as Fulani, Hausa, and Songhai in the west, and Maasai and Nubian in the

LEPSIUS.

KOELLE.

F. MÜLLER.

BLEEK.

ARCHDEACON D. CROWTHER
OF LOWER NIGER.

Figure 9　　NINETEENTH CENTURY AFRICANIST LINGUISTS

east. Some authorities grouped Hottentot with Bushman because of the presence of clicks in both; others included Hottentot within Hamito-Semitic because of the presence of a masculine-feminine distinction in nouns and pronouns. A four-fold classification of mainland languages into Bantu, Sudanic, Hamito-Semitic, and Bushman-Hottentot was the leading one until the end of the 1940's.

The criteria used in some classifications were often tenuous. For example, extraneous racial or cultural attributes of a certain group seem to have been at least sometimes decisive in determining that group's linguistic affiliations. One of the most blatant examples of this was undoubtedly Meinhof's conception of what can be called "maximal Hamitic", developed in *Die Sprachen der Hamiten* (1912). Despite little linguistic evidence, Meinhof tried to expand the Hamitic language family by fairly vague typological resemblances until speakers of "Hamitic" in his sense were largely coterminous with cattle-herding peoples and members of a basically Caucasoid stock—in Meinhof's view a *Herrenvolk* ("master race"). His theory necessarily entailed a good deal of mixing, both of races and languages. He assumed that Fulani represented a survival of the most archaic kind of Hamitic, that Bantu was a mixture of a Fulani-like language and a western Sudanic one, that Hottentot had a Hamitic base strongly influenced by Bushman, and that Maasai was typologically an ancient Hamitic form influenced by eastern Sudanic languages.

Such a view won fairly few adherents, although it was held for a while, at least in part, by so important an Africanist as Westermann. One of Meinhof's contemporaries, Albert Drexel,[31] rejected the scheme for sound linguistic reasons. But Drexel's own proposals, based essentially on the theories of the Kulturkreislehre, a school of anthropology now defunct, never gained wide acceptance.

The leading French theorists of the time were concerned with establishing the genetic unity of the languages of Black Africa. Delafosse[32] was content to state such an hypothesis while admitting that conclusive evidence for it was at present lacking. Lilias Homburger, one of his students, developed the Pan-African thesis in more detail, and in the opinion of most contemporary Africanists, to the point of absurdity. Her most notorious view is unquestionably the idea that all contemporary "Negro-African" languages are ultimately derived from some form of Ancient Egyptian. Some of these languages she derives from Koptic (e.g. Ewe and Mande); others from the mixed Egyptian-Ethiopian dialect spoken in the oasis of Ammon during the time of Herodotus, still others from a Nubian form of Egyptian. The vocabulary resemblances and other evidence offered by her as proof for this theory are deplorably loose and inadequate. Later she modified her view somewhat to include a Dravidian (Southern Indian) base.[33] With few exceptions, her theories have been dismissed by other linguists, but in fairness it should be recalled that she was one of the first to propose that Fulani was closely related to Serer and Wolof, and was not Hamitic [34]; this view is that now held by almost all Africanists.

An important accomplishment of this period was the attempted reconstruction of Proto-Bantu phonology and vocabulary by Meinhof in his *Grundriß einer Lautlehre der Bantusprachen* (1899, translated in 1932 as *Bantu phonology*). He also tried to reconstruct certain features of Proto-Bantu grammar in his *Grundzüge einer vergleichenden Grammatik der Bantusprachen* (1906). These attempts were quite successful and have survived essentially unchallenged until the present. Westermann's reconstruction of Proto-Western-Sudanic was less successful although he did establish significant sound correspondences between Western Sudanic and Bantu. Work on Proto-Semitic made considerable strides, and some work was done on Proto-Austronesian. But by and large, the reconstruction of protolanguages has played a relatively small role in African language study.

FROM 1945 TO 1965

The end of the Second World War saw increased interest in African languages and a greater internationalization of the field. German hegemony disappeared. To the old centers of linguistic work such as Hamburg and London, were added several others including East Lansing, Los Angeles, Leningrad, Moscow, Paris, and most appropriately in Africa itself: Dakar, Accra, Ibadan, Nairobi, among other places.

Decolonialization played a major role in this internationalization. The emergent nations were almost immediately confronted with problems of educational policy, national language problems, and the like, and engaged linguistics to gather basic information and to make recommendations. Foreign governments were also interested for various reasons. In the United States, the National Defence Education Act and such organizations as the Peace Corps and Teachers for East Africa focused attention on African languages to an unprecedented degree.

Such interest had generated a number of important developments, including:

(a) the appearance of technical journals devoted entirely to research on African languages, (e.g. Journal of African Languages, Journal of West African Languages, African Language Review, and Studies in African Linguistics);

(b) the creation of official orthographies for many hitherto unwritten languages as well as pedagogical materials for languages throughout the continent;

(c) the initiation of an encyclopaedic inventory of the field published by the International African Institute under the general title *Handbook of African languages*;

(d) the establishment in 1956 of the West African Languages Survey, in 1965 of the West African Linguistics Society, in 1966 of the Survey of Language Use and Language Teaching in Eastern Africa, and in 1967 of the Linguistic Circle of Accra.

Without question the most spectacular event of this period was the publication in 1949 and 1950 of a series of articles with the general title *Studies in African linguistic classification* by Joseph H. Greenberg, then of Columbia University, purporting to present a new and comprehensive genetic classification of all African languages. These articles occasioned a considerable amount of controversy partly because of the uncomprising tone in which Greenberg treated the views of highly repected scholars concerning, for example, the status of Bantu and the affiliation of socalled Nilo-Hamitic languages. In one instance, he branded as "sheer fantasy" Meinhof's argument for including Fulani within Hamitic.[35] Some critics have felt that comments of this sort bordered on invective; and one writer grudgingly characterized Greenberg's work as a "succès de scandale".[36] However the consensus seems to be, and rightly so, that the classification is correct on all major points.

Two problems dominated Greenberg's *Studies*: (1) the validity of Meinhof's concept of Hamitic, and (2) the relationship of Bantu to the group of languages called by Westermann Western Sudanic. Greenberg resolved the first problem by rejecting Meinhof's notion and even by dismissing altogether the notion of Hamitic—at least in the sense of a linguistic stock parallel to Semitic within a larger Hamito-Semitic phylum. In this instance, Greenberg followed up views already expressed by scholars such as Marcel Cohen. Greenberg established five co-ordinate groupings (Semitic, Egyptian, Berber, Kushitic, and Chadic) and labeled the phylum Afro-Asiatic. The inclusion of Hottentot in this phylum was denied; instead it was placed along with Bushman and a few other languages in a phylum called Click (later Khoisan). Maasai was set up in yet another grouping, a part of what had been called Eastern Sudanic by Westermann. Fulani was conclusively related to Wolof, Serer, and Biafada—languages of Westermann's Western Sudanic group.

Greenberg resolved the second problem by accepting Westermann's proposal that Western Sudanic and Bantu were genetically related. But he did not accept Westermann's view that they constituted co-ordinate units linked at a considerable remote time. On the contrary, Greenberg adduced evidence that Bantu was a fairly recent, low-level offshoot from a subgroup within Western Sudanic itself. This conclusion constituted perhaps the most controversial part of Greenberg's classification. It has been suggested (justly or not) that controversy lay not so much in Greenberg's data or methodology but rather in the fact that the new classifiçation seemed to diminish the status of Bantu studies and, hence, that of Bantuists themselves. Arguments for the soundness of Greenberg's position will be examined later on.

Greenberg's original classification was a generally conservative one, and 16 independent language families were set up for the continent as a whole (excluding Madagascar). In his 1963 revision (published under the new title *The languages of Africa*), he reduced this number to 4.

Greenberg's methodology was as important as his classification. The basic approach centered on what he called mass comparison, a method of lexical inspection used by the earliest classifiers of languages but never before made explicit. In the methodology worked out by Indo-Europeanists, only the establishment of sound correspondences was taken as proof of genetic relationship. The absence of detailed sound correspondences in Greenberg's supporting argument was indeed jumped on by a great many Africanists, [37] but curiously enough such critics have themselves rarely attempted to provide sound correspondences in support of their own classification. Thus, Tucker and Bryan, who maintain that vocabulary resemblances without sound laws can be used to prove just about anything, [38] have nowhere offered such correspondences for their Nilo-Hamitic (or Paranilotic) theory; rather, they resort to typological similarities. I think in light of linguistic experience we must agree with Paul Newman, who says:

The proof of genetic relationship does not depend on the demonstration of historical sound laws. Rather, the discovery of sound laws and the reconstruction of linguistic history normally emerge from the careful comparison of languages already presumed to be related. [39]

At least two other important developments occurred during this period. One of these is the introduction of a variety of sophisticated theoretical orientations into descriptive work. Several structuralist analyses have been attempted, and even a few tagmemic and generative grammars or grammatical sketches written.

The other development—an appropriate one to end this chapter with—is the fact that native speakers of African languages have begun to study their own languages. A notably example is Ayọ Bamgboṣe, himself a Yoruba and the author of a recent grammar of Yoruba, who was the first president of the West African Linguistics Society. Although, as was pointed out in the beginning of this chapter, Africans did not develop an independent tradition of linguistic analysis, it is clear that in the final analysis only a native speaker can produce a truly adequate study of his own language. The recruitment of African linguists is therefore a most auspicious development and should produce studies in depth the like of which we do not now possess.

Notes and References

1) *Geography* II.34.
2) *The history of Herodotus* (trans. by George Rawlinson, ed. by Manual Komroff), New York, 1928: IV.184.4 (p. 260).
3) *Natural History* V.8.8.
4) *Ibid.*
5) *History* II (p. 92).
6) *Ibid*, II.42 (p. 96)
7) C. K. Meek, 1960, The Niger and the classics: the history of a name, *Journal of African History* I.1.6.
8) Maurice Delafosse, 1912–14, Mots soudanais du moyen âge, *Mémoires de la Société de Linguistique*18.281.
9) Translation mine from the Delafosse quote (see fn 8).
10) C. M. Doke and D. T. Cole, 1961. *Contributions to the history of Bantu linguistics*, Johannesburg, 1.
11) Carl Meinhof, 1942, Pwani, *Zeitschrift für Eingeborener-Sprachen* 32:300–2. See also Ernst Zyhlarz, 1941–42, Das Land Pun.t, *Zeitschrift für Eingeborener-Sprachen* 32: 302–311. And B. Krumm, 1932, *Wörter und Wortformen orientalischen Ursprungs im Suaheli*, Hamburg.
12) Frumentius, the apostle to the Ethiopians, may have been a Persian or even an Indian (which could have significance in the development of the Ethiopic syllabary, see chapter 18), but he was also a disciple of Athanasius, a presbyter of Alexandria.
13) Carl Meinhof, 1919–20, Afrikanische Worte in Orientalischer Literatur, *Zeitschrift für Eingeborenen-Sprachen* 10:147–52. Other examples in this section are taken from sources already quoted: Delafosse (1912–14) and Doke (1938).
14) First published in R. Foulché-Delbosc, 1897, *Voyage à la côte occidentale d'Afrique*, Paris. Discussed in René Basset, 1913, Notes sur la langue de la Guiné au XVᵉ Siècle, *Academia das Sciencias de Lisboa, Separata do Boletim da Segunda*, Vol. 6, Coimbra. Also L. F. Brosnahan, 1965, A fifteenth century word list, *The Journal of West African Languages* 2.2.5.
15) Quoted in Doke and Cole (1961) 4–5.
16) *Ibid* p. 5.
17) This grammar, by Pedro de Alcala, is especially interesting because it dealt with the colloquial dialect of Granada unlike the traditional grammars of Arabic made by Arabs themselves, which considered only the classical language. For a discussion of this work, see Johann Fück, 1955, *Die arabischen Studien in Europa bis in den Anfang des 20. Jahrhunderts*, Leipzig, 31–2.
18) The translation given here is taken from Doke and Cole (1961), 54–5. See also M. D. W. Jeffreys, 1952, Corsali 1515 on Bantu and Sudanic languages, *African Studies* 11.191.
19) See P. Laurenz Kilger, 1935, Die ersten afrikanischen Katechismen im 17. Jahrhundert, *Gutenberg-Jahrbuch*, 257–264.
20) An English translation exists: H. Grattan Guinness, 1882, *Grammar of the Congo language as spoken two hundred years ago, translated from the Latin of Brusciotto*, London.

21) As quoted in Doke and Cole (1961), 18.
22) As reported in Joseph H. Greenberg, 1962, The history and present status of African linguistic studies, *Proceedings of the First International Congress of Africanists*, 87.
23) Robert G. Armstrong, 1964, *The study of West African languages*, Ibadan, 2.
24) But not published by Lepsius until 1855 in his *Das allgemeine Alphabet*.
25) P. 172. (Translation mine.)
26) William Marsden, 1782, Remarks on the Sumatran languages, *Archaeologia* 6.154–158.
27) Greenberg (1960), 89.
28) As quoted in Doke and Cole (1961), 56. See also A. Werner, 1929, English contributions to the study of African languages, *Bibliotheca Africana* 3. 199–200.
29) Greenberg (1960), 89.
30) In Eichhorn, 1781, *Repertorium*, vii 161.
31) Drexel, 1921–5, Gliederung der afrikanischen Sprachen, *Anthropos*.
32) M. Delafosse, 1920, Sur l'unité des langues négro-africaines, *Revue d'Ethnographie et des Traditions Populaires* 1:123–128.
33) See particularly Homburger, 1941, *Les langues négro-africaines et les peuples qui les parlent*, Paris.
34) See L. Homburger, 1939, Le serère-peul, *Journal de la Société des Africanistes* 9:85–102.
35) In 1964 revision, p. 29.
36) Pierre Alexandre, 1967, *Langues et language en Afrique noire*, Paris, 103.
37) E.g., István Fodor, 1966. *The problems in the classification of the African languages* (Studies in Developing Countries No. 5, Centre for Afro-Asian Research of the Hungarian Academy of Sciences), Budapest.
38) "The only conclusions which can be reached at this state is that mere vocabulary comparison, unsupported by phonology, may give rise to a variety of classifications, each as convincing as the other". A. N. Tucker and M. A. Bryan, 1956, *The non-Bantu languages of North-Eastern Africa*, London, xvi.
39) Paul Newman, 1970, Historical sound laws in Hansa and in Dera (Kanakuru), *Journal of West African Languages*, 7.1.39.

Part Four   AFRICAN LANGUAGE PHYLA

CHAPTER IX

Niger-Kordofanian

In this and the following four chapters a brief survey of the language phyla in Africa will be presented, following Greenberg's scheme. Controversial aspects of his classification will be discussed, and significant work on the groups will be outlined. Salient characteristics will be listed when practical.

The first group we shall consider is the Niger-Kordofanian phylum, proposed by Greenberg in 1963. It represents the gathering together of a number of previously established language families. The earliest of these was Bantu, first proposed in print by Lichtenstein in 1808, but probably formulated earlier by Marsden, as we have noted. The term Bantu itself (in the form **Bâ-ntu**) was coined in 1862 by W.H.I. Bleek, called the "father of Bantu philology" for his extensive work in the subject. An attempt to drop the ba-prefix (resulting in Ntu) sponsored by Wanger never gained many adherents.

Comparable groupings elsewhere in Niger-Kordofanian were rather late in coming. Many early scholars were, however, convinced that most if not all of the languages spoken by blacks in the Western Sudan were related, but whether their reasoning was based on linguistic information alone can be doubted because they lumped Hausa, Kanuri, and Songhai together with Yoruba, Fulani, and Mande. Müller and Cust labeled all these languages along with Nilotic, Nubian, and some others spoken in the Sudan region as the Negro Group. Lepsius modified the label (but not the group itself) to "mixed Negro" languages (*Misch Neger-sprachen*). In 1911 Diedrich Westermann attempted to marshal the evidence in support of such a phylum in his *Die Sudansprachen*, in which he maintained that all or most of the languages spoken between Dakar and the Nile were genetically related ("ein genetisch zusammenhängende Sprachfamilie"), e.g. Ewe, Twi, Gã, Yoruba, Efik, Nuba, Dinka, Kunama. In 1927, he made a much more detailed study, but ignored the Eastern Sudanic languages (Nuba, Dinka, Kunama) in an important work *Die westlichen Sudansprachen und ihre Beziehungen zum Bantu*. The significance of this book lies in the fact that it attempts to establish sound correspondences both within Western Sudanic and between Western Sudanic and Bantu. Furthermore, he established a subclassification that persists largely to this day: (1) Kwa, (2) Benue-Cross, (3) Togo-Remnant, (4) Gur (including Songhai, however), (5) West Atlantic (but minus Fulani), (6) Mande. Strangely enough, Westermann hedged on the question of whether Western Sudanic represented a true linguistic family. In 1927 he said his efforts were directed not as showing "that the contemporary Sudanic languages and groups had developed directly from some earlier undivided unity [Proto-Sudanic?] but ... that they had ... a common ancient heritage [einen altererbten Gemeinbesitz]".In 1940 he maintained that the Sudan languages were "languages of a common type, the genetic unity of which could only partially be demonstrated".[1] But in other works[2] he did state the ultimate genetic unity of Sudanic and Bantu, and in his review of Greenberg's proposals acknowledged that Greenberg's conceptualization was probably accurate.

The Greenberg scheme has already been sketched. He accepted Westermann's comparative data as sufficient evidence for genetic relationship in most instances. He added a subgroup of languages (including Zande) co-ordinate with Kwa, West Atlantic, etc., called Adamawa Eastern. Following Homburger and Klingenheben he placed Fulani in West Atlantic. These developments were set forth in his 1948 work, in which the largest units were Niger-Kongo (basically Westermann's Sudanic plus Bantu) and Kordofanian, considered as separate and unrelated. In 1963, the two were combined into one super-stock, Niger-Kordofanian. The result of this was that all the socalled class languages of Africa were now shown to be genetically related (with the sole exception of Mbugu).

JOSEPH H. GREENBERG

KARL MEINHOF

The crucial and certainly most controversial aspect of Greenberg's scheme was relegating Bantu to a subgroup of Sudanic. He did so because of various lines of evidence that showed Bantu to be set off from the other Niger-Kordofanian languages by what must have been relatively recent innovations. We have already mentioned the occurrence of m or n in noun/adjective prefixes where corresponding pronouns have none. Other innovations are found in vocabulary: cognates of some basic Bantu words occur widely in West Sudanic, but others not at all; e.g. Bantu *deme *tongue* has cognates in Fulani **ɗem-gal**, Mossi **zə-ləm-də**, Efik **é-démè**, Ewe **à-dé**, Twi **tɛk-rèmã**—whereas Bantu *bumo *belly* is not found outside of Bantu. On the other hand, and this is of special importance, certain West Sudanic words no longer exist as independent items in Bantu but as petrified stems: *bi, a common West Sudanic form for *child*, does not occur in Bantu except in a verb *bi-ala *give birth*, usually so obscured by sound changes that it has been submerged into the verb stem itself, e.g. Nyamwezi **vyala**, Swahili **zaa** (from *zala). In all these instances, the similarities are most economically and plausibly explained in terms of common inheritance from a single parent language, with the subgrouping as suggested by Greenberg.

However, Greenberg's position on Niger-Kongo has received vigorous attacks,

DIEDRICH WESTERMANN

Figure 10   TWENTIETH CENTURY AFRICANIST LINGUISTS

particularly (but not exclusively) from English Africanists. Guthrie for one has insisted most steadfastly that genetic relationship between Bantu and Western Sudanic has not been established.[3] He maintains that vocabulary resemblances may be due to borrowing, for one thing, and that most importantly sound correspondences have not been spelt out. Both these comments are somewhat surprising, however, since the vocabulary involved is generally considered most resistant to borrowing (items such as *head, ear, tongue, mouth, sun, stone, water, blood, two, three, I, he, we, you, they, go, be, eat, drink, sleep, die, large, black*) and Westermann long ago set up many sound correspondences between his own reconstruction of Proto-Western-Sudanic and Meinhof's for Proto-Bantu, as well as pointing out the similarities in class affixes in both groups; thus, an affix **ma** is used in both for liquids and mass nouns, **ku** as a locative and marker of infinitives, etc.

Interestingly enough, Guthrie's own position leads to a considerable number of implausible reconstructions for Proto-Bantu. For example, the present day distribution of the **ki**-class denoting things and taking regular concords in **ki** is less wide-spread than the **mu**-class denoting people and taking irregular concords in **yu** or **u**.[4] From the distributional facts for Bantu alone, Guthrie concludes that the **ki**-class itself, as well as regular concords, is a late development. By doing so he in effect abandons a reasonable model for Bantu concords and their development. And he fails to account for an unlikely co-incidence: the existence of affixes associated with essentially the same class meanings in other Niger-Kordofanian languages, as well as a person class in **u**-taking regular concords (the **m**- in Bantu, as we have already mentioned, seems most likely to be a Bantu innovation).

Westermann's original subgroupings have been modified somewhat, most conspiciously with reference to Kwa. Westermann and Bryan in their 1952 handbook excluded Kru and Idoma from Kwa, but they are now generally included by most scholars. The Togo Remnant languages were included by Greenberg under Kwa, as was Ịjọ, which he originally considered independent and co-ordinate with Kwa. As a matter of fact the validity of the separation of Kwa and Benue-Kongo languages (including Bantu) has seriously been questioned by scholars recently. The Kwa problem was one of the major topics of the Second West African Languages Congress held in Dakar, 1962.

Niger-Kordofanian languages are spoken by about 100,000,000 people—roughly half the total population of Africa. Of this, the Kordofanian branch claims only about 200,000 speakers. and Niger-Kongo the rest. The Bantu subdivision (about 400 languages) represents about 60,000,000 speakers. Of the 37 languages with 1,000,000 or more speakers found in Africa, 28 are Niger-Kordofanian, 15 are Bantu (see Appendix I).

With such a tremendous group, differentiated over a time span of surely at least 10,000 years, it proves difficult to provide a significant list of shared distinctive characteristics. This should be obvious enough when one recalls that former typological classifications usually described Bantu as agglutinating and Western Sudanic as isolating, so that typological resemblances within Niger-Kordofanian can easily be minimized. But throughout the phylum there are languages with a highly developed noun class and concordial system. The tendency towards an isolating structure devoid of noun classes in Mande, Ịjọ, and Western Kwa is undoubtedly secondary: granted the validity of the Niger-Kordofanian grouping, the protolanguage itself must have had a noun class system.

The classes and concords are normally but not invariably marked by prefixes. Permutation, which is only a secondary and as it were involuntary mark of class, is restricted to the West Atlantic and a few Mande languages such as Kpelle and Mende. The class meanings involved usually distinguish human, thing, plant, liquid, and animal categories but not masculine and feminine (which does occur exceptionally in Ịjọ, however). Quite frequently, some classes have no obvious class meaning.

Almost without exception, these languages are tonal, the major counterexamples being Swahili and Fulani. Clicks as normal phonemes are found in

Southern Bantu, presumably borrowed from Khoisan. Double stops are common in Western Sudanic but not elsewhere.

The basic word order is SVO except in Ịjọ, Mende, and Gur. In possessive phrases, the possessed precedes the possessor, except in Mende and western Kwa. Adjectives almost always follow the modified noun, except in Ịjọ, Ibibio-Efik, and Ogoni.

Practically nothing has been done on reconstruction except for Proto-Bantu, which was worked on extensively by Meinhof as well as Dempwolff and Bourquin. Guthrie has recently tried to bring reconstruction up to date in a truly gigantic study.

A phonemicization of Meinhof's consonant system for Proto-Bantu gives the following inventory:

p	t	k
b	d	g
m	n	
θ	s	
	z	

*/b d g/ represent [b d g] after nasals, [β l ɣ] elsewhere.[5] Westermann tentatively reconstructed a similar consonant system for Proto-Western-Sudanic; including at least:

p	t	k
b	l	g
m	n	

Note that Proto-Bantu *d had [l] as an allophone and Proto-West-Sudanic apparently used l to the exclusion of d. Double stops kp gb have not been reconstructed for the protolanguage because in most instances they seem to have developed from ku or gu.

Meinhof reconstructed a seven-vowel system for Proto-Bantu:

i	u
e	o
ɛ	ɔ
a	

in Meinhof's transcription: î i e a o u û (British Bantuists maintain this but use ị ụ for î û, respectively). However, a kind of vowel harmony occurs in many Bantu languages, the details of which suggest that at least in Pre-Proto-Bantu there was a nine-vowel system:

i	u
ɪ	ɷ
e	o
ɛ	ɔ
a	

Similar details from various Sudanic languages such as Yoruba, Igbo, and Ịjọ point to a comparable system at least for Proto-Kwa and probably Proto-Niger-Kongo.

A two-tone system has been reconstructed for both Proto-Bantu and Proto-Western-Sudanic.[6] This may well be the most plausible reconstruction even for Proto-Niger-Kordofanian.

Notes and References

Several important grammars and surveys have been published by such authorities as Alexandre, Ansre, Cole, Doke, Guthrie, Meeussen, Meinhof, Westermann. See also the various West African Language Monograph Series.

1) Hermann Baumann, R. Thurnwald, D. Westermann, 1940, *Völkerkunde von Afrika, Essen.*
2) D. Westermann, 1949, *Sprachbeziehungen und Sprachverwandschaft in Afrika*, Berlin. He apparently was unaware of Greenberg's position when he wrote this.
3) See particularly M. Guthrie, 1962, Bantu origins: a tentative new hypothesis, *Journal of African languages*, 9–21.
4) M. Guthrie, 1967, Variations in the range of classes in the Bantu languages, in *La classification nominale dans les langues négro-africaines (Colloques Internationaux du Centre National de la Recherche Scientifique*, Paris, 341–354.
5) Carl Meinhof, 1899, *Grundriß einer Lautlehre der Bantusprachen*, Berlin (trans. by N.J. von Warmelo as *Introduction to the phonology of the Bantu languages*).
6) J.H. Greenberg, 1948, The tonal system of Proto-Bantu, *Word* 4.3. 196–208.

CHAPTER X

Afro-Asiatic

The Afro-Asiatic phylum is essentially the long established Hamito-Semitic group with a few additions proposed by Greenberg mostly in conformity with suggestions by other scholars such as Marcel Cohen.

The term Hamitic used to be used for Egyptian, Kushitic, and Berber, which were thought to represent a family co-ordinate with Semitic. But it is now generally agreed that each of the three are co-ordinate with Semitic or at least that Hamitic is not a valid grouping. Consequently, most linguists have abandoned the term Hamitic altogether, although Murdock has suggested that it be used instead of Afro-Asiatic. Tucker and Bryan have suggested another alternant, Erythraic (because the languages involved surround the Red or Erythraean Sea). A proliferation of labels in this way is admittedly deplorable but in order to read the literature one must be aware of such variation.

The earliest notions of Afro-Asiatic stem from Biblical statements about the tribes descended from Shem and Ham (Genesis X). This account was reliable enough to provide a solid foundation for linguistic work, but was not entirely accurate, e.g., the Phoenicians (Canaanites)—who spoke a Semitic language—are stated to be descendents of Ham. The status of Hausa long posed many problems—no doubt owing to racial considerations in part, but also because few of the other Chadic languages are as well known. The Berber family, which was also not included in the Biblical account, was set up by Newman in the nineteenth century; he even tried to reconstruct the ancient language from Libyan inscriptions (see Chapter 16).

There are two controversial parts to Greenberg's classification. One of these involves the extension of Kushitic to include several languages in Tanzania and Kenya not in direct contact with the main Kushitic cluster: Iraqw, Mbulunge, Sanye, and the interesting Mbugu, discussed earlier. In an article published in 1963, Greenberg suggested the inclusion of yet another language, Mogogodo, into this Southern Kushitic branch.[1] More recently, Harold Fleming has added a few more, and all of these additions provide a chain in the geographical plausibility of the family.[2]

The other main problem was the validity of Meinhof's maximal Hamitic theory, which we have already discussed in some detail (Chapter 8). Greenberg's rejection of the theory occasioned no notable controversy, in large part because it had never gained much popularity in scholarly circles anyway.

In point of fact, Afro-Asiatic has proved to be the least controversial phylum in Africanist linguistics, apart from the peripheal question of the Nilo-Hamitic controversy (see Chapter 7).

The number of speakers of Afro-Asiatic languages is about the same as that for Niger-Kordofanian: c. 100,000,000. Of these, nearly 70,000,000 speak a form of Arabic, a Semitic language introduced into Africa after AD 600. The population breakdown for other groups is roughly as follows: Berber 11,000,000; Chadic 10,000,000 (of whom 9,000,000 or more speak Hausa, but some estimates run as high as 20,000,000 including nonnative speakers); Kushitic 6,000,000; African Semitic (Ethiopic) 7,500,000 (of whom some 6,000,000 speak Amharic). Egyptian, or in its more recent form called Koptic, is believed to be extinct although rumors persist that in some isolated villages in Upper Egypt it may still be spoken. It survives as the liturgical language of the Monophysite Christian church in Egypt, and some Kopts have even proposed reviving the language much in the manner of Israeli Hebrew. In the fifteenth century most of Upper Egypt was monolingual in Koptic; by the seventeenth century a European traveler there reported finding only a single speaker of it. In the eleventh edition of the Encyclopaedia Britannica, Albright mentions the possible existence of speakers of Koptic in 1927, and some prominent linguists including Carl Voegelin have assumed that this is still the case.

It may be appropriate to add a somewhat bizarre footnote on Egyptian. In a recent study of Teuso (or Ik[a]), spoken in Uganda and classified by Greenberg as Eastern Sudanic, Tucker was impressed with certain typological resemblances, particularly in the verb, between it and Ancient Egyptian. News of this, considerably garbled, somehow reached the *Times* of London and an article was written up stating that Tucker had discovered a group of "Ancient Egyptians", descendants of people who had fled from Thebes in antiquity and somehow had managed to establish and preserve a hidden kingdom to this day. Tucker wryly comments on the story that he only regrets not having intimated à la H. Rider Haggard that these Egyptians were ruled by a white woman called "She-Who-Must-Be-Obeyed".[3]

Of the five main divisions of Afro-Asiatic only two include tonal languages: Chadic (normally with two phonemic pitch levels) and Kushitic (usually with three). Certain sounds are almost entirely restricted to Afro-Asiatic, notably ħ and ʕ , technically pharyngeals (the ʕ resembles a "choked" æ; the ħ is the voiceless counterpart). They occur in Semitic (Arabic ع ح, Oriental Hebrew ÿ ח), Kushitic, Egyptian, and also Berber (but only in loan words from Arabic). A uvular q is equally widespread. Emphatic consonants (ṭ ḍ ḷ ṣ ẓ or ð̣ in the traditional analysis, but almost every consonant in some dialects have emphatic counterparts) are much more restricted. These sounds have no English counterpart

except that ļ resembles English l in *table*, as opposed (in some dialects) to l in
Lee. In some Chadic languages initial nasal stop clusters occur such as **mb-**;
Newman and Ma suggest that these clusters may have been due to the influence
of neigbouring Niger-Kordofanian languages.[4]

The structure of words commonly involves a consonant base, often three
consonants; cf. the following bases for *death, die*: Semitic, Egyptian, Berber
mwt (Chadic [Hausa] **mutù**).

Throughout the phylum, masculine and feminine genders are indicated in
both nouns and pronouns except for a few western Kushitic languages and one
subgroup of Chadic (the Plateau-Sahel branch in Newman and Ma's classification). The feminine marker is normally **t** or **at**, but may be some form of **a** in
nouns—presumably because of a loss of the **t**, as in Middle Egyptian and Modern
Arabic; e.g., Classical Arabic (**ʔal-**) **luɣatu**, Modern Cairene Arabic (**ʔil-**) **luɣa** *the
tongue, language*. A difference is commonly made between *you masculine* and
you feminine in the singular. Less frequently gender distinctions are indicated in
all the plural pronouns.

The basic word order in Semitic, Egyptian and Berber is VSO. In Chadic SVO
is usual, in Kushitic SOV.

Fairly elaborate case systems marked by suffixes occur in Kushitic and Semitic, often three in number: nominative, genitive, accusative, as in Somali and
Classical Arabic. A four case system (the above plus dative) occurs in Galla and
may have occurred in Proto-Semitic as well. Bilin and Awiya reportedly have a
seven case system including comitative, directive, and ablative cases. Information
concerning Ancient Egyptian is deficient but case does not occur in Koptic
(apart perhaps from the possessive construction). Chadic normally has no cases
although a defective locative sometimes crops up. Berber has a unique system of
independent and dependent noun not found elsewhere, whereby a genitive following the thing possessed, and a subject following the verb have the same form;
thus, **a-gellíd** *king* (independent or absolute form), but **tigimi u-gellíd** *house of
the king* and **iffúɣ u-gellíd** *the king went out* (both using the dependent form or
status annexus) — a variant of the verbal phrase with subject first in the independent form: **a-gellíd iffúɣ**.

Plurals frequently involve discontinuous or infixed elements, prominently
an -a- infix; e.g. Ethiopic **ʔəzn** *ear* pl, **ʔəz-a-n**; Berber **ŋgun** *belly* pl. **ŋgw-a-nen**;
Koptic **hime** *woman* pl. **hi-aa-me**; Hausa **askaa** *razor* pl. **as-àa-k-ee**.

Nouns in some languages, notably in Semitic but also a few Chadic languages,
require -n or -m suffixes when indefinite, but not definite; e.g. Classical Arabic
ʔal-waladu *the boy* but **waladu-n** *a boy*. In Semiticist jargon, this feature, which
occurs only in Afro-Asiatic languages, is called NUUNATION (or MIIMATION if
the suffix is -m).

Possessive phrases almost invariably take the order possessed-possessor, the possessed often having a special form, which may be due to stress factors. Adjectives normally follow the nouns they modify or else may either follow or precede.

In verb morphology, different constructions are often required for the perfective and imperfective. In Semitic the verb form itself normally shows ablaut, and the perfective requires concordial pronoun suffixes, the imperfective prefixes; e.g. Amharic *I* (1st person) perfective is **-hu** (a suffix), imperfective ə- (a prefix). In Hausa, a verb is used in the perfective, but a verbal noun (for most classes of verb) in the imperfective: **yaa zoo** *he came* vs. **yanàa zuwàa** *he is coming*.

A considerable amount of reconstruction has been done for Semitic, a little on Chadic, practically nothing for the other groups. The sound systems that have been reconstructed for Proto-Semitic and Proto-Chadic[5] are as follows:

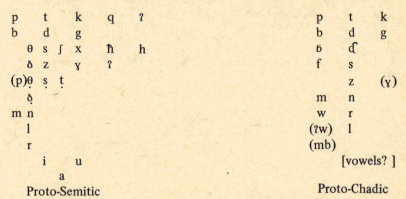

p	t	k	q	ʔ		p	t	k	
b	d	g				b	d	g	
	θ s ʃ x	ħ	h			ɓ	ɗ		
	ð z ɣ	ʕ				f	s		
(p)θ̣	ṣ ṭ						z	(ɣ)	
	ð̣					m	n		
m n						w	r		
l						(ʔw)	l		
r						(mb)			
i u						[vowels?]			
a									

Proto-Semitic   Proto-Chadic

No comparable reconstruction for Proto-Afro-Asiatic itself has been made except for studies by Greenberg[6] on the labial consonants. He reconstructs the following: p b f ɓ mb (as well as m w). Apart from an attempt to formalize sound correspondences between Hausa and Egyptian by C.H. Hodge,[7] almost nothing else has been done in comparative Afro-Asiatic apart from the extensive work on Semitic and Egyptian.[8]

Notes and References

Important works on the languages of this group are quite numerous and include studies by Abraham, Andrzejewski, Cohen, Greenberg, Hodge, Leslau, Parsons, and many others. A grammar of particular interest for methodological reasons is Paul Newman, 1970, *A grammar of Tera*. (University of California Publications in Linguistics, Vol. 57), Los Angeles.

1) The Mogogodo, a forgotten Cushitic people, *Journal of African Languages*, 2.1.29-43.
2) Flemming, (to appear) Asa and Aramanik: Cushitic hunters in Masai-land.
3) Personal communication. Colin Turnbell has recently produced a controversial anthropological account of this group in his *The mountain people*.
4) Paul Newman and Roxana Ma, 1966, Comparative Chadic: phonology and lexicon, *Journal of African Languages* 5.3.218-281.
5) *Ibid.*
6) J.H. Greenberg, 1958, The labial consonants of Proto-Afro-Asiatic, *Word*, 14.2/3.295-302, 1965. The evidence for */mb/ as a proto-Afroasiatic phoneme, in *Symbolae Linguisticae in Honorem Georgii Kurytowicz. (Biuletyn Towarzystwa Językoznawczego)*, Krakow, pp 88—92.
7) Carleton T. Hodge, 1966, Hausa-Egyptian establishment, *Anthropological* Linguistics, 8.1:40-57.
8) See the work of Calice, Ember, Cohen, and others.

CHAPTER XI

Nilo-Saharan

This phylum is the most controversial of all in Greenberg's scheme. For one thing, it contains the languages involved in the hotly debated Nilo-Hamitic controversy. And in addition it is comprised of several others that until Greenberg's 1963 revision were held by nearly everyone, including Greenberg, to be independent languages without known relatives.

The history of the classification of Songhai is interesting here. Delafosse grouped it with Mande in his Nigéro-Sénégalais family. Westermann classified it in his 1927 study as a member of the Gur branch of Western Sudanic. In 1952, he and Bryan set it up as an isolated unit unrelated to any other known language or Language Group. In his first study, Greenberg similarly set it up as an isolated language. In 1953, in a methodological paper published in the symposium *Anthropology today*, he suggested a relationship between Songhai and Niger-Kongo, presumably as co-ordinate units in a larger grouping. In 1963, it was integrated into a new grouping, the one considered in this chapter: Nilo-Saharan.

Nilo-Saharan is essentially comprised of that part of what Westermann called Sudanic when Niger-Kordofanian elements have been excluded. Greenberg's own thinking on the matter has been quite conservative. In his 1948 essay, he set up nine independent families that have since been labeled as Nilo-Saharan: Eastern Sudanic, Central Sudanic, Kunama, Berta, Central Saharan, Fur, Koman, Maban, Songhai. In a 1955 edition of these essays, he reduced this number somewhat by producing evidence which joined Eastern Sudanic, Central Sudanic, Kunama, and Berta in a group he first called Macro-Sudanic but later changed to Chari-Nile, following a suggestion by Welmers.

The most widely discussed controversy associated with this phylum, the status of Nilo-Hamitic, is actually one of quite recent vintage. The earliest writers on the subject, e.g. Murray and Müller in the nineteenth century, did not distinguish Nilotic and Nilo-Hamitic and so the Greenberg position represents a return to an earlier position.

Robert Shafer,[1] in a re-examination of the evidence for Chari-Nile, concluded that few systematic sound correspondences could be deduced from the vocabulary resemblances Greenberg suggested. Shafer rejected not only the Chari-Nile group as a consequence, but also the technique of mass-comparison to establish genetic relationship. Surely if the putative cognates were indeed cognates, then sound correspondences should be inherent in the data—granted the validity of linguistic theory. Shafer's inability to establish many sound correspondences in this instances may have a number of explanations. Greenberg could have been mistaken, but the total body of evidence he presents makes this unlikely. Or, Shafer may be requiring unrealistically strict correspondences without taking into account various secondary sound changes that tend to obscure correspondence. After all, Old English **oo** (ō) has something on the order of 16 different reflexes in modern English, as in *good* (u), *food* (uw), *blood* (ʌ), *don't* (ow), *soft* (o), *floor* (oh), etc. Historical reconstruction and the establishment of sound correspondences must be done in the light of realism and plausibility. Nevertheless, whatever the answer to the difficulties raised by Shafer, his work raises the important issue of eventually rigorizing the evidence for Greenberg's conclusions.

Nilo-Saharan languages are spoken by relatively few people as compared to the phyla already considered: about 11,000,000 in all. More than half of these speak Nilotic (including "Nilo-Hamitic"). The most important individual languages within the phylum include Kanuri, Luo, and Nubian, each with about 1,000,000 speakers.

Because the proposal of the phylum and of tenable groupings within it are of fairly recent age, and owing to the dearth of really basic and even elementary materials to work with—no adequate dictionaries exist for Songhai and Kanuri, for example, despite their importance—very little can be said about the phylum as a whole. The amount of superficial diversity from language to language would seem to be considerable from the available information.

The languages are almost invariably tonal.

Central vowels, otherwise fairly rare in Africa languages, are not uncommon; in Kanuri we find /ə/, and in many Nilotic languages as many as four centralized vowels occur. On the other hand, ejectives and double stops are quite uncommon.

Basic word order is most frequently SVO except for Nilo-Hamitic and a few other Eastern Sudanic languages with VSO. Adjectives tend to follow the noun modified, although there is a good deal of variation. In possessive phrases, the possessed usually precedes the possessor.

Noun gender is reported only for Nilo-Hamitic. In Maasai, for example, nouns are marked for gender by the prefixes **ol-** (masculine), **eŋk-** (feminine), and **e-** (locative); these prefixes are sometimes dropped, but never when the noun is cited in isolation.

Noun plurals seem in many instances to involve a suffixed pronoun *they* (at least historically) but quite frequently a considerable number of plural formations are reported, usually involving a suffix, however. In Saharan languages such

as Kanuri or Daza, on the other hand, the plural is marked quite simply by a
suffix -a.

Case systems are not infrequent, again usually marked by suffixes as in Kanuri, but also by internal changes such as tone, as in Nilo-Hamitic, or by vowel
changes of various kinds as in Nilotic.

Pronouns normally show what is called a block pattern: plural pronouns are
basically the same as the corresponding singular ones plus some additional element. For example, in Moru we find a prefix à- accompanied by tone changes:

	Singular	Plural
1	má	àmà
2	mí	àmì
3	ányà	ànyá

In Luo, there is a plural prefix (w- or g-, presumably from an earlier *g- in all
instances); in Kanuri, a plural suffix (-àndí)

	Luo			Kanuri		
	Singular	Plural		Singular	Plural	
1	án	w-án		wú {wí}	àndí	{w-àndí}
2	ín	(w)-ún		nyí {ní}	n-àndí	
3	ɛ́n	g-ín		ʃí {sí}	s-àndí	

(The Kanuri forms in braces are morphophonemic spellings of the phonemically
spelled words to their left.) The block pattern is not restricted to Nilo-Saharan,
however, but is also quite frequent in Afro-Asiatic, e.g., in Hausa and Iraqw:

	Hausa			Iraqw	
	Singular	Plural		Singular	Plural
1	n-ɪ {mi}	m-u		gàgár	gàràr-án
2	k-i	k-u		gàgád	gàgàd-á
3	ʃ-i {si}	s-u		gàgár	gàgàr-ír

(Feminine 2d and 3d person forms have been ignored here.) Gender distinctions
are nowhere in Nilo-Saharan realized in pronouns despite the fact that nouns
may be overtly marked for gender; e.g., Maasai with its three noun genders has
only a single third person pronoun singular: **nìnyέ** *he, she, it* (also *there*).

Aspectual distinctions in verbs are frequently expressed by tonal changes, but
this holds true for Chari-Nile languages mostly. Verbal derivation is extensive.

No serious attempts have been made so far to reconstruct protoforms.

Notes and References

Important works on this group of languages include the following:

J.P. Crazzolara, 1933, *Outlines of a Nuer grammar*, Wien.
A.N. Tucker and J. Tompo Ole Mpaayei, 1955, *A Maasai grammar*, London.
Carl H. Armbruster, 1960, *Dongolese Nubian: a grammar*, Cambridge.
Carl H. Armbruster, 1965, *Dongolese Nubian: a lexicon*, Cambridge.
R.P.A. Prost, 1956, *La langue Soñay et ses dialectes*, Dakar.
Johannes Lukas, 1937, *A study of the Kanuri language*, London.
A.N. Tucker and M.A. Bryan, 1966, *Linguistic analyses: The non-Bantu languages of north-eastern Africa*.
Oswin Köhler, 1955, *Geschichte der Erforschung der nilotischen Sprachen*, Berlin.

1) Robert Shafer, 1959, Phonétique comparée du Nigéro-Sénégalien (Mande), *Bulletin d'Institut Français d'Afrique Noire*, **21**, pp. 179–200.

CHAPTER XII

Khoisan

The Khoisan language phylum is still sometimes referred to as the Click phylum and was formerly called Macro-Khoisan. The current term was coined by L. Schultze apparently from the Hottentot's word for *person* (**kxoe**) and their name for the Bushmen (**sa-n**). The term was popularized by the anthropologist I. Schapera and Dorothea Bleek, one of the leading Khoisan language specialists.

The languages of this group are probably the least well studied in Africa and several have become extinct in modern times without adequate analysis, e.g., Grikwa Hottentot and /Kam-ka!ke Bushman.

The establishment of a Khoisan phylum has had a fairly straight-forward development. It may be recalled that as early as 1808 Lichtenstein divided South African languages into Hottentot and Kaffir (Bantu). Baldi in 1826 continued using the term Hottentot for both Hottentot and Bushman, apparently, presumably because of the scarcity of information about non-Hottentot Khoisan languages, and the comparatively greater amount of information available about Hottentot. After all, the first specimens of Hottentot were recorded as early as 1691 by Wreede and Grevenboek at the instigation of a friend of Leibniz's.

Müller, Cust, Lepsius, and Hahn among others were agreed that Bushman and Hottentot were related. A discordant note was struck by Lepsius, who classified them differently, subsuming them under Hamitic rather than considering them as an independent group. Meinhof compounded the discord by separating Bushman from Hottentot, setting Bushman up as an independent group, and subsuming Hottentot under Hamitic. All this very largely because of the occurrence of sex gender in Hottentot. However, Hottentot WAS admitted to be Bushman influenced. The facts are that vocabulary similarities between Hottentot and Afro-Asiatic are practically nonexistent. The affix similarities are flimsy indeed: Hottentot feminine suffix -s in singular, -ti in plural suggesting Afro-Asiatic feminine marker t; Hottentot masculine -b suggesting Kushite Bedauye masculine accusative -ba and the p and f of Egyptian demonstratives and possessive pronouns. The extreme position taken by Meinhof seems to be held by no one at present. However, some scholars cling to a modified view, as does Schapera, that Hottentot is basically Bushman with Hamitic features.

In addition to the South African Khoisan nucleus, two small groups in Tanzania constitute the remaining members of the entire phylum: Sandawe and Hatsa.

Both were discovered after 1900 and linguistic reports are fragmentary to say the least. The presence of clicks in both immediately suggested a tie up with the South African languages.

The position taken by Greenberg, which has remained almost entirely unchanged in the several revisions of his classification, has been severely criticized by Westphal.[1] The basis of this attack is largely that Greenberg uncritically accepted Bleek's classification of Naron as Bushman rather than Hottentot, which Westphal maintains it is, and that this vitiates Greenberg's Hottentot-Bushman comparisons. Westphal has apparently ignored the fact that Greenberg places Naron in his Central South African Khoisan group, along with Hottentot (the other Bushman languages are put in Northern and Southern branches). By doing so, Greenberg anticipated Westphal's own classification on this point.

Westphal further believes that the traditional notion of Khoisan actually encompasses five independent and unrelated language groups:

1) Hottentot (including Naron)
2) !Kung-Bushman
3) ≠Huang-Bushman
4) N/hu-Bushman (better known as ≠Khomani)
5) Kwadi (not mentioned by Greenberg at all and nowhere written up as yet).

Westphal's methodology in setting up these groups is typological. He says of Hottentot and "Bushman" (groups 2, 3, and 4), that any possible similarity between them

goes no farther than the... "click" sounds common to both, and *some* common vocabulary items. Their phonologies and their grammars are so divergent that they cannot be treated under the same heading. [italics mine EAG]

The kind of criteria Westphal himself proposes in establishing genetic groupings includes word order (which is SOV in Hottentot, SVO in Bushman), and grammatical gender (present in Hottentot, absent according to Westphal in all "Bushman" languages). The validity of such arguments should be clear from earlier discussions.

The Khoisan languages are spoken by a total of fewer than 75,000 people, making this phylum the smallest with regard to speakers in the continent. A few Khoisan languages or at least dialects have apparently become extinct quite recently and several languages have speech communities so small that they seem unlikely to survive the century, e.g. Korana Hottentot spoken by not more than 50 people; N/hu-Bushman, by not more than 10. Kwadi, spoken in Angola, of uncertain status but possibly Khoisan, has only a handful of speakers.

The most famous characteristic of the Khoisan languages is clicks, and no language of the grouped is reported as having fewer than three. Noun, adjective, and verb roots normally begin with a click. Even in Hottentot, which reportedly uses clicks less frequently than the Bushman languages, about seventy percent of such roots do begin with a click.

The other consonants tend to fall into a fairly skew pattern. In Nama, for example, we find the following.

p	t	k	ʔ
	s	x	h
	ts	kx	
m	n		
	r		
	l		

All the Khoisan languages for which there is adequate information are reportedly tonal. They were once discribed as having a contour tone pattern but recent work by Hagman suggests that this may be an error and that the languages really have a register system.

In Hottentot, Sandawe, and Hatsa, and also in Naron Bushman, grammatical gender occurs: in Naron, masculine and feminine; in Hottentot and Sandawe these plus common gender. When it occurs at all, gender is marked in both singular and plural as well as in pronouns.

Khoisan languages regularly distinguish a dual; a form of Bushman noted by P.W. Schmidt reportedly distinguishes a trial also, altogether unique in Africa.

Case systems have been reported for some Khoisan languages. In /Xam Bushman, a nominative and objective form may be identical, but an emphatic nominative also exists marked by a suffix **-kən** added to the simple form in most instances. The order in the possessive phrase varies. In some Bushman languages, the order is possessor possessed, with the possessor taking a suffix **-ka**. In Hottentot, the order is possessed-possessor with an intervening element (suffix?) **di**.

Almost nothing has been done on reconstruction. In a way, this is as it should be seeing that so little has been done on description.

Notes and References

Important works on Khoisan languages include the following.

Douglas M. Beach, 1938, *The phonetics of the Hottentot language*, Cambridge.
D. F. Bleek, 1929, *Comparative vocabularies of Bushman languages*, Cambridge.
D. Bleek, 1956, *Bushman dictionary*, New Haven.
R. Hagman, [1973], *A grammar of Nama Hottentot* (unpublished PhD dissertation, Columbia University, N.Y.).

1)   E. Westphal, 1962, A re-classification of southern African non-Bantu languages, *Journal of African languages* 1.1–8.
2)   In A. N. Tucker and M. A. Bryan, 1956, *The non-Bantu languages of north-eastern Africa*, Oxford, 166–7.

CHAPTER XIII

Residual Topics in Classification

AUSTRONESIAN or MALAYO–POLYNESIAN

Malagasy spoken on the island of Madagascar represents the sole example of the Austronesian phylum with relevance for students of African languages. It is believed to be the only language spoken on the island with the possible exception of what has been called Beosy, as yet unstudied, spoken in the Bemará mountains not far from the west coast. Beosy may turn out to be Bantu (but this is unlikely) because Luis Mariano, who traveled to Madagascar in 1613-1614 reported that an African language was spoken on the west coast. Malagasy contains a great many loan words taken from Bantu, but the reverse does not seem to hold true, although an occasional word or two does appear on the mainland, e.g., variations on **fiotsy** *banana*.

The resemblances of Malagasy to languages spoken in Indonesia, Malaya, the Philippines, and neighboring areas are so striking that even superficial familiarity would suggest close ties between them. The traveler Mariano, mentioned above, maintained that the people had migrated there from Malacca and based his hypothesis on the great similarity between the languages. In 1708, a Dutch scholar Hadrian Reland published a comparison of Malay and Malagasy, and included sound corresponces in his discussion. J. R. Forsyer, a German member of Captain Cook's expedition of 1772–1775, compared Malagasy with Malay and Javanese, concluded that they were descendents of an ancient language, and vaguely suggested the existence of the Austronesian phylum. This phylum was really first proposed by William Marsden in 1780 (published 1782). However, the beginning of comparative Austronesian studies is usually dated from the publication of Wilhelm von Humboldt's posthumous publication, *Über die Kawi-Sprache* (in 3 volumes, 1836-1839). In this work he attempted to prove once and for all the relationship of Malagasy to Indonesian and Polynesian, ignoring for the most part the scholarly work that preceded his. He concluded that Malagasy was closer to Philippino languages than to Malay, as had previously been thought.

The most recent classification of Malagasy by Isidore Dyen, following an hypothesis by Otto Chr. Dahl, aligns it most closely to Maanyan spoken on the island of Borneo. In Dyen's view the two languages form a distinct subgroup, the

Malagasy Cluster, which is fairly closely related to languages of western Indonesia such as Malay, Javanese, Balinese, and Minangkabau. By the way, although the terms Austronesian and Malayo-Polynesian have usually been used as synonyms in the scientific literature, Dyen has introduced a distinction, making Austronesian the more inclusive term, and Malayo-Polynesian a subgroup within the Austronesian phylum.[1]

Since all the closest linguistic relatives of Malagasy are about 2000 miles away in Indonesia and the South Pacific area, one can only surmise that Austronesian speaking peoples are not indigenous to the island, but have migrated to it. The journey itself is not an implausible one since trade connections along the Sabaean Lane in the Indian Ocean are attested from very early times and coins of Alexander the Great have been found in the Philippine islands. The consensus is that the migration took place about the start of the Christian era and that up till that time Madagascar was uninhabited.[2] Mainland African language influences therefore represent a later increment rather than a substratum. The relatively insignificant linguistic impact by Malagasy on the mainland is all the more curious because innovations of considerable importance to Africa apparently accompanied the migrations, e.g., the introduction of yams, taro, bananas, sugarcane.

Malagasy is spoken by about 6,000,000 people in several dialects all quite similar and mutually intelligible. The Merina dialect, written in Latin script, has been the official language since 1820. Since Malagasy is only one of about 500 Austronesian languages spoken almost entirely in another geographical area, no attempt will here be made to summarize general characteristics of that group, or to consider any aspects of the fairly extensive reconstruction that has been made.

Malagasy is nontonal. The phonemic inventory has been reported as follows for the standard dialect:

m	n	ŋ		i	u
p	t	k		e	a
b	d	g			
v	z				
f	s	h			
	l				
	r				

(o occurs in some dialects; tr and dr are found and may represent unit phonemes, as may prenasalized stops mp, nt etc).

Basic word order in VOS with an indefinite object, VSO with a definite object. An adjective follows the noun modified. The possessive phrase has the order possessed-possessor.

Nouns do not overtly show case or number, but pronouns indicate number.

Gender classes do not exist. Verb phrases can be transformed into a number of passive constructions not otherwise found in African languages and difficult to render in English: passives of instrument, place, etc.

MEROÏTIC

Meroïtic is known from hieroglyphic inscriptions from Meroë in the Sudan, once the capital of an empire that flourished just before the beginning of the Christian era. About 300 inscriptions have been found, the first by Cailiand in 1820. Lepsius discovered perhaps the most important of these: an inscription on the base of a statue written mostly in Ancient Egyptian but with the names of Meroïtic kings and queens written in both languages. By means of this F. Ll. Griffith succeeded in demonstrating the alphabetic nature of Meroïtic script and in assigning certain sound values to the various symbols. However, to this day, because of the absence of more extensive bilingual texts, the language itself has not been deciphered.

On these grounds, Greenberg and other scholars have offered no classification at all. Speculation has not thereby been stopped. Marcel Cohen thought it was Kushitic, particularly close to modern Beja. Homburger considered it a late form of Egyptian—not surprisingly in light of her theory of an Egyptian base for African languages in general. Zylharz, who has written up the most complete account of the Meroïtic problem, considered it to be early Nubian or closely related to Nubian.

The most promising approach has been that of Bruce Trigger.[3] In much the same way that Grotefend was able to decipher cuneiform, Trigger has attempted to translate certain incriptions by guessing at possible linguistic formulae, especially on funeral stele that might be in imitation of Egyptian ones. His tentative conclusion is that Meroïtic is indeed related to Nubian, but he goes no further than to say it is Eastern Sudanic.

Further work is being done by East German scholars, among them Fritz Huitze, who has stated that a definite breakthrough now seems in sight.

PIGMY LANGUAGES

At present all African Pigmies speak the languages of their neighbors. Thus, some Pigmy groups speak Bantu languages; others, other Niger-Kordofanian languages or Nilo-Saharan; e.g. the Mbuti and Twa speak Bantu; the Efe, Central Sudanic. No independent Pigmy language exists nor is there any evidence that one has ever existed. Nevertheless, a great many scholars have assumed that an original Pigmy language has now been lost.

The argument for this rests largely on racial considerations. The traditional racial groupings can be broadly correlated with the language phyla: caucasoids speak Afro-Asiatic, negroids speak Niger-Kordofanian or Nilo-Saharan, bushmanoids speak Khoisan. Of course, exceptions occur and they are important: the negroid Bergdama speak a Khoisan language; and Chadic (a subgroup of Afro-Asiatic) is spoken by predominantly negroid peoples also. But these examples can perhaps best be explained as instances of borrowing. In the traditional view, Pigmies represent a race and they should, therefore, be associated with a distinct language or languages as well. And presumably African Pigmy language(s) should be related to those spoken by Pigmies elsewhere, such as the Andaman Islanders, and the Semang of Malaya. Greenberg has offered the hypothesis that these non-African languages are indeed genetically related but related also to Papuan and Australian spoken by non-pigmoid groups.

The traditional view is shaky on many points but very largely because it is questionable that Pigmies represent a race. They may well be short because of dietary and other factors. Murdock, who accepts the theory of an original Pigmy language, has suggested that even if adaptation of this sort had really taken place, it would have involved such a considerable amount of time, that the degree of difference between the speech of Pigmies and their neighbors should be far greater than it is now, if they originally spoke the same language. Hence, the Pigmies must have borrowed neighboring languages whatever their history.

However, modern racial and genetic theory suggests that such an adaptive radiation or modification can readily be accomplished in a few generations. As a matter of fact, the earliest Pigmy remains are fairly recent and have not been discovered in the earliest sites. These considerations suggest that there is no need to posit the existence of an ancestral Pigmy language at all.

LARGER GROUPINGS

From time to time groupings are suggested that are more extensive than those proposed by Greenberg. In some instances these hypotheses seem plausible enough, but the evidence is inadequate.

Many of the more implausible suggestions fall into well recognized categories. For example, Basque, Sumerian, and Dravidian are non-African languages of unknown genetic affiliation despite extensive attempts to find linguistic relatives. Mukarovski has recently tried to link up Basque with Fulani via a Mauretanian substratum. Wanger attempted the same thing with Bantu and Sumerian. In addition, Kanuri has been linked up with Sumerian, and both Bantu and Sumerian with Dravidian, a language family spoken in southern Indian. Most of these attempts concern themselves with single languages or subgroups of more inclusive groupings and fail to consider the larger implications, e.g., if Fulani is really related to Basque then so are all the Niger-Kordofanian languages. A similar argument applied in our discussion of English-Hausa relationships.

Perhaps the most famous, or rather notorious, superphylum is that proposed by Lilias Homburger. As we have already mentioned, all the languages of Black Africa are in her opinion derived from Egyptian. That means, that in some sense all the languages of Africa (with the possible exception of Khoisan) are Afro-Asiatic, although Homburger herself never quite spelt it out in this way. In later versions of her theory, she added a Dravidian base as well. The evidence she presents, however, is uneven and she even includes in her comparative word list items such as *cow* and *horse*: these could not by any stretch of the imagination been part of the ancestral language of her proposed group because they were unknown in Africa until quite late, the horse being introduced about 1000 BC, cattle somewhat earlier, about 5000 BC—but too late for any realistic proto-language such as she proposed.

Several attempts have been made to relate Afro-Asiatic to other phyla. At one point Greenberg entertained the idea of an ultimate affiliation with Chari-Nile, but this has apparently since been abandoned after the establishment of the Nilo-Saharan phylum. Several linguists have proposed linking Afro-Asiatic with Indo-European, which is comprised of English, German, French, Russian, Greek, Armenian, Hindi, etc. Herman Møller, a Danish linguist, made the most thorough-going examination of the evidence to date and concluded that they were related. But the evidence he accepted was of a typological and hence typically vague nature, such as the occurrence of gender and vowel ablaut in both. Few scholars accept his evidence although his conclusion may be correct. One linguist who did accept it was the world-famous Louis Hjelmslev. In a little book published just before his death he set up the most comprehensive scheme of genetic relationship so far proposed by any reputable linguist. He accepted not only Møller's theory about the relationship of Afro-Asiatic with Indo-European, but also Homburger's (pre-Dravidian) theory of African languages as well as the view of Holger Pedersen, another Dane, about the unity of Indo-European and Uralic (which includes Finnish, Hungarian, and Samoyed). Hjelmslev called this superphylum Nostratic. Needless to say, Nostratic is still to be established to everyone's satisfaction.

A certain amount of evidence suggests a tie-up between Niger-Kordofanian and Nilo-Saharan. I call the resulting superphylum Kongo-Saharan. The main work that has been done on this subject is that of Margaret A. Bryan, who was not building a case for Kongo-Saharan, but rather trying to salvage the distinctiveness of "Nilo-Hamitic" against Greenberg's onslaughts. She investigated certain elements she designated as T, K, and N in forming singulars and plurals in nouns, pronouns, and demonstratives in several East African languages. Rather than setting up a macro-family (which she regarded then as a macro-monstrosity), she talked instead of a T/K and an N/K substratum, and hinted somewhat vaguely at a complicated Mischsprache situation, the details of which are now lost and perhaps unknowable. An examination of the languages she considered shows that all are members either of Nilo-Saharan or Niger-Kordofanian, with the exception of Iraqw. But the inclusion of Iraqw must be rejected, since it lacks K and N elements altogether, and uses T in only two out of four possible ways.

Some of the evidence that might be adduced for Kongo-Saharan follows (NK:Niger-Kordofanian, NS:Nilo-Saharan).

1) A singulative in **t.** Cf. NK Koalib **t-au** *pl. y-au drop of water* with NS Nubian **wɔl-tu** pl. **wɔl** *piece of charcoal.*

2) Plurals in **-k** (or **-ŋ** derived from ***-kʔ**), particularly with interrogatives, kinship terms, pronouns. Cf. NK Nyimang **ŋa** pl. **ŋa·ni** *who?* —NS Fur **kii** pl. **kii-ŋ** *who?*

3) The **t/k** singular-plural alternation. This was listed as a NS trait by Greenberg, especially of Chari-Nile. It may be related to the NK Proto-Bantu prefixes ***de-*ga**. In NK Kadugli-Krongo the **ta-ka** prefixes are used with noun agents and members of a tribe; in NS Tama and Eranga, **t-k** is reported particularly for "ethnic names".

4) The **n/k** singular-plural alternation. In NK Katcha verbs take **n** in singular, **k** in plural; eg. **n-asalaʔa** *I look at* pl. **k-asalaŋa** *we inclusive look at*. In NS Maba and Teso, an **n/k** alternation for singular vs plural action is a common device. Greenberg includes **n/k** as a NS trait, and lists verb plurals in **k** as another.

5) A **li** or **di** prefix for body parts. This is the common NK form and is found in various NS Central Sudanic languages.

6) Third person singular pronoun in **o/u** or (particularly as nonsubject form) **e**, NK Ewe **o** or **e** alternation for subject,—**e** for object, NS Meje **o** subject, **-ɛ** possessive.

A number of vocabulary items also support the Kongo-Saharan hypothesis. Interestingly enough if the hypothesis proves valid it would mean a greater correlation between language and race since most of the negroid peoples of Africa would speak Kongo-Saharan.

A few details point to a link between Niger-Kordofanian and Afro-Asiatic.[5] In Arabic the word for *blood* is **dam** ending on an **-m** as do two or three other words denoting liquids. This is reminiscent of the Niger-Kordofanian **ma** affix used with liquids. In the Hausa word **sárkíi** *king*, emir, the **-kíi** is known from comparative evidence to be a suffix, as is perhaps the **-kìi** in **dookii** *horse*. This suffix may be related to a Niger-Kordofanian **k** element found in pronouns, the prefix in **kabaka** *king* (Ganda), and the Fulani suffix **-ko** as in **gor-ko** *man*. Again the details are tantalizing, but insufficient and in this instance even less clear than in the Kongo-Saharan material.

AFRICAN LANGUAGES ABROAD

Despite the vast population movements associated with the slave trade, few languages were exported out of Africa. It was the policy of slave traders in many cases to break up families and to render the individual slave linguistically isolated. Some West Africans did travel to Europe on their own, and it is known that several West Africans went to London as early as 1554 to study English, but it is unlikely that their linguistic influence on the natives was great.

No African languages really survived in North America. The interesting Gullah dialect of English,[6] spoken by former slaves and their descendants on islands off South Carolina and Georgia and on the coast nearby, preserves many Africanisms but from a variety of sources. Individual words (in particular names) have been identified from a number of West African languages including Igbo, Vai, Ewe, Hausa, Yoruba, and Kongo. With regards to syntax the Gullah dialect often seems to translate literally from African constructions (a technique known as CALQUING), and we find such typically African idioms as **'e tall pass una** *he is taller than you* [he (is) tall surpasses you], and **dey fa go shum** *they went to see her* [they take go see-her]. A number of words of African origin retained in Gullah have become quite common in other varieties of English; e.g. **cooter** *tortoise* (Bambara, Malinke **kuta**), **goober** *peanut* or *groundnut* (from Kongo **ŋguba**), **gumbo** *okra* (Luba **ci-ŋgɔmbɔ**, Umbundu **oci-ŋgɔmbɔ**), **tote** *carry* (Kongo **tota**, **tɔta** *pick up*, Umbundu **tuta** *carry*), **juke** (**box**) (Wolof **jug** *lead a disorderly life*, Bambara **jugu** *wicked, violent*).

In Latin America, the situation was considerably different, particularly in the province of Baía in Brazil where several African languages were spoken until the end of the nineteenth century. In about 1880, Nina Rodriguez was able to collect fairly extensive word lists in Yoruba, Ewe, Hausa, Kanuri, and a few other languages.[7] No such speech communities appear to have survived to this day, however, although a ritual use of Yoruba (known as Nago) is reported in several possession cults such as Umbunda and Candamblé. The high priests of these cults know the language quite well and in one instance at least (which I know of personally) a priest who went to Nigeria was able to communicate by means of it to speakers of African Yoruba. (Miss Ebun Ogunsanya, herself a native speaker of Yoruba, has told me of meeting in 1969 a 90 year old man from Baía who actually spoken Yoruba fluently and had never been to Africa.) A similar retention of Yoruba as a ritual language in various voodoo cults has occurred in Cuba, where it is known as Lucumí. Apparently no one speaks this language natively any more. A language known as Coromanti, derived from some West African language was spoken in Jamaica around 1800, but has apparently disappeared.

Extensive and intimate connections have long existed between East Africa and India and as a consequence, Swahili is sometimes found spoken along the Indian West Coast. The speakers are occasionally referred to as the Seedee. Of course at present, Africans speaking a wide variety of native languages can be found in England, France, the Soviet Union, China, the United States, and elsewhere as part of diplomatic corps, as students, or in a number of other capacities.

That African languages have made an impact on other languages of the world is shown by many loan words. There are few educated people in the world who are not familiar with the Swahili terms **bwana** and **safari** and the word **gorilla**, discussed before (Chapter 8), presumably of West African origin.

Among African words that have become part of English and many other languages we find the magical or mysterious terms **zombi** (cf. Kongo **zumbi** *fetish*), **voodoo** (Ewe **vodũ**), **mumbo jumbo** (perhaps from Mende **mama dyambo** the name of a god), **juju** (Hausa **jùujuu** *spirit*). African words for objects include **assagai** (a kind of spear, ultimately from Berber) and perhaps **banjo** (cf. Kimbundu **mbanza**, a musical instrument similar to a banjo) although the etymology is uncertain: the word is usually said to be a corruption of *bandore*, from Spanish or Portuguese, but this seems to be a mistake. Other words that have been said to be of African origin (frequently Malinke or Wolof) include: **hep** (or **hip**) and **hep-cat**, **boogie-woogie**, **jam** (in **jam-session**), **to jive**, **to goose**, **to bug** someone, to **dig** (meaning to understand, appreciate), to **lam** (meaning to go), **uh-huh** and **uh-uh** (for yes and no), **ofay** and **honkie** (both terms for white man), **cocktail**, **guy**, and **bogus**.

The expressions **to do one's thing**, **to be with it**, and perhaps some others, seem to be calques from widely used phrases in West Africa. The expression **O.K.** has also been attributed a West African origin, but this is not widely admitted.[8]

At least three important plants have names with African etymologies: **kola** (as in *coca-cola*; from Temme **kola** or a neighboring language), **okra** (? Twi **nkru-man**) and **yam** (from a West Atlantic language such as Fulani or Wolof where **nyam** means *food* or *eat*).

A large number of African loan words deal with animals native to Africa. Thus, we find **chimpanzee** (Kongo), **gnu** (Bushman **nqu**), **kudu** (Kafir **iqudu**, ultimately from Hottentot), **tsetse (fly)** (Sesuto **ntsi(ntsi)** *fly*, via Afrikaans), **impala** (Zulu), **okapi** (mbuba), **tenrec** (a kind of monkey); **tandraka** (Malagasy via French). Terms for antelopes of various kinds are especially prolific, although not all are in common English use: **bongo** (Kele or Mpongwe), **dibatag** (Somali), **dikdik** (Ethiopian), **kob** (Wolof), **tiang** (Dinka), **topi** (Bantu, cf. Swahili **tope**).

Figure 11   YORUBA DRUMMER
The drum pictured is an hour-glass tension drum often used in "talking".

TRADE LANGUAGES, PIDGINS, AND CREOLES

Several African languages have been adopted as a second language primarily for commercial reasons. Such a language is a TRADE LANGUAGE or LINGUA FRANCA. Examples include Swahili, Hausa, Fulani, Kongo, Sango.[8]

Sometimes a consciously simplified form of a language is used, and this form is not native to any of the speakers who use it. Such a language is a PIDGIN (from a Chinese-English pidgin word for *business*). A number of pidgins are reported from Africa, based on both native African languages and European ones; e.g. Pidgin English, (Kos Ingilisi or Wes Kos) an English based pidgin spoken throughout West Africa and perhaps the most practical means of communication in that area; Français-tirailleur (or Français-tiraillou), a French based pidgin spoken in the formerly French West African territories (although often referred to as Petit Nègre in Europe, this term has little currency in Africa itself); Up-country Swahili (or Kisettla), a Swahili based pidgin spoken largely in Kenya; Kitchen Kafir (IsiPiki, Basic Bantu, Fanagolo, Chilapalapa, Chilololo, etc.), a Zulu based pidgin spoken in South Africa; Lingala, a Kongo based pidgin spoken in Zaïre and Congo, an Ngbandi based pidgin spoken in Central African Republic and Southern Chad; and a Camerounian pidgin with the intriguing name Pidgin A-70 (so called by Pierre Alexandre with reference to Guthrie's alpha-numeric classification of Bantu languages; also called Ewondo populaire, Bulu bediliva, Bulu des chauffeurs), a Bulu based pidgin.

Most of these languages have, apparently, a very greatly reduced morphology, "syntax by position", and widely varying phonological realizations, often involving loss of tonal contrasts. The prestige of pidgins varies considerably. I have found that educated Ghanaians tend to deprocate the use of Pidgin English, whereas educated Nigerians find it amusing and often slip into it in informal situations. Sango has become the official language of the Central African Republic.

What is for one generation a pidgin sometimes becomes the native language for succeeding generations. Such a language is a CREOLE. An example of this is the creole English of Freetown, Krio, which is almost identical with the Pidgin English of neighboring areas. A Portuguese Creole (Kriyol or Purtugues) is spoken on the Cape Verde Islands (where the indigenous languages have been lost), Gambia, Portuguese Guinea, part of Senegal, and the island of São Tomé.

Pidgins and creoles have posed a number of problems for language classification. The problem boils down to what criteria for classification are chosen. Suzanne Sylvain, for example, used syntactic criteria and concluded that the French Creole spoken on the island of Haiti is really Ewe with French words. Since, however, grammatical characterizations—no matter how transparent—are less tractable than specific vocabulary resemblances, most linguists are agreed that even with regard to pidgins and creoles with their high degree of direct translation (calquing) from one language to another, the usual criteria of genetic affiliation must apply, and hence Haitian Creole must be regarded as a variety of French, Wes Kos a variety of English, Kisettla a variety of Swahili.

The development of pidgins and creoles is now believed to have occured much more frequently than was formerly thought to be the case. The processes of pidginization and creolization have become a matter of considerable theoretical interest and we can expect a number of intensive studies in the near future.[9]

EUROPEAN LANGUAGES SPOKEN IN AFRICA

The languages of the former colonial administrations have remained of considerable importance in Africa. They have even begun to play a crucial role in the social structures of the independent countries since one of the distinctive and unifying features of the ruling elite is their ability to speak the same European language. The continuing importance of these languages stand in marked contrast to the fate of Turkish, which effectively disappeared from the North African scene at the dissolution of the Ottoman Empire even after many centuries of Turkish rule. There seem to be many reasons for this, including the fact that Turkish was competing with Arabic, which had the tremendous prestige of Islam behind it. Furthermore, the governmental organization was such that Turkish was a necessity only at the very highest administrative levels, which were not open to non-Turks; hence, a knowledge of Turkish could not be relied on to further personal advancement. [10]

A number of European languages are spoken in Africa, the most important being English, French, and Portuguese. One language in particular should be singled out as especially interesting: Afrikaans, an official language of South Africa since 1925. It is a Germanic dialect, interintelligible with Dutch, but characterized by considerable morphological simplification, having lost noun gender and personal verb endings.

The various European languages spoken in Africa have come to differ in detail from those spoken in the mother countries, in accent and idiom. The English spoken in South Africa is a case in point. It has been influenced by Afrikaans as well as Zulu and other African languages, e.g. working class people often pronounce p t or k without the aspiration that accompanies them in standard English, perhaps because of Afrikaans influence where corresponding consonants are not aspirated. South Africans normally pronounce words such as Xhosa, Cetewayo with clicks (x as C, c as ʔ). And of course, vocabulary shows Khoisan, Bantu, and Afrikaans influences; e.g. **goga** (Hottentot **xoxo-n**) *any sort of insect*, **bansela** (Zulu) *tip*, **enkosi** (Kafir **inkosi** *chief*) *thank you*, **baas** (Afrikaans) *master, boss,* **vlei** (Afrikaans), *low-lying land where water collects in wet season.*

Particularly interesting is the variety of basically standard English spoken as their native language by many West Africans, who may even have lost fluency in some indigenous tongue, but who still are influenced by the idioms and metaphors of these languages as well as by pidgin. Of cource, some terms have been created within the dialect itself; so, apparently the expression **been-to** meaning a person who has been to England, etc. Other terms are borrowed directly from pidgin; e.g. **dash** *tip, bribe.*

In the growing West African English literature—a constant source of delight for the linguist—an enormous number of very interesting forms may be found, some apparently calques from native languages, others high-falutin mock learned terms, still others colorful analogical formations. The following are a few examples of these.[8]

> I turned and double fasted back to the room.
> He has pregnanced her daughter.
> money-monger (a person too much interested in money)
> foot-break-pot (an ungrateful person).

Here is a story about West African English told to me by David Ames, an anthropologist. It may be apocryphal but it suggests the kinds of language interference that might be encountered in such a complex language situation. A European doctor was examining a woman who complained of pains in her stomach. He asked her whether she had the pains often. She answered, "Every now and every then". The doctor concluded her condition was not grave and gave her some relatively mild medicine. When he returned the next week, he learnt that the woman had died. He had incorrectly diagnosed her sickness because he assumed the woman had meant to say "every now and then", that is, "once in a while". But what she did mean was "always"—which is what "every now" and "every then" would add up to!

Notes and References

1) Isidore Dyen, 1965, *A lexicostatistical classification of the Austronesian languages*, Baltimore.
2) Some scholars believe that Pigmies once inhabited the island, but there is no evidence of this.
3) B.G. Trigger, 1964, Meroitic and Eastern Sudanic: a linguistic relationship?, *Kush*, 12.188−94.
4) Louis Hjelmslev, 1963, *Sproget En introduktion,* København.
5) Here as so often throughout this book I am indebted to Professor Greenberg for much of the information.
6) Written up in Lorenzo Dow Turner, 1949, *Africanisms in the Gullah dialect*, Chicago.
7) Nina Rodriguez, 1932, *Os africanos no Brasil*, São Paulo.
8) See Bernd Heine, 1970, *Status and use of African lingua francas*.
9) Taken from Henry Drewal, unpublished term paper. Recently a number of studies of West African English have appeared, notably in John Spencer, ed. 1971, *The English language in West Africa*.

Part Five   LANGUAGE AND THE NONLINGUISTIC

CHAPTER XIV

Language and History

Although little is known of the history of African languages, they in turn have proved to be of considerable importance in reconstructing African culture history.

The main, but by no means sole, reason for this stems from the notion of genetic relationship between languages discussed earlier. By definition, genetically related languages comprise diverging continuations of a single ancestral language. This protolanguage was presumably spoken at one time by a single speech community living within a restricted geographical area. Examination of situations with known histories make this clear enough. At present, Romance languages—French, Italian, Spanish, Portuguese, Roumanian, etc.—are spoken in an enormous area including western and southern Europe, Central and South America, and elsewhere. All these languages represent a continuation of a single ancestral language, Latin, originally spoken by a speech community in a relatively small area in and around Rome. By analogy we can make reasonable reconstructions about the spread of languages without written records by examining present day distributions.

A clear example that such is the case is provided by Murdock.[1] At present, Kunama and Barya are spoken in Eritrea, on the Red Sea. Their closest linguistic relatives are located further inland along the Nile. Murdock assumed the two languages in question must have split off from their relatives and moved away from their ancestral home. Later he found confirmation of his reconstruction in an Arab account from the eighth century describing the Kunama and Barya as in fact living along the Nile at that time.

Whether languages or language families have been geographically split up because of migrations or some intrusive group is not always clear. From European history, we know that Hungarian speaking peoples cut through the Romance language area and severed direct ties between Roumanian and its related languages. A similar explanation seems most plausible to explain the present distribution of Khoisan languages. A commonly held hypothesis is that bushmanoid peoples, most likely speaking Khoisan languages, inhabited the savannah lands in Africa south of the equator sometime before the Christian era. Today, Khoisan languages are spoken mostly in southern Africa and by two small enclaves in Tanzania. Invading Bantu and Sudanic speaking peoples apparently broke up the original contiguity of the Khoisan language area and the resulting isolated groups were eventually pushed into relatively inhospitable places, most notably the Kalahari desert. A similar breaking up of the Berber languages in North Africa occurred partly as the result of invasions by Arabic speaking peoples, first as a result of the Islamic conquests of the seventh century, and later by the socalled Hillalic invasion, a mass migration of Beduin Arabs into the area about AD 1200.

As a rule, competing hypotheses about migrations, or intrusions, and even the routes taken during these movements can be evaluated as to plausibility by counting the number of "moves" that the hypotheses require.[2] Consider the Afro-Asiatic languages. Let us assume that Greenberg's analysis is correct and that there are five co-ordinate language families within the phylum. Because of the fact that Semitic is "based", as it were, in Asia—and especially because of certain Judeo-Christian traditions or emphases—it has often been assumed that Asia represents the homeland of Afro-Asiatic. Such a view was, moreover, not unreasonable given the earlier subgrouping that made Semitic co-ordinate with the other four groups (Egyptian, Berber, Kushitic, Chadic) taken as a single branch, Hamitic. But in the Greenberg scheme, an Asian origin must be ruled out. If the four groups are really independent and each is co-ordinate with Semitic, then positing an Asian homeland would mean setting up four distinct moves into Africa. But if we assume that Proto-Afro-Asiatic originated and became differentiated within Africa, only a single major move is required: that of Semitic into Asia. (The Arabic and Ethiopic migrations are of course of a much later date and have no bearing on the question at hand.) The simplicity of the second reconstruction makes it the more plausible.

Consider a much lower level problem of the same general type. Fulani is spoken in an enormous area stretching from Dakar on the Atlantic to Adamawa province in Nigeria. A number of accounts of the origin of this language have been conconcted, the most fantastic (and facetious) perhaps being that of M.D.W. Jeffreys, who suggested it was invented arbitrarily by playful children.[3] With regard to the place of origin, the most pertinent fact is that the languages genetically closest to Fulani, viz. Serer, Wolof, and other members of the West Atlantic subgroup of Niger-Kongo, cluster in or near Senegal. Since it is inconceivable that Fulani should have originated *ex nihilo*, it most likely became differentiated in the general area where its relatives are located and then spread from there.

The highly controversial question of the origin of Bantu can only be answered in the same general way. If Greenberg is right, and Bantu represents a fairly low-level subgroup of Benue-Kongo, which in turn is one of six co-ordinate phyla within Niger-Kongo all centered in West Africa, then only one reconstruction seems tenable: that Bantu originated in West Africa (probably in or near

modern Cameroun) and spread out from there. The argument for such a reconstruction is the same as that discussed for Afro-Asiatic. In addition, as a general
rule of thumb, whenever we find very little linguistic differentiation over a large
area, we can usually infer fairly recent language expansion, and conversely, a high
degree of linguistic diversity within an area suggests long term, permanent settlement. The Germanic languages in Europe (German, Dutch, Skandinavian) have
been spoken in more or less the same areas for nearly 2000 years and are now
quite distinct, with a high degree of dialect differentiation within each language.
English, a West Germanic language, is spoken over an area many times the area
of all the other Germanic languages put together, but has spread only within the past 500 years and is quite uniform. The same sort of thing is true
for Russian, and for Bantu. Although Bantu no longer constitutes a single
language, the similarities between contemporary Bantu languages are so striking
and obvious that despite the enormous area covered, and the large number of
people who speak them, a relatively recent spread of Bantu must be posited.
West Africa, the presumed homeland of Bantu, is at present an area where
related languages are so different that the fact of relationship has long been
disputed.

I think no one would seriously doubt the basic validity of such a reconstruction if it were not for disagreement about the classification of Bantu to begin
with. The foremost critic of this scheme is Malcolm Guthrie of the School of
Oriental and African Studies in London. What he challenges is not the methodology of reconstruction, which he himself makes use of in other contexts, but
the crucial assumption that Bantu is a Niger-Kongo language. Guthrie believes
that genetic relationships between Bantu and other languages have not been
demonstrated. In line with his view that vocabulary and other resemblances
between Bantu and Western Sudanic languages can be accounted for in terms of
borrowing, he posits a Pre-Proto-Bantu homeland to the north of the area where
those Western Sudanic languages formerly called Semi-Bantu are now spoken,
i.e. near Lake Chad.[4] At present, no Bantu or even Niger-Kordofanian languages
are spoken in this region at all, and his reconstruction seems untenable.

The actual reconstruction of a protolanguage (more accurately, of course, the
attempts to do so) by means of the comparative method can also provide information for historical inferences. If a word can legitimately be reconstructed as
part of the vocabulary of the protolanguage, the historian can often find clues as
to the cultural repertory of the speakers of that language. This kind of approach
has been labeled as the Wörter-und-Sachen (lit. words-and-things) hypothesis.
The hypothesis is often difficult to apply in practical situations, but seems
reasonable and basically valid because speakers of a language use words to talk
about only those things they know, in some sense. We do not expect people to
invent words for things they have no inkling of simply because the things are

conceivable. For example, if in a given language we find lexical items such as *wine*, *beer*, *cocktail*, *whisky*, *gin*, *bar*, *drunkard*, and the like, we can safely assume that liquor, its use, and the consequences of its use are not unknown to the speakers of that language. (In a slightly different way we should assume that unicorns and mermaids were "known" to a people—as part of their mythology perhaps—if words denoting these things existed in the language, but we need not, of course, conclude that such things existed in the real world.)

In line with these considerations, reconstructed words for a protolanguage can supply hints as to levels of technological development, kinds of economy, geographical habitat, diet, religious practices, etc. For Africa, the Wörter-und-Sachen hypothesis has rarely been applied, but one linguist, Father G. Fortune, has suggested that the following inferences about Proto-Bantu speakers can be made on the basis of reconstructed vocabulary: they were familiar with elephants and giraffes as well as domesticated dogs and chickens; raised beans and melons, made beer and porridge; smelted iron; prized cowry shells, carved drums, hunted with spears and arrows; had chiefs and medicine men, and venerated their ancestors.[5] In a more controversial vein, it should be noted that one can apparently also reconstruct with a high degree of certainty a Proto-Bantu word for *cow* (*-gɔmbɛ) and *goat* (*-bodi) and possibly even a word for *cattle pen* (*-taŋga); these reconstructions follow Guthrie's monumental work in that field and suggest that the Proto-Bantu speakers were familiar with and probably practised animal husbandry involving cattle. This particular inference is at variance with other reconstructions based on nonlinguistic grounds. Murdock, for one, believes that the early Bantu speaking people traveling from West Africa emerged from the tropical forest cattleless and only acquired cattle from Nilotic or Kushitic speaking pastoralists very recently, about AD 1000—perhaps two millenia after Proto-Bantu was spoken. Since a plausible reconstruction of the prehistory of any area requires that the various lines of reasoning underlying the reconstruction should not be contradictory, this sort of problem must obviously be re-investigated in light of the very high degree of probability that the linguistic forms are correct.

The most spectacular application of the hypothesis in reconstructing African culture history has been made by Christopher Ehret in his book *Southern Nilotic History: Linguistic Approaches to the Study of the Past* (1971). Here Ehret has tried to trace the most likely origin for scores of culture words of particular interest for students of East African history, such as *milk*, *goat*, *circumcize*, *iron hoe*, *age set*. Among the more significant of Ehret's substantive findings is his assertion that cattle herding in East Africa is at least one thousand years earlier than Murdock's reconstruction, if not several thousand, and that his postulated "Megalithic Kushites" must be rejected as a significant cultural group responsible for various megalithic ruins scattered throughout East Africa.

LANGUAGE DIFFUSION IN AFRICA

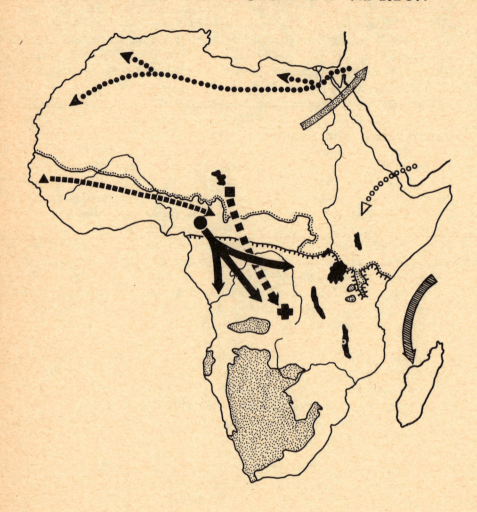

■   Pre-Bantu homeland according to Guthrie
■ ■ ➤ Migration of Pre-Bantu-speaking peoples according to Guthrie
✚   Proto-Bantu homeland according to Guthrie
●   Proto-Bantu homeland according to Greenberg
➡   Initial spread of Bantu according to Greenberg
⋯⋯⋯   Approximate boundary of Niger-Kongo languages
ⲧⲧⲧⲧⲧⲧ Approximate boundary of traditional Bantu
▲   Proto-Fulani homeland
■■■■➤ Migration of Fulani-speaking peoples
▨▨▨▷   Initial spread of Semitic
∘∘∘∘∘∘▷ Migration of Semitic-speaking peoples into Ethiopia
••••••➤ Migration of Arabic-speaking peoples into North Africa
▨▨▨▨▷ Migration from Indonesia of Austronesian-speakers
▨▨▨   Areas in which Khoisan languages are spoken

Figure 12   LANGUAGE DIFFUSION IN AFRICA

It is clear that the Wörter-und-Sachen hypothesis can validly be applied only when accurate linguistic reconstructions are available in the first place. Far too often, the linguist is unable to provide them. On the other hand, he has sometimes reconstructed untenable forms and the more blatant errors can even be caught by the historian. This is the case with the forms for *maize* and *peanuts* reconstructed by Bourquin for Proto-Bantu. Since these New World crops are known to have been introduced into Africa no more than 500 years ago, no Proto-Bantu forms for them are possible. A re-examination of Bourquin's evidence shows that it is insufficient to support his reconstruction. Similar difficulties seem to exist with Newman and Ma's reconstruction of a word for *horse* in Proto-Chadic, which was probably spoken before the introduction of horses into Africa from Asia (perhaps by the Hyksos invaders of Egypt about 1700 BC). The situation here is particularly difficult, however, because the reconstructed form (*d-wk) may well have existed in the protolanguage but with a different meaning (in Ancient Egyptian an apparently related form meant *hippopotamus*).

A different kind of historical inference based on genetic classification is provided by glottochronology, first formulated by Morris Swadesh in the early 1950's. Initially greeted with considerable enthusiasm, this theory has encountered many devastating (or near devastating) critiques in later years. Although it still numbers some celebrated linguists among its devotees, their ranks have diminished greatly. Swadesh was led to formulate his theory by analogy with a dating method suggested for archaeology by the physicist, W.F. Libby. Libby's method exploited the fact that certain radioactive materials deteriorate at a constant rate; once this rate is determined, objects containing the radioactive materials can be dated absolutely, i.e., given a precise date. Swadesh believed that within a language, the basic vocabulary also deteriorates at a given rate. Basic vocabulary was defined by listing (although the lists themselves varied from time to time) and included such words as *I, two, this, sky, arm, woman, father, feather, ash*; these words were assumed to be the most impervious to loss in the total vocabulary of all languages. By examining a number of languages where adequate records existed over a considerable time span, Swadesh concluded that the rate of loss, i.e. replacement, of items in the basic vocabulary for all languages was approximately 20% per 1000 years—provided that interference because of conquests, migrations, and the like was minimal. Swadesh argued that two related languages would presumably lose different words but the same percentages; thus, if these languages split off from each other 1000 years ago, they would share about 66% of their basic vocabulary. Clearly such a device if reliable would be invaluable. As a matter of fact, a number of very tentative dates have been suggested for African languages, e.g., c. 8,000 BC for Proto-Niger-Kongo.[7]

However investigations by other scholars for languages with known histories have challenged some of the basic premises of the theory. Surely if the calculations do not work for languages with known histories, application to languages lacking historical documentation should be even more questionable.

A number of African languages with adequate records going back several hundred years do exist and could be used to test the hypothesis further. Ancient Egyptian and Koptic have actually been compared, but the results are hardly compelling seeing that the a margin of error of 1000 years was recognized for a time differential of less than 3000 years.[8] Armstrong has compared a form of Yoruba recorded more than 100 years ago with a modern dialect. Although the time depth was not great, the virtual identity of the two lists prompted Armstrong to conclude that the rate of change was "glacial".[9] On the other hand, Olmsted found quite unexpected results in his comparison of African Yoruba and a Cuban ritual language, Lucumí, identified as a Yoruba dialect. Since the New World variety could not have been introduced into Cuba more than 500 years ago, there should be relatively little difference between the two. Olmsted found considerable difference, enough in the usual calculations for a separation of 1500 years.[10] The case is interesting and may have several explanations. Unfortunately, Olmsted did not publish the actual word lists he used so that independent corroboration is not possible. I have myself compared African Yoruba with the ritual Yoruba (Nago) found among Brazilian cult groups known as Umbunda; differences are very slight. However, in neither instance are the ritual languages spoken as the native languages of any living speakers.

A few extensive word lists of African languages exist from the sixteenth century: Kongo, Malagasy, and Nubian. Records of Nubian also survive from the eighth century or earlier but only a very defective basic vocabulary can be culled from them. Information for Ge'ez from the fourteenth century at least is adequate enough to be compared with modern Tigrinya. I have myself examined a great many of these. The results vary, but in general are tolerably close to Swadesh's estimates; inaccuracies in the compilation of the word lists themselves may account for much of the residual discrepancies. The very least they suggest is that the rate of vocabulary loss in preliterate speech communities is not noticeably different from that in literate groups. In short, the use of glottochronology can probably be justified out of desperation if nothing else.

A significant source of historical inference not derived from genetic classification is provided by tracing the spread of loan words, and of words dealing with introduced cultural items in general. A considerable amount of work on this has been done with regard to Hausa; a very important finding made by Greenberg [11] based on such work was that Islamic influence probably entered Hausaland first from the east via the Kanuri rather than from the west, the previously accepted theory in line with Hausa tradition as recorded in the Kano chronicle.

Several ways of giving names to cultural innovations have been practised. In most African languages borrowing seems to be extremely common. Sometimes calquing is resorted to; thus, *blackmarket* is quite frequently rendered by native words that actually mean *black* and *market*, e.g., Swahili **soko nyeusi**, Hausa **báƙár kàasúwáa**. Another device involves modifying an already existing word. For example, in some languages it has been reported that the expression for *horse* is literally *European cow*. Two historical inferences can be made immediately from this phrase, which in this instance we know to be correct: (1) horses became known after cattle; (2) horses were European innovations.

In tracing the path of loanwords, one may encounter many difficulties not the least of which is the direction of borrowing. In a few instances, the linguistic forms themselves give adequate clues. Compare Nupe **kə́rə́w**, Kanuri **káɽáw**, and Hausa **káɽáw** *glass bracelet*. Only the Hausa form has a ƙ (an ejective); but Hausa also has a k sound. It is difficult to imagine that a Hausa speaker would use a k in imitation of a ƙ (having both), but it seems likely that a ƙ would be imitated with k in languages with k but without ƙ; hence, the Hausa origin of the word is clear. On the other hand, in the triad Nupe **tùmbi**, Kanuri **tìmbí**, Hausa **tùmbíi** *stomach*, there are no obvious formal clues as to origin. In this case, comparative evidence seems conclusive: languages related to Nupe or Kanuri have no cognates for these forms, whereas Hausa has; again Hausa must be the source. In the same vein, certain "Nilo-Hamitic" and Kushitic languages share a word for *ten* generally on the order of **tomon**. It has usually been considered as a loan from Kushitic into Nilo-Hamitic. However, cognate forms are not found in any languages related to Kushitic, but an apparent cognate is found in Nubian, a Nilo-Saharan language related to Nilo-Hamitic. The direction of transmission seems clear enough.

Occasionally it is possible to identify layers of word borrowings. The idea is to identify words borrowed before a certain change took place and so were subject to that change as opposed to others borrowed later, and hence were unaffected. [12] With luck it may be possible to create an extensive seriation grid permitting ready identification of different time depths for borrowing. A minor example is provided in Luo, where a ***b** between vowels at one stage became **w**. No native Luo words contain a **b** in this position, but in recent loan words from Swahili and other languages such a **b** does occur: **kitabu** *book*, **msalaba** *cross*. They presumably were borrowed after the sound change took place. In a few instances, Luo has **w** in words presumably foreign in origin where neighboring languages show **b**; e.g. **ndawa** *tobacco*, common forms in neighboring languages being **taba** and the like (Acholi **taba**)—an earlier Luo form perhaps ***ndaba**. More elaborate grids have been worked out for a number of Western Sudanic languages. [13]

A seriation grid based on considerations of this sort can provide simple but effective tests of statements about the relative age of borrowings. For example, it has been alleged that the Hausa words **lifidii** *quilted horse armor* and **sirdii** *saddle*—and the objects denoted—are among the earliest Hausa borrowings from the Arabs. [14] This can hardly be the case because a number of Arabic loans were clearly subject to sound changes that have not affected these two items, e.g. **d** and **s** before **i** became **j** and **ʃ** respectively. These words retain the Arabic **d** and **s** and so must be placed at a later level of borrowing.

Practically all the instances where language data have relevance for historical reconstruction stem from the comparative method, as has already been said: either the fact of genetic relationship or reconstruction of particular linguistic forms. At one point linguists had hoped the comparative method might also shed light on the origin of language itself. Since Africa now appears to be the cradle of mankind (from the accelerated archaeological finds being made there), it may well have been the cradle of human speech also. For this reason, the question of language origins is especially pertinent here. However, the earliest protolanguages reconstructable by means of the comparative method seem in no essential ways to be different from contemporary languages in terms of complexity or structure. These reconstructable stages are presumably not early enough to be relevant for the problem at hand.

They have some value, as far as the question of origin goes, nevertheless. Several theories have been advanced as to characteristics of the first human language. Van Ginneken has suggested, for example, that its sound system must have differed considerably from that of languages spoken today. [15] Clicks figure prominently in his hypothetical phonology, as do other contemporary phonological "oddities". But there is some indication both from internal reconstruction and comparative data that clicks in Khoisan may have developed out of originally nonclick consonant combinations. And in practically all instances double stops such as ƙp or ɓd can readily be accounted for as reductions of whole syllables, e.g. ku—or bVd-, respectively. In light of such reconstructions, van Ginneken's suggestions appear fanciful.

The linguist Roman Jakobson has long been identified with another position based on observations of the acquisition of speech by children. He asserts that certain phonemic contrasts are learnt much later than others by children, whatever the language involved. Thus the opposition b-d, is always achieved prior to b-g. All the "oddities" of a language's phonemic repertoire are among the last items to be acquired. It is interesting to note in this connection, as Jakobson does, that Hottentot tales for children are almost devoid of clicks. Consequently, Jakobson argues that the phonological structure of even the most primitive language must have been fairly close to structures existing at present because of the way in which such structures are first learnt. [16]

Obviously what the original language (or languages) of mankind was like will always remain a matter of speculation. However, increased knowledge of the communicative systems of apes and other subhuman animals—together with certain developments within linguistic theory itself—has revived interest in a subject that was once literally tabued in respectable linguistic circles. Among archaeologists, the question has really never been dropped—or rather, at least part of the question, that of the age of language. For want of other lines of evidence, archaeologists have tended to assume that the ability to "make tools to a set and regular pattern" could be correlated with the capacity for speech. The celebrated archaeologist L.S.B. Leakey followed such an argument with regard to a fossil type known as *Homo habilis*, found by him at Olduvai Gorge in Tanzania and dated at something like 1.8 million years or more before the present. Leakey maintained that its jaw formation would have permitted speech and that all known specimens are associated with tools made to a set and regular pattern. [17] However, the cranial capacity of *Homo habilis* (i.e. a measurement of part of the skull that contains the brain) is at most a little more than 720 cubic centimeters, about half that of modern man. Some physical anthropologists have doubted that such pre-men or ape-men forms had sufficient intelligence to be able to speak, seeing that normal children begin to talk with a cranial capacity of about 1000 cubic centimeters. The relationship of brain size to various forms of intelligence is not clear cut, however, as is evidenced by the fact that nanocephalic (i.e. dwarf-headed) idiots can acquire language.

Gordon Hewes has recently argued that language began with gestures and developed along with increased manual dexterity involved in tool-making and tool-using. A gesture origin theory goes back to Lucretius but Hewes arguments are quite attractive, although perforce speculative,[18] especially in light of that fact that recently chimpanzees have been taught to use correctly 60 or more of the manual symbols for the deaf.

The facts are these. No direct evidence exists demonstrating the existence of language for any ape-man or even prehistoric man that did not belong to the variety *Homo sapiens*, the only form of man alive today. Some theorists have denied speech even to Neandertal man, an early kind of *Homo sapiens* that mostly likely interbred with peoples capable of language.

Furthermore, from studies of human children and anthropoid apes, various kinds of thought seem clearly preverbal. The ability to produce rudimentary tools also appears to be preverbal. On the other hand, the creation of symbolic forms almost certainly was accompanied by language, e.g. cave paintings believed to have magic or religious significance, burial of the dead with various ceremonies such as covering the body with red ochre, mutilations presumably associated with initation rites of various sorts such as the removal of teeth (as found in a fossil skull discovered near Singa on the Blue Nile). If this is so, language was unquestionably known to the Upper Pleistocene peoples of about 50,000 years ago, and this date may perhaps be taken as a minimal age for human speech.

Notes and References

1) G. P. Murdock, 1959, *Africa: Its peoples and their culture history*. New York, 43.
2) For a theoretical justification of such a strategy, see Isidore Dyen, 1956 Language distribution and migration theory, *Language* 32: 611–626.
3) Jeffreys, 1947, Speculative origins of the Fulani language, *Africa* 17: 47–54.
4) See, for example, his 1962 article, Bantu origins: a tentative new hypothesis, *Journal of African Languages* 1.1: 9–21. A more detailed exposition of his view is found in volume 1 of his *Comparative Bantu* (1968).
5) G. Fortune, 1962, The contribution of linguistics to ethnohistory, *in* E. T. Stokes (ed.), *Historians in tropical Africa*, Salisbury, 28. See also N.J. von Warmelo, 1930, Early Bantu ethnography from a philological point of view, *Africa*, 3:31–48; E. Gregersen, 1968, Words and things in African prehistory, *Anthropological Linguistics*, 10.3: 1–4; Christopher Ehret 1971, *Southern Nilotic history*.
6) P. Newman and R. Ma, 1966, Comparative Chadic: phonology and lexicon, *Journal of African Languages*, 5.3: 244–245.
7) By Robert G. Armstrong, 1964, *The study of West African languages*, Ibadan, 12–13. For a detailed (and favorable) account of glottochronology, see D. H. Hymes, 1960, Lexico-statistics so far, *Current Anthropology* 1. 3–44. For a somewhat different view, with an Africanist slant, see Roger W. Wescott, 1967, African languages and African prehistory, *in* Creighton Gabel and Norman R. Bennett, (eds.), *Reconstructing African culture history*, Boston, 47–54.
8) Robert B. Lees, 1953, The basis of glottochronology, *Language* 29. 113–27. Interestingly enough, Lees was one of the early proponents of the hypothesis but has now abandoned it.
9) Robert G. Armstrong, 1962, Glottochronology and African linguistics, *Journal of African History*, 3.2: 283–290.
10) David L. Olmsted, 1957. Three tests of glottochronological theory, *American Anthropologist* 59: 839–42.
11) Joseph H. Greenberg, 1960, Linguistic evidence for the influence of the Kanuri on the Hausa, *Journal of African History*, 1.2: 205–212.
12) It may be that certain classes of borrowed word in any given language will not be subject to the same sound changes that native words are, but for the most part this seems not to be the case.
13) See Joseph H. Greenberg, 1947, Arabic loan-words in Hausa, *Word* 3.1: 85–97; and Edgar A. Gregersen, 1967, Linguistic seriation as a dating device for loanwords, with special reference to West Africa, *African Language Review* 6: 102–108.
14) As is done in M. Hiskett, 1965, The historical background to the naturalization of Arabic loan-words in Hausa, *African Language Studies*, 6.21.
15) J. van Ginneken, 1939, *La reconstruction typologique des langues archaïques de l'humanité.*
16) R. Jacobson, 1962, *Collected works*, Vol. 1, p. 531.
17) For a summary of Leakey's approach, see his *The progress and evolution of man in Africa*, London (1961).
18) Gordon W. Hewes, An explicit formulation of the relationship between tool-using, tool-making and the emergence of language (unpublished talk given at the American Anthropological Association annual meeting 1971, New York).

CHAPTER XV

Language and Culture

Language can be studied not only with reference to its formal properties, as has been done throughout most of this book, but also with regard to its relationship to the lives and thoughts and culture of the people who speak it. I shall try here to sketch ways in which this has been attempted. This is in effect a catch-all chapter that tries to suggest areas of interest falling under the broad—and not often clearly delineated—fields of ethnolinguistics, psycholinguistics, and sociolinguistics. In addition, a few language derivatives and the like of special interest to the Africanist are considered.

Language expresses values and is itself a value. This is obvious from the attempts to revive Hebrew and Gaelic, the struggle to have Afrikaans recognized as an official language, the policy of spreading Arabic at the expense of other languages. Furthermore, in the same vein it is clearly not enough that a word refer to something, it must convey appropriate sentiments. Thus, a garbage collector tries to improve his status by changing his label (but not his job) to sanitary engineer. To forget a dictator more readily, Stalingrad becomes Volgagrad. But what is acceptable one generation turns to a bone of contention in the next as we see in the current struggle over the labels Colored-Negro-Black-Afro-American in the United States.

In Africa, an important question has arisen of what to do with geographical names because in some instances the colonial connotations associated with them are felt to be intolerable or at least inappropriate. In 1966, the names of the three most important cities of Zaïre, formerly the Democratic Republic of Congo, and before that the Belgian Congo, were changed: Leopoldville becoming Kinshasa; Stanleyville, Kinsangani; and Elisabethville, Lumbumbashi. Similarly, the main road in Nairobi, originally Delamere Avenue, was changed after Kenyan independence to Jomo Kenyatta Avenue—not only to honor the first president of the country but also to show disfavor with Lord Delamere who through his successful policy to restrict the Kenya Highlands exclusively to white Europeans was a catalyst in setting off Mau-Mau. Even when a name is relatively innocuous, a more prestigious one may push it aside, as was the case with the former Gold Coast. In 1956 it became the first country in Black Africa to be freed from colonial rule, and a rechristening was felt to be in order. The name chosen, Ghana, the name of the earliest of a number of famous Sudanic king-

Figure 13 WOMAN WITH LIP PLATES

The woman is identified as a Mokonde or Mohonde. A number of groups in the Ubangi-Chad area (e.g. several Sara-speaking peoples) followed the fashion of inserting large disks into holes cut into the lips of women. The fashion is dying out and is now found only among the old. With such labrets, speech is very much modified and the production of labial consonants such as p is rendered impossible.

Courtesy of the American Museum of Natural History

doms in the Middle Ages, was geographically somewhat inappropriate (Old Ghana was located several hundred miles away from the boundaries of the modern state) but symbolically and emotionally more than fitting. Similarly in 1975, Dahomey was rechristened Benin.

The vocabulary of a language will normally show correlations with cultural need and focus. It is hardly any surprise that the Eskimo have dozens of words to differentiate various kinds of snow, but the Bantu living in the equatorial rain forest have none. Or on the other hand, an extensive vocabulary denoting camels is found among the Tuareg of the Sahara, but is altogether lacking among the Australian aborigines. Now terms like these may represent technical jargon, as for example the various words in English denoting horses (*palomino*, *roan*, *pinto*, etc.) associated with the horsey set or addicts of Westerns. But in Nuer society, an extremely rich vocabulary dealing with cattle exists shared by all the people who live in the traditional cow-oriented Nuer way. The reason is extra-linguistic. The Nuer have been said to think and talk cattle: scarcely any aspect of life exists into which cattle do not enter and play an important part. Evans-Pritchard writes that the Nuer define all social processes and relationships in terms of cattle and that their social idiom is a bovine idiom.[1]

Quite obviously, too, the organization of a society, its religious beliefs, its economy are reflected in words. Peoples on the very lowest technological levels, hunters and gatherers without herds or animals—who apparently seldom find it necessary to count large sums—sometimes have distinctively rudimentary number systems. In New Guinea, a few languages have the numbers *1*, *2*, *(3)*, and *many*— such languages having an associated singular, dual, (trial), plural inflection of nouns. In no known African languages is such a system actually found today, but a 2-base system occurs in Bushman; thus, the basic numbers are *1* and *2*; the word for *3* can be analyzed as *2 + 1*, *4* as *2 + 2*, etc.

A semantic or lexical "field", i.e. semantically definable subdivision of vocabulary, of special interest to anthropologists, is that of kinship terminology. This is a linguistic universal. But what is not universal is the way various kinsmen are lumped together under a single label. Specific assignment of particular kinsmen to classes of kinsmen would seem basically to reflect the facts of social organization. For example, a common institution in African social organization is the sib (or clan). A person inherits his membership in a sib through the male or the female line and usually cannot marry other members of his sib. Among the Ruanda and Rundi, for example, the inheritance is through the male line. As a consequence marriage with a man's father's brother's daughter is forbidden (since she is in the same sib he is), but not with a man's mother's brother's daughter, who is actually the preferred wife for a man among the Rundi. In English, both girls would be given the single label of *cousin*. Among the Ruanda and Rundi, two separate terms exist. It is obviously of considerable importance in a society to deter people from committing what they consider to be incest and so it is no wonder that the kinship terms would be different.

By the same token uncle-aunt terms can be realized in a number of ways. Among the Amhara, Teda, Gā, and !Kung Bushman two words are used to distinguish *father*, *father's brother*, and *mother's brother*, following the English pattern. Among the Sandawe, Zulu, and Lango two words are also used but with a different arrangement: the same term is used for *father* and *father's brother*, but a different one for *mother's brother*. Among the Naron Hottentot, Herero, and Malinke, all three are differentiated with separate terms. Among the Jukun, Serer, and pagan Hausa (but not Muslim Hausa), one term is used for all three. These systems are obviously not dependent on what language family is involved (as the Hausa example unambiguously shows), but for the most part on sociological considerations.

Color terminology is another semantic field that has received a considerable amount of attention, and the findings have sometimes been played up as indications of profound differences in human perception. Be that as it may, it is clear that the spectrum of colors, which in nature involves a continuous gradation, is broken up in ways that vary considerably from language to language. In Shona there are, besides the terms for black and white, three basic color terms (and of course many other terms that can be subsumed by these): **cicena** covering generally what would be called *yellow* and *green* in English, **citema** *blue*, and **cipswuka** *orange*, *red*, and *purple*. In Bassa, spoken in Liberia, there are two basic color terms: **hui** *purple*, *blue*, *green* and **zīza** *yellow*, *orange*, *red*. Gleason has tellingly pointed out that on objective grounds no one set of color terms is inherently better than the other: for different purposes, different systems are more useful than others. For example, botanists have found the English color terms not sufficiently general for describing flower coloration because yellows, oranges, and many reds are found to constitute one series; blues, purples, and purplish reds another. Two technical terms have therefore had to be coined: *xanthic* and *cyanic*. These are basically equivalent to the Bassa **hui** and **zīza**, and in Bassa the botanist would have had no need to create new words at all.[2]

In light of examples such as these the question has been raised as to whether speakers of different languages do not actually perceive the external world in different ways according to a kind of perceptual straitjacket provided by their language. The most famous exposition of the position that one's world view is determined by the structure of one's language is associated with Benjamin Lee Whorf, and his stand is often referred to as the Whorfian hypothesis. From a comparison of certain American Indian languages with European ones, Whorf concluded that the

concepts of "time" and "matter" are not given in substantially the same form by experience to all men but depend upon the nature of the language or languages through the use of which they have been developed.[3]

He seems to have held essentially the same position regarding the notion of space, but admitted that to a certain extent "the apprehension of space is given in substantially the same form by experience irrespective of language".[4] In short, by means of a kind of linguistic original sin, the speakers of a language are doomed to perceive the world as the first speakers apparently did. Among the many difficulties generated by such an hypothesis is the problem of how change can occur, both in language structure and world view. This problem is hardly ever considered by proponents of the hypothesis.

There are of course many variants of the hypothesis. The extreme form may be compared with a situation concocted by Ionesco in his *La cantatrice chauve* (*The bald soprano*) in which all the members of a certain family, men and women alike, were called Bobby and hence could never be told apart. The weakest variants say merely that people can discriminate perceptions and concepts more readily if their language provides handy words for them.

The evidence for variants of the theory other than the weakest are not compelling. For example, it is frequently alleged that speakers of Bantu do not distinguish the categories of time and space—at least not in the same way as Europeans. The only real evidence offered is linguistic, e.g. the fact that certain grammatical elements (particles such as **ku, mu, pa**) refer to both time and space. No corroborative study of a nonlinguistic sort is provided. And so the argument is as circular as it is unconvincing in light of the common extension of space metaphors to time situations in many if not all languages such as English: *a* LONG (or SHORT) *time*; *the time* IN *which*; etc.

Even the color terminology differences discussed before do not prove to be so irreconcilable as once thought. A recent cross-cultural study by Berlin and Kay[5] suggests that the value of color terms are less arbitrary than had been maintained even though systems differ in having as few as two or as many as eleven basic terms. Their important finding is that the foci or "truest" values assigned to terms will be essentially the same. In languages with five basic color terms, for example, these five will always have their foci at the same points, which we can designate as white, black, red, green, yellow—never, say, brown, purple, grey, pink, chartreuse. Languages with six basic terms will retain the five term foci and add a term with a focus at blue. This study is however, fraught with methodological problems and requires considerable outside confirmation.

The theoretical orientation associated with recent generative research also does not support the Whorfian position. Some theorists hold, for example, that the underlying structure to be posited for a sentence is simply the logical structure, which means that the logically equivalent sentences of different languages can probably best be considered as differing merely in surface realization rather than in some quinessential way. If true, this would offer no support for the Whorfian hypothesis at all—on the contrary.

The Whorfian hypothesis is provocative but probably false. And it should be realized that it is the product of a period of linguistic theorizing when overt differences in grammatical structure between languages were emphasized almost to the exclusion of the fundamental similarities that pervade all languages.

In a great many specific ways, religious and other cultural conventions have had an obvious influence on language. Various kinds of tabu are important examples. We are all familiar from English with tabus on certain words dealing with sex and excretion. Similar tabus are universal in Africa but the severity of the tabu varies considerably from group to group. Another fairly common avoidance has to do with the names of dangerous animals.[6] Among the Ila, for example, the "real" word for *lion* cannot be used in the bush; instead a euphemism is required: **sikunze** *the outsider*. In Bena, spoken in South West Africa, the word for *lion* is **ingalupala**, but in actual usage **nonunyalibondo**, *the one who lives in the gorge* occurs more frequently. Similar customs obtain in many languages for leopards, hyaenas, and snakes—as they have done in European languages for wolves and bears.

A similar custom is the common African practice of naming a child whose mother has lost several other children with a name indicating its worthlessness—presumably in order to trick or confuse evil spirits in much the same way that dangerous animals are confused when their true name is not mentioned. Names for such children often include the following: *Dog, Stick, Dung-heap*. In Hausa, we find **À-jéefás** *Let-it-be-thrown-away*, **À-bár-shì** *May-he-be-spared*, **À-mântáa** *Let-her-be-forgotten*, **À-júu-jíi** *On-the-dung-hill*, **Báywáa** *slave*.

The widespread use of a phrase *hand-for-eating* to refer to the right hand seems also to be due to a tabu: very commonly it is considered offensive to use the left hand for eating or handing something to another person because it is with that hand one cleans oneself after defecation. The idiom is found in Swahili, Kanuri, Nyamwezi, Zulu, and almost universally in long Islamized groups (in Muslim culture this distinctive use of the left hand is traditional). In Nilotic *hand-for-eating* refers to the LEFT hand. The reason is not clear.

One of the functions of verbal tabus is to show respect. The dead are frequently not mentioned, or only by periphrasis. In-laws also often require language avoidance of various kinds. Among the Zulu and related groups, such avoidance customs, known as **hlonipa** *shame*, are highly developed. A woman is not to speak to her father-in-law at all except in dire necessity. And she may not even refer to him or even her son-in-law. As a matter of fact, she must also avoid words that sound like their names. For example, if her father-in-law were called **uManzi** *Waterman*, she would be obliged to use another word for *water* in normal discourse. A hypothetical parallel in English would involve substituting words for *brown* (meaning the color) if one's in-law were called *Brown*. How the **hlonipa** words are chosen or devised is often unclear. In Zulu, the consonants of the original word are often merely changed to clicks; it has been suggested that this custom has played an important role for intrenching clicks in the language (they seem originally to have been borrowed from Hottentot). The Zulu also developed a royal name avoidance: since one king was called Mpande, the similar sounding word **impande** *root* could no longer be used, and the word **imbaxo** (where x represents ɓ) was substituted (apparently derived from **ibaxa** *fork or crotch in the branch of a tree*).[7]

Of course, the precise details of avoidance vary from society to society, although when it occurs it nearly always is directed towards in-laws. Among the Hausa, on the other hand, a man avoids using the name of his father, his senior wife, and his eldest child. Nor does he mention to these relatives the name of someone who has the same name they have, but rather says *your namesake* or some similar phrase. The verbal avoidance rules reflect areas of potential friction within the Hausa family, and an eldest child (to whom a parent traditionally shows no public affection) is frequently adopted by some relative avoidance is not appropriate with.

We have already mentioned a few customs regarding naming. The whole subject is fascinating and worthy of extensive studies in its own right. In Africa, as elsewhere, names are frequently changed according to some significant event in a person's life. In many West African societies as among the Yoruba, the custom of teknonymy occurs whereby a person who becomes a parent is not called by his own name but rather as *Father of so-and-so*. The obverse custom of using a patronymic (calling a person *Child of so-and-so*) is perhaps even more widespread, but of course does not accompany a change in status. Among the Acoli and related groups war names are given for special acts of bravery, a custom reminiscent of the Plains Indian in North America. In Acoli such names include: **Nekomoy**, *He who killed many in war*, **Lolaamoy**, *He who has been the first to kill when in war*, **Laywemoy** *He who freed his fellow countrymen from fear through an extraordinary deed*.

Among the Central Bantu, two or more names are given to a person, one a spirit name said represent the reincarnated soul of a dead person. In West Africa, "secret names" are quite frequent: names that count as the real names of people but are nearly never uttered for fear that maleficent powers may gain control of the bearer's spirit by knowing it. Instead, nicknames of various sorts are used.

A common source of names is some division of time. In many groups, including the Nilotes, the reference may be to the season one is born in or the time of day. In West Africa, reference to the day of the week is frequent. A person is really called Monday, Wednesday, etc.—but frequently with modifications to indicate sex. As a matter of fact, gender distinctions are the rule for names even though gender is not marked in other nouns; thus, In Luo the **o**-prefix indicates a man's name, an **a**-, a woman's: **Otieno—Atieno** *Person born at night*.[8]

Among the Nuer, men often assume the names of their favorite oxen, which seems appropriate in light of their cultural focus on cattle.

Islamized groups use the names of Muslim holy persons (prophets, kalifs, relatives and friends of Mohammed) much like the Christian use of saints' names. Very frequently, however, although these count as a person's real name, he may go through life with some other appelation, e.g., a name denoting occupation or origin, or a day name, as in other African groups.

Personal names have not escaped the visicitudes of nationalism. President Mobutu Sece Soko of Zaïre insisted in 1972 on the Africanization of Christian names and threatened the prosecution of Catholic priests who refuse to give "authentic" Zaïrian names to children at baptism. He himself abandoned his own Christian name Joseph Désiré. Furthermore, names of newspapers have been changed. *Le Progrès* has become *Salongo* ("return to work") and *Courrier d'Afrique, Elima* ("a person who inspires fear"). Similar Africanization policies have been begun elsewhere, e.g. in Congo and Chad in 1974.

Language can function as a technique to indicate social distance. The various avoidance customs mentioned earlier constitute extreme forms of this. In European languages there are frequently two forms for *you*: one indicating intimacy or social superiority, the other distance or inferiority. In a few areas of Africa, similar honorific–nonhonorific forms may be found. Where they do occur, the special polite or honorific pronouns are identifiable as an extension of either *you plural*—as in Yoruba, Mende, and Sukuma—or, more rarely, of *he*— as in Sotho. In a few languages *they* is used, but to indicate a higher degree of reverence than *you plural*, with which it almost invariably co-exists. The honorific dimension is rarely if ever maintained in the plural. And for reference rather than address there are seldom any special honorific third person forms, except in a few Ethiopian languages.

In no African language to my knowledge (unlike several Indonesian languages) are there any deferential first person pronouns, which would indicate humility and denigration on the part of the speaker, and could be rendered in English by *I, your most abject servant* or some similar variant. But in a few central Bantu languages, an HONORIFIC *I* occurs (literally *we*), e.g. among the Lamba, Lala, and Nsenga. It is used by elders who would be addressed as *they* (other adults normally being addressed as *you plural*). In Nyamwezi, a different usage obtains: an adult in conversation with someone else he would address with an honorific *you plural* refers to himself as *we*, but not normally otherwise. The use of an honorific plural thus becomes a feature of the discourse in general. A similar sort of thing has been reported for Mossi where honorifics are used to everyone when a chief is present even though in other situations these same people would be addressed familiarly.

Remarkably enough, a royal *we* rarely occurs even in the many African groups with "divine" kings. On the other hand, one might distinguish for African languages between a royal *my* vs. a plebian *our* because a widely found convention dictates that *my people*, *my village*, and so on is appropriate only in the mouths of chiefs, commoners saying *our people*, *our village*, etc. Such holds true for Zande, Hausa, and Nyamwezi, and many other languages.

In the central Bantu area and sporadically elsewhere, nouns in the plural are used to denote singular referents honorifically. For plural referents, however, no honorific dimension is regularly possible. As a matter of fact certain words denoting kinsmen such as *grandfather*, *father's brother*, and many in-law terms hardly ever occur except in the plural.

In Yao, spoken in Mozambique, we find the closest thing to an honorific in the plural reported for Africa. The original prefix for nouns denoting human beings par excellence, viz. **vá** (from Proto-Bantu ***ba**) is used almost exclusively as an honorific singular, and a new prefix has been developed for the plural, **acáá-**, whether honorific or not. Thus, *woman* informal is **jwá-mbúmba**, honorific **vá-mbúmba**, and the plural for both is **acáá-mbúmba**. Occasionally the formal-informal distinction can be realized in the plural also, but there seems to be no consistent pattern; e.g., *man*: singular **jwám-lúmé**, plural, **acáá-lúmé**, honorific singular **váá-lúmé**, honorific plural **vaa-lúmé** (**acáá-lúmé** is also possible).[9]

Precisely why these and other similar forms developed is not clear. We must undoubtedly rule out a single origin for, say, honorific pronouns and assume that the notions of plurality or third person are vivid enough in themselves in conveying the notion of social distance to permit multiple convergence in many parts of the world.

With one exception, honorific language levels such as those of Japanese, Javanese, and Balinese are not found in African languages. In the East Asian examples, extensive parallel sets of vocabulary and sometimes even of morphological resources have been developed, the appropriate use of which depends on the relations between the speaker and the addressee and on the status of the person who is the subject of discourse. The only example in Africa (apart from Malagasy, related to Javanese and Balinese) that even remotely resembles the Asian conventions is found among the Shilluk, who are one of the many African groups having a divine king complex with an extensive class of nobles. In addressing the king, and to a lesser extent in addressing any noble, certain everyday words and phrases are avoided and replaced by euphemisms and circumlocutions. For example, verbs of motion and some others when used in addressing nobles are replaced by phrases implying divine intervention or agency; thus, *to get up* is construed as *to be lifted up by God*, *to enter the house* is *to be stuffed into the house by God*, *to exist* is *to be nursed by God*, and so on. But *to sleep* is *to go out to graze.* A remarkable feature of other vocabulary substitutes is that they tend to refer to an object less exalted than what is actually being talked about—something on the order of a Gilbert-and-Sullivan mock-Japanese: *my worthless house*, etc. For example, the head of the king is always referred to by a word that otherwise means *pebble*; *beer* is called *water* in addressing nobles; *donkey* is *dog*; *pipe* is *mud.* [10]

Occasionally in the Africanist literature references are made to dialects peculiar to some nonlocalized subgroups. One of these is the socalled woman's language, which is a "language" only in the freest sense. The differences between the language of men and that of women are seldom great and may consist merely of preference for or avoidance of certain words. Among the Kele of Zaïre the custom that women wear lip-plugs and men do not has in and of itself produced a distinction: because of the presence of a labret, women cannot pronounce labial sounds such as **p** or **b** well. One consequence of this is that the word **libwa** *nine* is not used by women, who say **iseke** instead—the reason being that their pronunciation of the word would sound too much like a magical curse **lilwa**, which can be uttered only by men who are members of a special secret society. A Kele chief, upon hearing that girls in a European school were being taught a song containing **libwa** in the text, personally undertook the day-long journey to forbid the singing of that song and insisted on its removal from the school song book. [11]

Rehse has reported on a special language used by women among the Zinza of Tanzania, which they are taught before their marriage. This language apparently cannot be understood at all by people who have not been taught it. Mansfeld mentions a special woman's language called Mboandem used in the Cross River area of Cameroun by a "higher class" of women. The main characteristic of this language is that certain words are replaced by vivid phrases: *fish → water-animal, snake → long-meat, mirror → see-the-face*, etc.

Special royal or courtly languages have been reported from a number of African groups. King Nʒoya (Nʒшəya, often Anglicized as Njoya) of the Bamum of Cameroun consciously invented a secret palace language in imitation of neighboring kings largely by borrowing words from French, English, and German and redefining them; e.g. **ganson** (French *garçon*) *good*, **inklan** (English *England*) *head*, **ornun** (German *Ordung*) *our*. [12]

A priestly language has been reported for the Zinza, used during possession. This is perhaps a kind of glossolalia (speaking in tongues) found in various parts of Africa and perhaps familiar to Europeans and Americans from Pentecostalist and other Christian sects. A secret language, Rúcuzi among a caste of smiths is said to exist among the Ruanda. An entirely separate language, Buso, is reportedly spoken by smiths in Bousso (Chad). Smiths quite frequently represent submerged groups of one sort or another and so a special language is not unexpected. But Rúcuzi seems basically to be Ruanda plus changed word order and periphrasis.

Secret languages are especially associated with initiation groups and of course secret societies. A few of these been described in some detail. Tessmann has made a grammatical sketch of two cult languages, To and Labi, used by the Baja of the Cameroun hinterlands; he asserts that they were originally two real languages replaced in ordinary conversation by Baja. A secret cult language, Yehwe, used in southern Togo and Dahomey—mostly among the Ewe—is described by Westermann as a complete language in its own right but with a grammar like Ewe. The Kele secret language already mentioned, called **lioi lya lokonda** *language of the forest*, seems to be used across tribal and language boundaries as is the associated **libéli** rite; the Zande **nebeli** is probably related.

According to Huber[13] ritual specialists among the Yaka of Zaïre must learn a language called Ngombu (or Kingombu), used only in divination. From the examples that Huber gives there seems to be no straightforward relationship between Ngombu and normal Yaka, at least with regard to vocabulary.

	NGOMBU	YAKA
father	kipfuila	tata
mother	malambo	mama
child	kindende	mwana
sister	khete	pangi
fire	mulemo	mbau
water	madibu	mamba
house	zambisina	nzo
to dance	kukini sina	kukina

Among the Nyoro, diviners substitute a double d for other consonants while imitating the voice of a particular spirit. Beattie[14] reports that one diviner imitating a spirit called Irungu said to a woman: **Muddana wandde, ibadda ddyawe niddyo ddiha** "My girl, what is your name?" The normal Nyoro form would be: **Muhara wange, ibara lyawe niryo liha**.

Secret languages on the order of English pig-Latin are probably a cultural universal. In Swahili quite a few exist. One, called Kinyume, involves placing the final syllable of a word at the beginning: **sanduku** *box* becomes **kusandu, nyumba** *house* becomes **mbanyu** (note syllable division); **utakwenda** *you will go* becomes **ndautakwe** (which is interesting because some scholars maintain that correct word division should be **u ta kwenda**). In another type of Swahili pig-Latin, Kilabi, **-kiri** is introduced after every syllable: **maneno mengi** *many words* would be transposed to **mákiri nékiri nókiri mékiri ngíkiri** (the stress pattern is unlike that of normal Swahili, where the next to the last syllable almost without exception receives the stress). In yet a third, Kilagwi, the vowel of the next to the last syllable is changed to a, and the final syllable ends on -wi; thus, **kitabu kipo hapa** *the book is here* becomes **kitabwi kapwi hapwi** (Cf. Kinyume **bukita paki paha**; Kilagwi **kíkiri tákiri búkiri kíkiri pókiri hákiri pákiri**).

Little information is available about what happens to the tones of tonal languages in such permutations. In one type of Hausa pig-Latin, **záuráncíi** (basically like the Kilabi of Swahili), the tones and vowel lengths of the underlying forms are ignored; thus **káashíi** *excrement*, **káashìi** *junior person*, **káshìi** *heap* would all be realized in the same way. If the suffix were **-ruwaruwa** we should find **káruwaruwa shíruwaruwa**. Ignoring underlying tone, stress, and similar features may be common with African languages (and register tone systems to begin with), but is certainly not linguistically universal since certain varieties of Chinese pig-Latin are said to keep the underlying tones. [15]

With regard to language derivatives and associated fields, only a very few aspects can be considered here. African literature fits into this category but obviously encompasses a vast field in itself. We can note, however, that although fables, proverbs, riddles, and tongue-twisters are pan-African, rimed poetry is not. [16] All those groups that use rime fall in the northern half of the continent, and undoubtedly they borrowed it from Arabic—as seems to be the case for European rime as well. In point of fact, many other poetic devices such as alliteration, syllable count, and meter are also not generally found outside this area. There are two known exceptions. One is that the Somali may have developed a native system of alliterative poetry—with very lax rules indeed, viz., that one particular consonant must occur at least once in every line of the poem.

The other exception is the Efik tone-riddle (in Efik **ukabade iko** *change of words*). [17] The correct answer to the riddle must have the same number of syllables and the same sequence of tones as the question; e.g.

Q.	àfák	ɔ́kɔ̀k	kéták	útɔ̀ŋ
	putting	chew-stick	under	ear

R.	èsín	ényìn	kéŋk͡pɔ́	ówò
	putting	eyes	in-thing	of-person

The Luvale are also reported as having tone riddles, perhaps an independant invention (the Efik living in Nigeria, the Luvale in Angola with no reported intervening examples of languages with tone-riddles).

One of the most remarkable language derivatives in the African field is surely drum talking. Communication—or at least the transmission—of a text by drumming follows the same basic principles everywhere in Africa that it is used, and these principles have not been reliably reported for any other part of the world. A Morse-code type of signaling is not used. Rather, a drummer actually tries to reproduce the tones of the underlying verbal text. Normally two distinctions of pitch (more rarely of stress) reproduce the tones and a frequent set-up involves a slit-gong having one lip thicker than the other. The distinct pitches are usually

Figure 14   NARMER PALETTE

Line drawings of slate palete from Hierakonpolis near Thebes in Upper Egypt, possibly 1st Dynasty. Several of the symbols (e.g. the design between the horned heads on the top) are believed to represent names using early hieroglyphic conventions.

Figure 15   TABLET OF MENES

Line drawing of an ebony tablet from Abydos, Egypt, c. 3400 BC. One of the earliest known examples of the use of hieroglyphs.

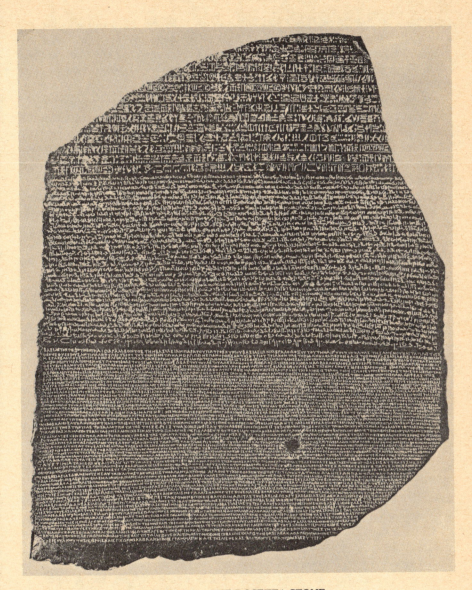

Figure 16   THE ROSETTA STONE

The stone with bilingual inscription was found July 1799 near Rashiid in the Western Delta of the Nile in Egypt by Bouchard, a French officer of Engineers, during Bonaparte's Egyptian campaign. The bottom is written in Greek, the top in two forms of Ancient Egyptian: hieroglyphic (first 14 lines) and demotic. Its discovery led to the eventual deciferment of Ancient Egyptian by François Champollion in the 1820's.

referred to as masculine (low) and feminine (high). Less often two separate and differently tuned drums are used, or two bells. Quite obviously in those languages with more than two phonemic pitches, a Procrustean accommodation takes place of necessity: a single drum-pitch will have to make do for two or more spoken pitches.

Another set-up involves the tension drum, where the number of pitches that can be played is practically unlimited. Despite this, actual sentence intonation is almost invariably ignored as it is with the other drums. This may indicate a single origin for the whole talking drum complex (which is quite likely) or else it may show that such drumming is akin to chanting. In Zulu eulogistic recitation (isiɓongo), for example, the same convention is observed.

The conventions of African drumming necessarily entail an enormous amount of ambiguity in reproducing the verbal text. Since in drumming the consonants and vowels of a word are ignored and only the tones and syllable lengths are indicated, the possibilities for confusion are great. Two approaches with regard to this problem have been taken. One is to ignore it altogether, as is usually the case with panegyric drumming: although an underlying verbal text exists, the drumming is taken as a piece on its own, having a value much like that of a Wagnerian leitmotif. The other approach certainly does not get rid of ambiguity, but helps to reduce it. Instead of drumming out a simple word, say *camel*, one would beat out *ship of the desert* instead, i.e., a longer, conventionalized—and often archaic—phrase (or KENNING) with less chance for misunderstanding.

Drum communication can cut across language boundaries only if the drummers involved are bilingual. This is often the case, and in point of fact Ewe drumming is invariably done to an underlying Twi text, suggesting a Twi origin for the Ewe drumming complex in the first place. [18]

Whistling and humming, as well as other musical instruments such as elephant tusk flutes, are often employed in basically the same way. It should be realized that the development of such techniques is enormously sophisticated and requires a linguistic analysis of sorts that is quite remarkable. Nevertheless, even professional drummers engaged in drum-talk are usually at a loss to explain accurately what principles are involved.

Other forms of language derived communication in Africa, with one exception (viz. writing), have been poorly described. Labouret describes the use of smoke signals among the Dan and the Ube (Oube) of the Ivory Coast, but the precise conventions followed are not stated. [19] A cross-tribal sign language of the significance and extent of the American Indian systems appears nowhere to be found in Africa, although hand signals for numbers have been standardized in many areas cross-cutting language boundaries. Thus, in the Western Sudan, among the Songhai, Hausa, Nupe, and Kanuri, *one* is usually represented by touching the little finger of the left hand to the palm, *two* by touching both little and ring fingers to the palm, *five* by a clenched fist, and so on.

The most significant language-derived means of communication, writing, is so important and of such interest that the following chapter will be devoted to it entirely.

Notes and References

Many topics associated with sociolinguistics, the ethnology of communication, and the like have not been dealt with here in part owing to the paucity of information specifically African. Some interesting articles dealing with areas not specifically covered in this chapter include the following.

Ethel M. Albert, 1972, Culture patterning of speech behavior in Burundi, in John J. Gumperz and Dell Hymes, eds., *Directions in sociolinguistics*, New York.

W. W. Whiteley, 1964, Problems of a lingua franca: Swahili and the trade-unions, *Journal of African Languages*, 3.3:215–225.

E. Ojo Arewa and Alan Dundes, 1964, Proverbs and the ethnography of speaking folklore, in John J. Gumperz and Dell Hymes, eds., *The ethnography of communication*, *American Anthropologist*, Special publication 66.6.2:70–85.

1) E. E. Evans-Pritchard, 1940, The *Nuer*, Oxford.
2) H. A. Gleason, 1961, *An introduction to descriptive linguistics* (rev. ed.), New York.
3) John B. Carroll (ed.), 1956, *Language, thought, and reality: Selected writings of Benjamin Lee Whorf*, New York, p. 158.
4) Ibid.
5) Brent Berlin and Paul Kay, 1971, *Basic color terms: Their universality and evolution*, Berkeley.
6) Many of the examples given here are taken from D. Westermann, 1940, Afrikanische Tabusitten und ihrer Einwirkung auf die Sprachgestaltung, *Abhandlungen der Preußischen Akademie der Wissenschaften*, Jahrgang 1939, (Philos-histor. Klasse), Nr 12.
7) See Alice Werner, 1940-5, The custom of "hlonipa" in its influence on language, *Journal of the Royal African Society*, 4.112–116.
8) However, people are sometimes named for others who have recently died—not always of the same sex. The name given indicates the sex of the deceased.
9) K. Mbaga and W. H. Whiteley, 1961, Formality and informality in Yao speech, *Africa* 31, 135–146.
10) M.E.C. Pumphrey, 1937, Shilluk "royal" language conventions, *Sudan Notes and Records*, 20:319–321.
11) These and most of the following examples of cult languages are taken from Westermann's summary. (see fn 6).
12) Maurice Delafosse, 1922, Naissance et évolution d'un système d'écriture de création contemporaire, *Revue d'Ethnographie et des Traditions Populaires*, 8:11–19.
13) Hugo Huber, 1965, A diviner's apprenticeship and work among the Bayaka, *Man* 65:46–47.
14) John H. Beattie, 1967, Consulting a Nyoro diviner: the ethnologist as client, *Ethnology* 6:57–65.
15) The functional load of tones probably plays an important role, and nowadays also the official spelling.
16) Joseph H. Greenberg, A survey of African prosodic systems, in: Stanley Diamond, 1965, *Culture in history: Essays in honor of Paul Radin*.

17) D. C. Simmons, 1955, Specimens of Efik folklore, *Folklore* 66.417–24; also D. C. Simmons, 1960, Ibibio tone riddles, *Nigerian Field*, 25.132–4.

18) The literature on drumming is quite extensive. See George Herzog, Drum signaling in a West African tribe, reprinted in Dell Hymes ed., 1964, *Language in culture and society*, New York, 312–323 (plus extensive bibliography 323–329).

19) H. Labouret, 1923, Language tambouriné et sifflé, *Bulletin du Comité d'Etudes Historiques de l'Afrique Occidentale Française, pp. 120–158.*

CHAPTER XVI

African Writing Systems

African systems of writing not based on the Roman alphabet are few in number and normally limited in use. But they are fascinating—not only in their own right, but also for the light that they can perhaps shed about the evolution of writing systems in general.

Writing cannot, of course, be equated with language, but is merely language DERIVED. Any language could be written in a variety of ways and some in fact have been, e.g. Swahili in Arabic, Roman or even Devanaagarii (an Indian script); Ge'ez in Sabaean, unvoweled Old Ethiopic script, and the modern Ethiopic syllabary. Hence, writing properly constitutes a marginal interest for the linguist. But because no comprehensive study of all relevant African systems exists, the present chapter deals with the subject somewhat more fully than might be expected.

The boundaries between writing, art, and various kinds of memory aid are sometimes difficult to distinguish. Some authorities, for example, suggest that rock-paintings associated with the Bushmen really function as a kind of rudimentary writing rather than as merely an aesthetic exercise. For West Africa we have the attempt by Kathleen Hau to prove that carvings on ivory tusks from Benin are not only decorative but comprise a written text employing writing conventions that ultimately originated in Crete and were brought to Benin via the Sahara "hundreds of years before Christ".[1] Most scholars consider such suggestions far-fetched.

The problem with pictures and other quasi-artistic items is that we do not always know if a language text is even implied. Mnemonic devices, on the other hand, pose other difficulties for defining writing because a text is quite frequently associated with them. Among the Ewe, objects are used to call to mind proverbs and songs—a threaded needle, for example, suggesting the proverb "the needle sews great cloth" (more or less the equivalent of the English "great oaks from little acorns grow", for which an acorn would presumably be an appropriate reminder). Mary Kingsley reported finding native singers in West Africa who carried round with them in a net bag objects indicative of their repertoire.[2] Zahan as a matter of fact talks of "three dimensional" writing in reference to brass gold-weights, illustrating proverbs, used by Akan-speaking peoples, as well as certain wooden message discs, with proverbial scenes in relief, used in the Lower Congo.[3]

A more abstract use of objects, comparable to the wampam of North American Indians, occurs among the Zulu and the Swazi of South Africa. Love notes and evil messages are conveyed by "bead letters", the symbolic value of each bead determined by its color and degree of translucency. Thus, an opaque white bead indicates all that is good; an opaque red bead, blood; a glass red bead, fire or anger.[4] Cowries are used among the Yoruba in somewhat the same way although meaning differences are accomplished by the number and spacing of cowries on a string. Two cowries close together signify *relationship and meeting*; placed apart they signify *separation and enmity*. Meanings sometimes depend on homophony: the word for *six* **efa** in Toruba also means *attracted; eight* **eyo** also *agreed*. A string of six cowries from a boy to a girl, and a reply of eight cowries is romantic effusion at its most succinct.[5]

None of these forms of communication can qualify in a strict sense as writing, which involves visible marks of some sort used as arbitrary symbols to represent (at least some) linguistic elements in a productive way. It is not enough that a proverb can be "read" off from object. In true writing, any and all normal utterances can be represented, even though certain features of the utterance may be systematically ignored (e.g. vowels are not indicated in Arabic as a rule, nor is tone shown in the official orthographies of most tonal languages in Africa). The marks used in any particular system may represent phonemes, syllables, words, or a mixture of these elements. A system based on the representation of phonemes is called alphabetic and its repertory of symbols, an alphabet. A system based on syllables is called syllabic and its repertory of symbols, a syllabary. A system based on words is called logographic (sometimes also, but less precisely, ideographic) and its symbols, logograms (or ideograms). Alphabetic systems often depart from a strictly phonemic representation for a morphophonemic one. Using these terms, the present official spelling of English is alphabetic with strongly morphophonemic tendencies, representing as it does phonemes as in *ten*, *pit*, *man* but frequently distinguishing different morphemes (*site*, *sight*, *cite*) or keeping a morpheme shape constant (*nature* with /ney-/, but *natural* with /næ-/); in addition, a small number of logograms are used: 1 2 3 4 & # $ £, etc. In Africa, representatives of all these systems can be found.

Some theorists have argued for the existence of yet another type of writing system, based on whole sentences. The picture "writing" (pictographs) of the Plains Indians in North America, which are tribally understood with fairly stereotyped "readings", at least approaches such a system. The closest thing to sentence writing is of essentially the same order as objects used as a mnemonic devices. For example, the Ewe sometimes use drawings of objects rather than the object itself to suggest proverbs: a picture of a threaded needle serves the same function as a real needle. These drawings seem to be idiosyncratic and understood only be the person who made the drawing or at best to some of his close friends. A similar use of pictures for recording proverbs has been reported by Dennett for some parts of Zaïre.[6] A highly systematized set of pictographs is used by the Dogon for purposes of divination.[7] Similar graphic symbols occur in other groups of the Western Sudan such as the Bambara and Bozo. The **nsibidi** signs used by secret societies in various language groups in southern Nigeria, e.g. the Igbo, Efik, and Ekoi, have been considered by some to be of a similar pictographic nature, but others have maintained it is true writing, based on either a logographic or syllabary system. Although **nsibidi** signs were first discovered by T. D. Maxwell as early as 1904, published accounts remain fragmentary and the available evidence seems insufficient to decide the matter one way or another. Adams adds an interesting detail that might be mentioned, viz. that the Arochuku people of this same general area and probably users of **nsibidi**, sent messages between villages by painting them on the bodies of the messengers themselves.[9]

Two main divisions of writing traditions can be distinguished in Africa: (a) the North African scripts, all of which seem ultimately derivable from Ancient Egyptian (this would include Semitic and Greek scripts); (b) West African forms of recent development, which may be related, but which seem in large part an attempt to imitate Latin or Arabic writing.

The origins of the Ancient Egyptian script are still obscure but it apparently developed out of an earlier rebus pictograph tradition, perhaps influenced by Sumerian writing. The earliest example of Egyptian writing is sometimes considered to be found on the palette of Namer from the first dynasty (c. 3000 BC), but the readings (of various names) are dubious. The writing system lasted essentially unchanged until the Christianization of Egypt, after which it was soon replaced by a modified form of the Greek alphabet.

The signs of the Egyptian system occurred in a number of styles. The oldest style, which persisted in formal inscriptions in temples and public buildings, is called hieroglyphic. A more cursive style, hieratic, developed quite early and by the eighteenth dynasty (c. 1400 BC) was employed in all normal texts. About the twenty-third dynasty (c. 730 BC) an even more rapid form appeared, demotic. The direction of writing generally went from right to left, but sometimes also from left to right (the direction in modern normalized printed texts), and, in inscriptions, in vertical columns read from top to bottom. Those signs representing persons, animals, and others with distinguishable fronts and backs function as nearly infallible guides for determining the direction of reading: if a face points to the right, one starts reading from the left, and vice versa.

The system had two basic kinds of units: logograms and syllabic signs. The latter have often been called a consonant "alphabet", since vowels are not indicated. But the structure of the syllable in Ancient Egyptian is basically CV and so a sign specifying a consonant also implies in most instances a following vowel. In other clear-cut syllabaries, not all syllable types have distinct symbols. In Akkadian and Assyrian cuneiform, for example, many signs can represent syllables ending on either **i** or **e**: **li, le** shared a single symbol, despite the fact that **la, lu**, were distinguished. A few signs represent a consonant plus any vowel: **w^v**, **y^v, ʔ^v**. This sort of thing played a minor role in Mesopotamian systems, but in Egyptian all vowel distinctions were neutralized and only the position of a vowel was generally predictable.[10] Consequently a sequence we could transcribe as **tm** might represent **tama, tima, tuma tumu**, etc. but apparently never **utma** or the like, which was assumed to be the case by earlier Egyptologists.

The actual syllabary contained 24 symbols representing a single consonant plus vowel such as ⬭ **r^v**, ◿ **q^v** ⬬ **m^v**. About 80 signs are biliteral, representing two consonants plus vowel(s) such as ⊏⊐ **p^v r^v**, ⚹ **m^{v}r^v**; a few are triliteral such as ⚱ **n^{v}f^{v}r^v**. No known signs represent four or more consonants. The purpose of multiliteral signs was economy in writing and indeed abbreviations of various kinds including "summary writing" where inflections are ignored are perhaps more common than full spellings.

Logograms had two functions: to serve as word signs in their own right and further to act as a generic determiner. The word for *sun*, which can be transcribed **r^{v}ʕ^v**, may be represented by the logogram ⊙ alone, or with syllabic spelling plus logogram serving as a determinative, thus (transliterated) **r** ʕ⊙. Because of the ambiguity inherent in a system that did not specify vowels, such determinatives were hardly luxuries.

The Egyptian writing system was apparently never used directly for any other language, African or not, with one exception. Although the Egyptian Empire at its widest extent went as far south as the town of Napata near the fourth cataract on the Nile, and must have encompassed a great many groups that did not speak Egyptian, no attempts have been attested that their languages were reduced to writing with the aid of hieroglyphs. Egyptian was the only official language of the Empire. It is not surprising, therefore, that the one exception should have involved a group living outside effective Egyptian political control, but near enough to be familiar with Egyptian culture. This group was the people of Meroë, which lay between the fifth and sixth cataracts, about 150 miles north of modern Khartoum. Even here, the Egyptian writing system was completely transformed, although the symbols used were basically unchanged. Logograms were abandoned, and four vowel signs were developed, thus creating a true alphabet. Two styles were maintained: hieroglyphic for monumental use, and demotic for other writing. Word division was regularly indicated by three dots in hieroglyphic style, by two (like a colon) in demotic. Writing went from right to

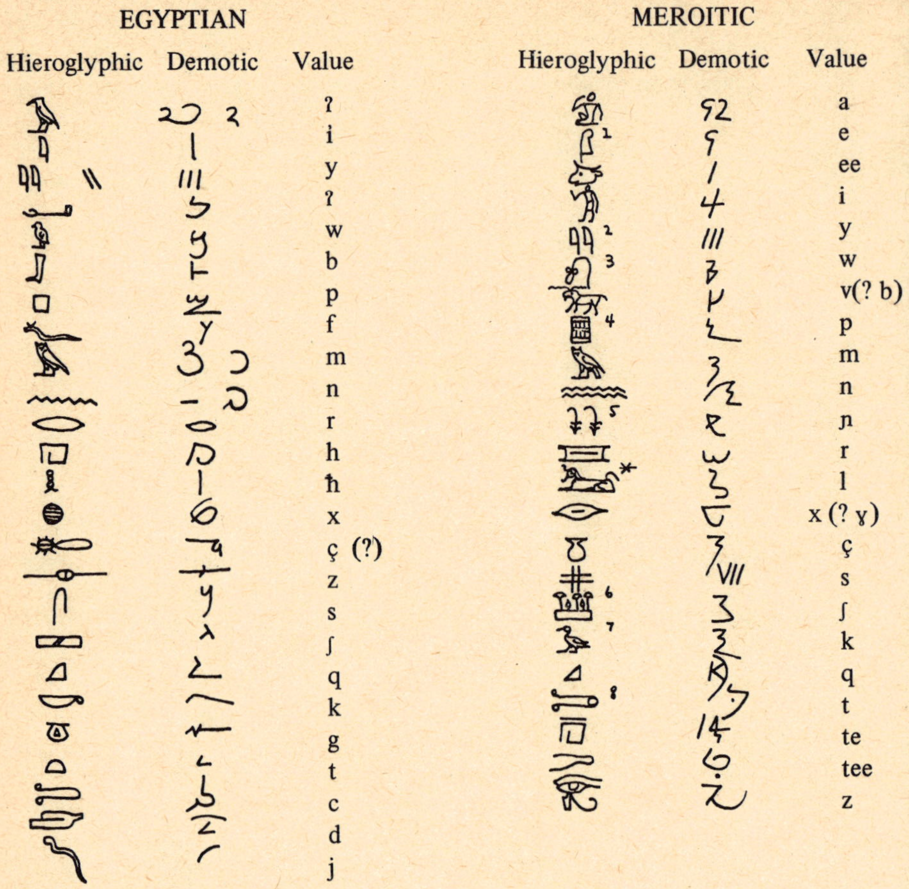

EGYPTIAN			MEROITIC		
Hieroglyphic	Demotic	Value	Hieroglyphic	Demotic	Value

EGYPTIAN Value column: ?, i, y, ?, w, b, p, f, m, n, r, h, ħ, x, ç (?), z, s, ʃ, q, k, g, t, c, d, j

MEROITIC Value column: a, e, ee, i, y, w, v(? b), p, m, n, ɲ, r, l, x (? ɣ), ç, s, ʃ, k, q, t, te, tee, z

1. Cf. Eg. ß ʃw (perhaps confused with 𝌆 i).
2. Cf. Eg. y.
3. Cf. Eg. 𐦀 wʔ Demotic ℓ.
4. Cf. Eg. ▫ p.
5. Cf. Eg. ⳥ nn.
6. Cf. Eg. ⳥⳥ ʃʔ late Eg ʃ, Demotic ℥.
7. Cf. Eg. ⳥ sʔ.
8. Cf. Eg. c.

* Late Eg. ⳥ *lion* had the value of 1, Demotic ⅄ .

Figure 17 EGYPTIAN AND MEROITIC SCRIPTS.

left, more rarely from top to bottom. The number of phonetic symbols used was 23 including the four vowel signs (with apparently rather vague values), and two syllabics representing **te** and **tee** (or **too**). The values of these signs are sometimes directly borrowed from the Egyptian, or with a slight modification: thus, **y p m n q** have the same values in both. Occasionally a biliteral Egyptian sign is reduced to its first consonant, etg. Meroïtic **w** and ʃ are derived from Egyptian wʔ and ʃʔ respectively. And sometimes a wholly new value has been given to a symbol: Egyptian **nn**, ʃw, and possibly also **pn** were used for ɲ, **e**, and x respectively in Meroïtic. Meroïtic writing began about the first century BC and died out after the fall of Meroë in the fourth century AD, but a few of the Meroïtic demotic signs persisted, having been borrowed by the Nubians to supplement the Greek (Koptic) alphabet they used. [12]

Some of the developments in Meroïtic actually had Egyptian antecedents. For example during the Saïte period (c. 650–525 BC), the use of determinants as well as of multiliteral signs was markedly reduced; some multiliteral signs were reduced to the first consonant value. Elsewhere, the Western Semitic scripts, which seem to be a continuation of the principles of Egyptian writing without necessarily preserving Egyptian symbols, had previously thrown out nonuniliteral symbols altogether, in a development the anthropologist Alfred E. Kroeber has called reduction-segregation. [13] These scripts, which include Hebrew, Arabic, Aramaic, and Phoenician (which is ancestral to Greek), have played an important role in the history of writing in Africa. In point of fact the earliest known inscriptions in a related and possibly ancestral script namely Proto-Sinaitic, [14] have been found in the peninsula of Sinai in Egypt, but they are not yet well understood.

From about the second century AD inscriptions in the socalled Libyan or Numidian [15] script appear from Sinai to the Canary Islands. A similar script, Turdetanian, [16] used for inscriptions on coins, has been reported from southern Spain from about the same period. Libyan is believed to be a derivative of a West Semitic script, probably Phoenician: many of the grafitti found written in Libyan come from the area round Carthage and six letters seem to be taken directly from Phoenician script. The grafitti themselves have so far not been translated and so the underlying system is not well understood. There are apparently twenty-five phonetic symbols; vowels are not represented. A remarkable number of choices existed for the direction of writing. Lines may be written from left to right to or right to left, or with an alternation of the two in a style called *boustrophedon* (i.e. in imitation of the rows plowed by a bull). The lines themselves are usually arranged so that the bottom line is read first, but the opposite way (as in normal English writing) is also found; even spiral inscriptions exist. The reason for such variation is not clear. But since most of the inscriptions are found on rocks, the variation may be a function of the material; we need only recall that neon signs often require English writing, normally written from left to right, to be written from top to bottom.

Libyan is thought to be the lineal ancestor of a kind of writing currently found among the Tuareg called **tifinaɣ** (usually spelt **tifinagh**; the word is evidently a berberization of the Latin **puunica** *Punic* or some related form, the **ti-** being a prefix). Indeed of its 24 main symbols, nine are the same in form and, presumably, value as the Libyan counterparts. Vowels are not normally indicated although they may be at the end of a word. Direction of writing varies; although left to right predominates, vertical and other directions are possible. The writing itself is used mostly for rock inscriptions or on objects such as bracelets or other jewelry. Although few Tuareg men are literate, all Tuareg women reportedly can read and write this script.[17]

A Semitic script of considerable practical and historical importance in Africa is the Ethiopic, used in writing Ge'ez, Amharic, and Tigrinya. Texts in Galla in

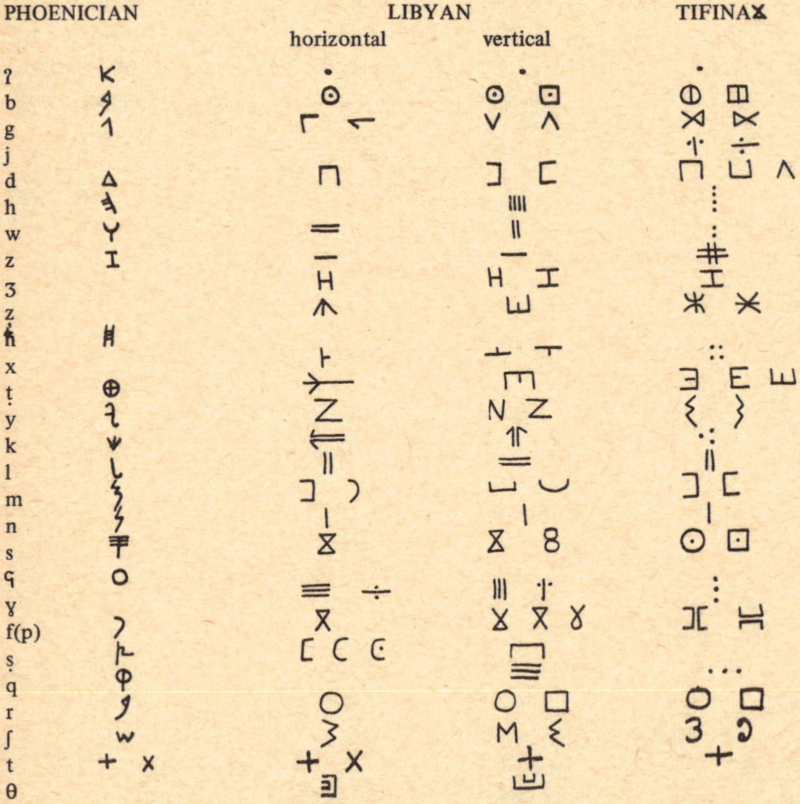

PHOENICIAN		LIBYAN		TIFINAɣ
		horizontal	vertical	

Figure 18   PHOENICIAN, LIBYAN AND TIFINAɣ SCRIPTS.

this script have been prepared by European missionaries but have proved to be inconsequential from a practical point of view. The Ethiopic system represents a development of a South Arabic type. As a matter of fact, some scholars (notably Littmann[18]) have suggested that Ethiopic was produced by a conscious reform of Sabaean (or Himyaritic) script, in which the earliest inscriptions in Ge'ez were written. Both scripts have 24 letters in common. Ethiopic dropped four others that occured in Sabaean and created two new ones, for **p'** and **p** (the latter perhaps a modification of Greek Ψ or Π). The oldest form of Ethiopic

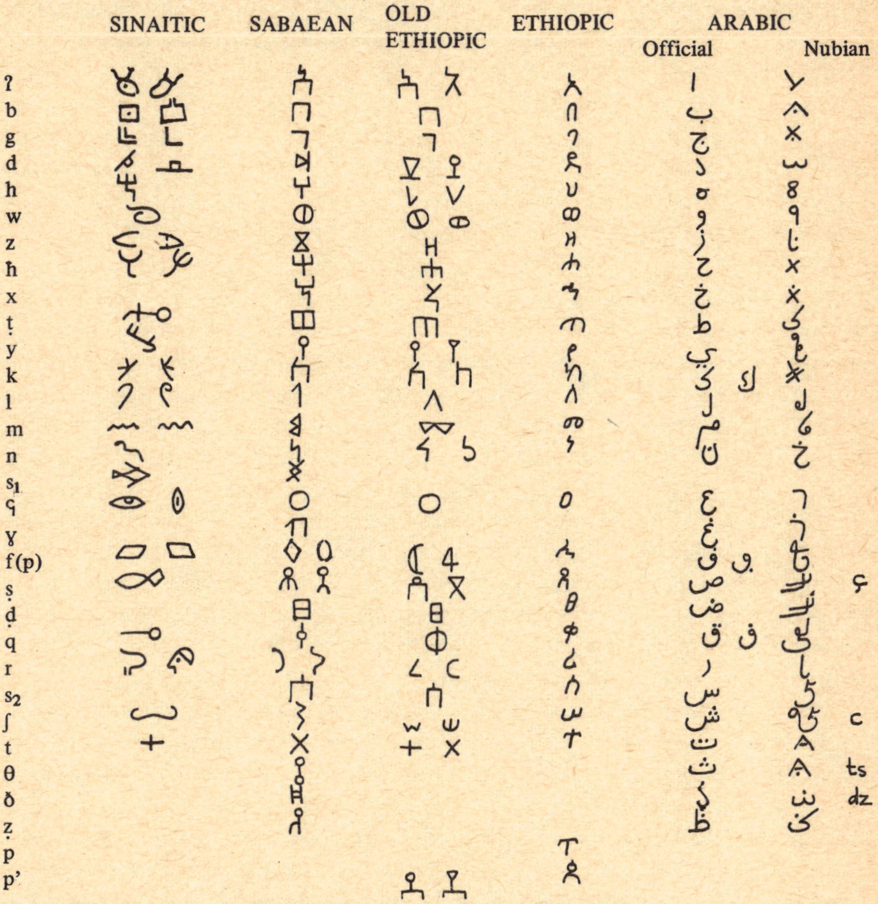

	SINAITIC	SABAEAN	OLD ETHIOPIC	ETHIOPIC	ARABIC Official	Nubian
ʔ						
b						
g						
d						
h						
w						
z						
ḥ						
x						
ṭ						
y						
k						
l						
m						
n						
s₁						
ʕ						
ɣ						
f(p)						
ṣ						
ḍ						
q						
r						
s₂						c
ʃ						
t						ts
θ						
ð						dz
z̧						
p						
p'						

The order of the Arabic signs in eastern usage is (from right to left):

ا ب ت ث ج ح خ د ذ ر ز س ش ص ض ط ظ ع غ ف ق ك ل م ن ه و ي

The order of the Arabic signs in Maghrebine usage is (from right to left):

ا ب ت ث ج ح خ د ذ ر ز ط ظ ك ل م ن ص ض ع غ ف ق س ش ه و ي

Figure 19   VARIOUS SEMITIC SCRIPTS.

script, in inscriptions from about AD 300, is vowelless. Remarkably enough, and contrary to several centuries of Semitic writing tradition, a full system of vocalization appeared about AD 350. The vowel signs were incorporated directly within a base consonant symbol, which by itself had the value of consonant plus the vowel a (which otherwise was unmarked). A consonant not accompanied by a vowel in pronunciation was represented by a consonant plus a "dummy" or zero vowel indicator. These details parallel exactly certain writing systems found in India such as the Braahmii and the derived Devanaagarii. Because of the rarity of such a syllabary type (being confined to India and Ethiopia), independent invention seems unlikely. The Indian syllabaries originated as early as the third century BC, some 600 years before the Ethiopic, and so an Indian stimulus for the Ethiopian development, rather than the other way round, must be reckoned with.[19] But no Indian scripts have themselves actually been used in writing other African (or even Semitic) languages except for some recent sporadic attempts to write Swahili in Devaanagarii within the Indian community in East Africa. Precisely how the idea of such a system could have found its way to Ethiopia remains uncertain. But interestingly enough, the apostle to the Ethiopians, Frumentius, consecrated bishop of Aksuum in 326, may provide a link. His own origins are obscure. He has been called Phoenician, Persian, and even Indian. According to Hommel,[21] he was the student and possibly a relative of an Indian[22] philosopher Meropius and because of his presumed knowledge of Indian writing and his great prestige among the people of Aksuum it has been suggested that Frumentius was responsible for the introduction of vowel writing. The problem of origin is fascinating, whatever the solution.

Ethiopic differs from other Semitic scripts in that the direction of writing is regularly from left to right, except for the earliest inscriptions where the normal Semitic right-to-left direction was maintained. Change in direction may be due to Greek or Koptic influence. As a matter of fact, Greek forms were adopted for numerals and one of the special Ethiopic letters may be derived from the Greek alphabet, as has already been mentioned.

Yet another Semitic scripts, Arabic, has undoubtedly played the most important role in African writing in general, apart from the Roman alphabet. In its inception and still today in ordinary use, Arabic is a vowelless syllabary. Even before the introduction of Islam, however, a method for representing vowels had been devised and by the eight century AD, the present system of vowel diacritics written above or below a sign representing a consonant that precedes in speech was current. This system with full representation of vowels is used in editions of the Koran and in elementary readers but not normally elsewhere. With vowels, the writing is truly alphabetic.

In its normal form, there are twenty-eight consonant signs, and three vowel diacritics. Absence of a vowel following a noninitial consonant is indicated by a dummy vowel diacritic. Curiously enough, the sign for one consonant, the glottal stop (Arabic *hamza*) is also a diacritic, which usually requires a dummy consonant, an alif, to support it. Long vowels are analyzed as short vowel plus consonant, e.g. ii is i plus y, aa is a plus alif. Direction of writing is almost invariably from right to left.

Arabic script has been adopted with greater or lesser degrees of success to an imposing number of African languages: Swahili, Hausa, Kanuri, Malagasy and sporadically to Nubian, Berber, Songhai, Nupe, Bambara, Malinke and perhaps a few others. In most instances the resources of the script prove to be inadequate for the borrowing language. In Swahili, for example, the fit is poor indeed. There are only three vowel signs for the five Swahili vowel phonemes. There are no signs for the consonants v p g ŋ c [23]; and consonant clusters such as ŋg or nd, which are not normal in Arabic itself, are frequently simplified. As a result an incredible degree of ambiguity results. Words as distinct as yaŋgu *mine* and yako *yours* are spelt identically *yaku* (the ŋg simplified by dropping the ŋ; a single letter used for both g and k, and another for o and u.) In the 1930's Sheikh Al Amin bin Ali of Tanga [24] proposed a reform which—if accepted—would have made the Arabic script spelling of Swahili superior to the official Roman one by even accommodating coastal speakers with an Arabic biasis; separate symbols for the marginal phonemes ṣ ḍ ṭ ḥ x p ʔ exist, whereas in the Roman form they are sumed under the symbols for s ð t and h (=h ḥ x), or else not represented (p ʔ).
The reform never really caught on, however, and since the Zanzibari revolution of 1963 publication of Swahili in any form of Arabic script has ceased. It must be admitted that the fit with some other languages, e.g. Hausa, is much better but never perfect (in Hausa ɓ and b, u and o are confused, and tone is systematically ignored).

In northwest Africa a distinctive Maghrebine style of Arabic script developed and spread throughout the western Sudan. This style is characterized by square-shaped letters with elaborate final flourishes, some variation in the other of letters within the alphabetical listing, and the use of ڢ for f instead of eastern ڧ, and of ڧ for q instead of ڧ.

In normal Arabic handwriting and printing, consonant sings are joined together within a word in much the same way that letters are joined in common Roman handwriting conventions. But in some areas, especially for magical purposes, special scripts with nonattachable consonant letters are used. MacMichael has in fact called attention to two alphabets of this kind, which have been used to write Nubian. [25]

In 1920—2, an alphabetic writing in part influenced by Arabic script and writing conventions was invented for Somali by ʕIsmaan Yuusuf Keenadiid. This script, known as Somalia writing (Far Soomaali) or the Ismanya (Osmania) script, has twenty-nine letters including 10 vowel signs. The order of the consonants is essentially that of the eastern Arabic alphabet. Direction of writing is from left to right, however. In 1932, Cerulli [26] reported that long vowels were indicated after the Arabic pattern as short vowel plus consonant; a later study, by Maino in 1951, [27] indicated that long vowels were represented by special symbols, which were modifications of those used for the corresponding short vowels; Maino noted that the inventor himself denied ever having used the system reported by Cerulli. The shape of the letters of the alphabet seem to have been invented freely. Some authorities have suggested an Ethiopic inspiration, but again Maino reports that the inventor denied knowing Amharic. He did know both Arabic and Italian, however, and influences of both are obvious in his creation.

Somali writing has no official status although it is being promoted by the Society for Somali Language and Literature, in Mogadiscio, and an estimated 20,000 or more people use it in private correspondence and in bookkeeping. Several books have been published in it, as is a fortnightly journal *Horseed* (anglice, *Vanguard*), all cyclostyped. A variety of other scripts have been developed for Somali, perhaps as many as twenty—most of them used only by their inventors and a few friends. The best known of these is the Gadabuursi script used at present by about a hundred persons, probably fewer. [28] Such a remarkable proliferation of scripts is due in large part to the even more remarkable fact that whereas Somali is the native language of nearly all the people in Somali, it is not that country's official language and has no official orthography in any script. [29]

The Greek alphabet, itself a derivative of Phoenician, was used in a modified form to write Koptic and Old Nubian. The major difference between the Phoenician and Greek scripts was the development of separate letters for vowels in the latter—usually from consonants that had no Greek analog. Even in Phoenician and Ancient Egyptian vowels were occasionally indicated by related semivowels such as y for i or w for u; thus a syllable ti could be written in the normal way as t^v or with a semivowel reminiscent of the vowel: t^v-y^v. Such conventions probably developed from analogy with petrified spellings for words in which certain original vowel consonant combinations had become reduced, e.g. aw → o but indicated as w. When consonants are used in this way to suggest vowel timbres, the writing is called *scriptio plena* or plene [full] writing, as opposed to normal vowelless writing or *scriptio defectiva*. The consonants used to indicate vowels are known technically as *matres lectiones*. Examples of plene writing among the Egyptians are believed to occur as early as the Pyramid Texts of the Old Kingdom; the device was fairly common later on in writing foreign place names. What the Greeks did was to reinterpret a plene writing such as t^v-y^v which they found in Phoenician to mean simply t-i and then to write in the vowels consistently. By such a process of reduction, the Greeks were the first to achieve an alphabetic system of writing.

The Koptic and Old Nubian scripts followed the normal Greek conventions. The actual shape of the letters used differs from the modern Greek printed forms, being in the style prevalent before the tenth century AD known as uncial, i.e. majuscule script with somewhat rounded letters. Only one size of letter was used, the distinction between capitals and small letters (or technically majuscule and minuscule) not appearing until much later in the Greek world. In Koptic script six letters taken from demotic Egyptian writing were added to represent

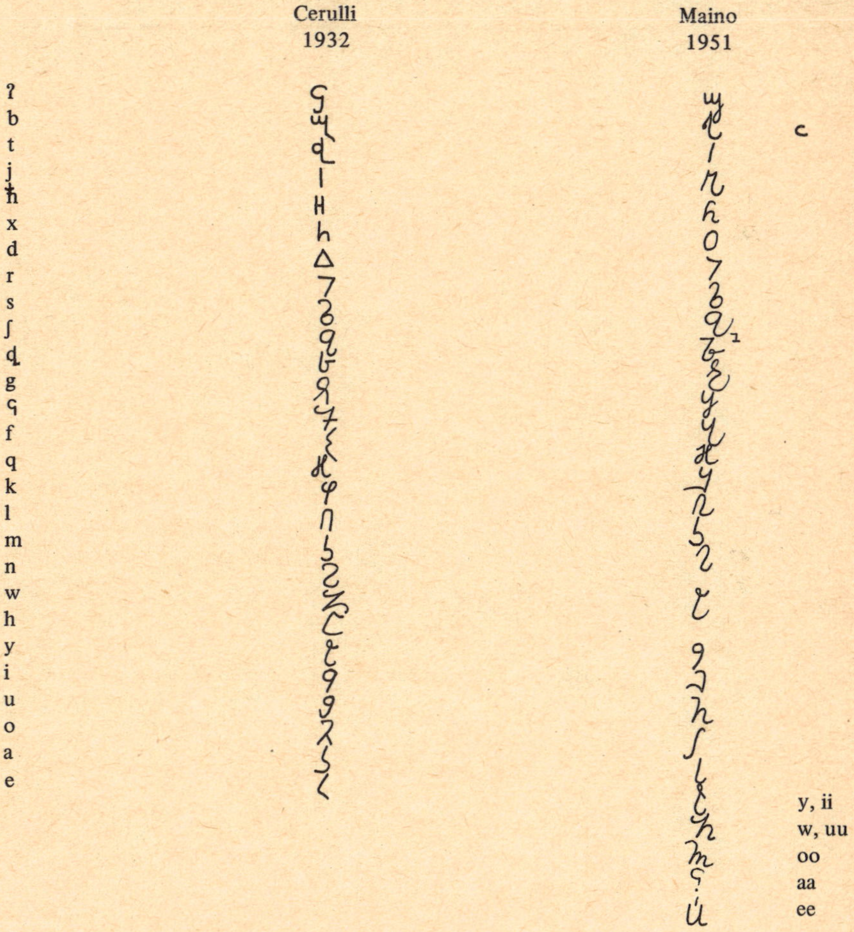

	Cerulli 1932	Maino 1951	
ʔ			
b			
t			c
j			
ħ			
x			
d			
r			
s			
ʃ			
ɗ			
g			
ʕ			
f			
q			
k			
l			
m			
n			
w			
h			
y			
i			
u			
o			
a			
e			
			y, ii
			w, uu
			oo
			aa
			ee

1. In Maino's ɗ and g are reversed.

Figure 20 SOMALIA WRITING

phonemes with no Greek correspondents: ʃ f x h j c; a seventh new letter represented the syllable **ti.** The consonant **h** was written with a separate letter and not as a diacritic as in later Greek conventions. The Nubians in turn borrowed two of the Koptic letters, **h j,** and added three others derived from Meroïtic: ŋ ɲ **w.**

All the writing systems discussed so far belong to the division earlier labeled as North African. They all seem ultimately derivable from Ancient Egyptian.

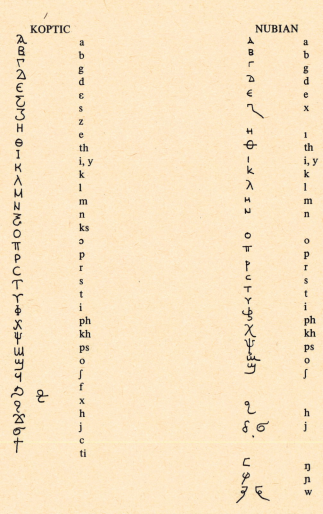

Figure 21   KOPTIC AND NUBIAN ALPHABETS

The members of the second large division, here called West African, are not known to be related although some sort of relationship is likely in many instances. [30]

We have already mentioned various pictographic systems in the Sudan. We may also note that a pre-Islamic tradition of writing is reported by Leo Frobenius for the Nupe. [31] He maintains that historical accounts were written down on the skins of animals but that these records were buried with the Nupe King Zado (AD 1850) to prevent them from falling into the hands of the Muslim Fulani. No corroborative evidence has so far been adduced in support of Frobenius's report.

The West African writing system that has received most publicity is the Vai script, [32] used in Liberia and Sierra Leone. It was apparently devised about 1833 by Mɔmɔlu Duwalu Bukɛlɛ. At any rate the script was reported as early as 1834 by two American missionaries, J.L. Wilson and S.R. Wynkoop. A two-page manuscript in Vai script from about 1850 exists in the British Museum, the earliest known original manuscript in any of the indigenous West African scripts. Some authorities have suggested a considerably earlier date for its invention—Delafosse for one suggesting the beginning of the sixteenth century AD. No evidence supports such contentions. The script came to the attention of the academic world because of reports by F.E. Forbers and S.W. Koelle, who even visited the inventor and received a detailed account of its origin. Bukɛlɛ said the script was revealed to him by divine inspiration in a dream: a tall, venerable looking white man showed him the writing in a book. However, Bukɛlɛ admitted that he and some of his friends were forced to invent signs because he could not remember the ones in the dream.

The Vai script is a syllabary using up to 212 characters in its modern form. It is now written from left to right but in the mid-nineteenth century was sometimes also written from right to left, or from top to bottom. Tone is not indicated. Unlike the Ethiopic syllabary, the Vai script does not indicate vowels by predictable modifications of a basic consonant sign. Rather, every syllable is normally represented by a unique underived sign, which only sporadically represents variations on a thematic consonant; thus **bi ba bu be bɛ bɔ bo** are represented as

respectively. However, some characters do seem to be derived from others by means of diacritics; but it is consonant, not vowel, variation that is so indicated and most often consonants produced at the same point of articulation. Thus, **ju cu nju yu** share an underlying character, as do the **s-z** series, the **ɓ- mɓ** series, and the **f-v** series. This detail suggests some sort of accommodation to a consonant permutation system like that found in Fulani, but oddly enough not in Vai.

Vai writing has proved to be remarkably popular. By 1899 most of the Vai were said to be literate in the script. The Vai of Liberia continue its use to this day, mostly in informal correspondence. Professor A. Klingenheben even had a set of type in the syllabary prepared in Germany; the type has never been used, however. The script reportedly has currency among the Kpelle, the De (who speak a Kru language) and various other neighboring groups but it is not clear whether they write in Vai or in their own languages. Klingenheben noted that in 1927 some Mende in Gene (in Liberia on the Sierra Leone border) were trying to apply it to their own language.

A number of fairly minor changes have occurred in the script since the first descriptions of it appeared: the shape of some letters has changed; punctuation marks have been introduced, as well as new characters for foreign sounds found in loan words. Most of these innovations were introduced by a Vai called Momolu Massaquoi—and Klingenheben, who was fascinated by the subject.

The true origins of the Vai script remain obscure. The presumed inventor, Bukɛlɛ, is known to have been acquanted with Roman script, which he learnt from missionaries as a boy. Some knowledge of Arabic script also seems likely for a number of reasons. For one thing, the syllabary is usually referred to as **A-ja-ma-na** in Vai itself, a term reminiscent of the Sudanic names for (Arabic) script (Hausa **àjàmi**, Fulani **ajemi**, etc). And in Bukɛlɛ's dream, he was instructed by the white man (an Arab or a European?) that those who learnt the writing should not eat dogs, monkeys, or animals that have not had their throats cut—familiar Islamic injunctions. Some scholars, notably Kroeber,[33] have held up Bukɛlɛ's invention as a prime example of stimulus diffusion; i.e. of an instance of where the *idea* of a culture trait (in this instance, Roman or Arabic writing) is spread, but not the trait itself. On the other hand, an older pictographic or logographic system may have provided some sort of stimulus. The remarkable thing is that although the Ethiopic syllabary must probably be ruled out altogether as a source for the Vai sillabary, a writing system that appears on the face of it to be a much more unlikely source cannot: the American Indian Cherokee syllabary invented by Sequoya between 1820 and 1824.[34] The underlying principles of both scripts are the same: every syllable normally has a unique underived symbol to represent it. We have already considered examples of this for Vai. Here is an example from Cherokee, which is structurally identical:

W	Ꮥ	Ꮖ	Ᏺ	M
ta	te	ti	to	tu.

The Cherokee system, itself a clear cut instance of stimulus diffusion (having borrowed Roman letters but assigning total new values to them), was sponsored by the American Board of Foreign Missions shortly after its invention. The possibility of a connection between the two scripts lies in the fact that this same missionary group was also active in Liberia, and its journal, the *Missionary Herald*, published an account of the Cherokee syllabary in 1827 and 1828. Furthermore, Wilson, who together with Wynkoop was the first to report the existence of the Via script, was an agent of that mission group. Precisely what all this adds up to is unclear and even the likelihood of a connection between the two writing systems has yet to be demonstrated.

A number of other scripts have appeared in neighboring areas in Liberia, Sierra Leone, and Guinea. With few exceptions they are syllabaries of the same general type as the Vai. Since they are all more recent than the Vai script by at least 80 years and since in most instances the inventors are known to have visited Vai country or to have had access to samples of Vai writing, a Vai influence or stimulus is probable. In three instances, a supernatural origin or inspiration is cited, which suggests a knowledge of Bukɛlɛ's dream.

The Mende script,[35] referred to as **Ki-ka-ku**, is believed to have been invented by Kisimi Kamara, a tailor, in 1921. It is written from right to left (the only West African syllabary to be so written) and uses about 195 characters. Tone is not indicated. The system differs somewhat from the Vai in that diacritics are sometimes, but not invariably, added to a basic consonant sign to idicate a following vowel; e.g.

$$\gg \quad \dot\gg \quad \acute\gg \quad \gg.$$

| ni | na | nu | nɛ |

(but nɔ is :|:). Kisimi could speak Vai and apparently visited Vai country. The fact that he was a Muslim and had a certain knowledge of Arabic may account for the direction of writing. Details of the invention of the script are unclear. The inventor reportedly was inspired by a dream or vision (in all events he was reputed as having "second sight"). The script was never used outside of a few Mende speaking communities in Sierra Leone and is now falling into extinction.

The Loma script[36] was invented by Widɔ Zoɓo who was aided in devising signs by a friend, Moriba—like Kisimi, a tailor. The writing runs from left to right and has a total of at least 185 characters. Tone is not indicated. Variation on a consonant base sign to indicate vowels or other consonant does not occur. Tradition maintains that the syllabary was inspired in a dream in which Widɔ reproached God for not having given the Loma writing; after some discussion and a promise by Widɔ that the Loma would not desert traditional ways, God agreed to give them writing provided that Widɔ never teach it to a woman. At present the script is little used but was at one time popular among Loma speakers in Liberia and Guinea, particularly on a Firestone plantation in Liberia where Widɔ himself worked.

The Kpelle (or Guerzé) script[37] was probably invented by Gbili, a Kpelle chief, in the 1930's. The direction of writing is apparently from left to right although a great flexibility seems to exist. The syllabary uses 88 characters, some of which may be moved 90°, others 180°. A point or small circle is used to indicate a low tone; this tone mark may not have been part of the original system but rather a subsequent modification suggested by conventions in the Bassa script (discussed below). A striking feature of the Kpelle syllabary is the fact that certain consonant pairs are subsumed under the same character; e.g. **pi** and **bi** are written with a single sign—so also **ti** and **di**, **ki** and **gi**, **fi** and **vi**, etc., for all vowel combinations. The mostly plausible explanation of this is that the members of these consonant pairs enter into regular alternations with each other; the spelling would thus be partially morphophenemic. The script is now very rarely used although at one point it enjoyed some currency among Kpelle-speaking groups in both Liberia and Guinea.

The Bété script [38] was invented by Frédéric Buly-Bouabré, a civil servant from the village of Zeprigue in the Ivory Coast, about 1956. The script is written from left to right and employs 401 signs (including punctuation marks). Monod, who first reported the existence of Bété script, has published a remarkable account of the principles underlying the writing system along with copious examples written by the inventor himself. The point of departure, as it were, for the creation of the script was the use of special stones (apparently a variety of prismatic crystals) used in children's games and for divination in the town of Gbekola. Buly-Bouabré considered the use of these stones as a kind of "writing" and was inspired to create a systematic and comprehensive writing for more normal purposes. The syllabary he evolved is basically of the Vai type, where every syllable has a separate and nonderived form. However, in the Bété system, reduplication of one sign to form another commonly occurs within a consonant vowel series. Thus, the sign for **gu**, $\lambda\lambda$, is a reduplicated form for **gɔ**, λ; so similarly **ku** is a reduplicated form of **kɔ**. But this devise is not developed systematically: both **vɔ** and **vu** are separate and underived, as are **tɔ**, **tu**, etc; and other patterns may emerge for any particular consonant set: **vi** and **vo**, **ti** and **to** are unrelated, but **go** is a reduplicated form of **gi**. Syllables beginning with consonant clusters such as **zr-** or **gl-** are considered as single units and treated like other syllables. Special logograms for some numbers were also invented but complete details are unavailable. The extent to which the system is actually used is not known. The inventor maintains that several people have learnt to write it and that some of its signs were even painted on the walls of a house. In all events, Buly-Bouabré says that his whole village has become very much interested in the project.

The Bassa script, [39] found in Liberia, also known as the Vah script or **Nni-ka-se-fa**, is believed to have been invented by Dr. Thomas Flo David Gbianvoodoh Jidah Lewis in the 1920's. Unlike the other West African scripts considered so far, this one is an alphabet consisting of 30 letters (7 representing vowels) plus 5 diacritics indicating tone, which is truly the remarkable feature of the script.

Using the vowel sign for a, the tones are shown as follows: ⼞ á (high), ⼞ à (low), ⼞ a (mid), ⼞ a (low-high), ⼞ â (high-low). Writing goes from left to right.

According to Bassa tradition, the script is a refinement of an earlier ideographic writing (also referred to as Vah), simplified and improved by a man called Dirah about 1800. Owing to the fact that he had an adulterous love affair with the head wife of the paramount chief of the Bassa, Dirah was sold into slavery by the chief—eventually arriving in the United States where he kept

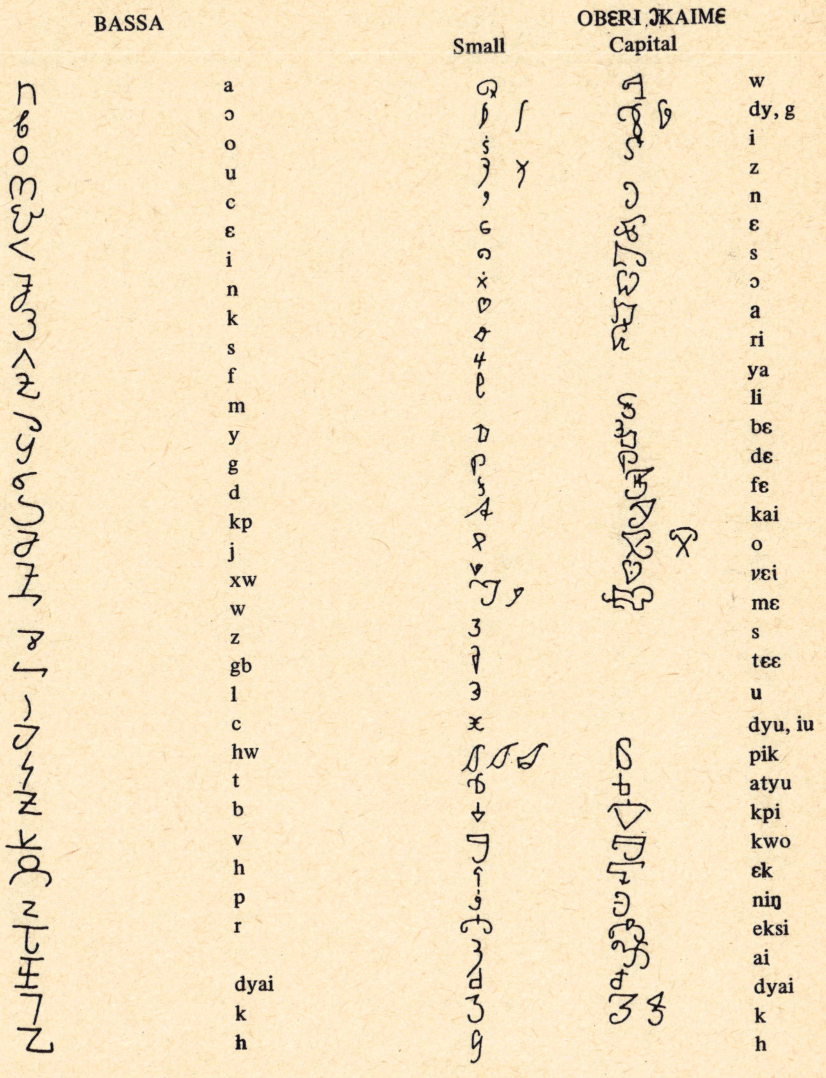

BASSA		OBERI ƆKAIME		
		Small	Capital	
	a			w
	ɔ			dy, g
	o			i
	u			z
	c			n
	ɛ			ɛ
	i			s
	n			ɔ
	k			a
	s			ri
	f			ya
	m			li
	y			bɛ
	g			dɛ
	d			fe
	kp			kai
	j			o
	xw			vɛi
	w			mɛ
	z			s
	gb			tɛɛ
	l			u
	c			dyu, iu
	hw			pik
	t			atyu
	b			kpi
	v			kwo
	h			ɛk
	p			niŋ
	r			eksi
				ai
	dyai			dyai
	k			k
	h			h

FIGURE 22   BASSA AND OBERI ƆKAIME ALPHABETS

up the work of improving the script. His son, Jenni Dirah, continued the work after his father's death and it was from him that Lewis learnt Vah. Whether Lewis actually modified the script further is not clear. In any event it is said that he eventually published an account of it, and taught the script to hundreds of Bassa on his return to Liberia. How well this tradition reflects history is another matter. When the script was devised is also open to question. Another tradition records the use of the (unreformed?) Vah script in the 1820's in connection with Bassa aid to the recently formed settlement of freed slaves from the United States. However, as Dalby has pointed out, it must be borne in mind that "in view of the dominant position in Liberia which the Americo-Liberian descendents of the Colonists still hold, it remains politic for the indigenous tribes to recount 'traditions' of how they gave support to the early Colonists".[40] The earliest reliable reference to the script was apparently made by Klingenheben in the early 1930's; another early reference, published in 1936, occurs in Graham Greene's *Journey without Maps.* The problem of what ties the Bassa script might have with Vai also remains uncertain. Some of the Bassa letters are reminiscent of Vai forms; cf. Bassa Ɜn(i) and ∧k(a) with Vai Ƨni and Иka. The very name Vah suggests some sort of connection.

The Bassa Vah Association, whose aim is promoting the use of the script, was established in 1959. Type for the script seems to have been produced by a missionary group, but Pichl in 1964 was unable to find any but a few remains of it. No printed materials in the script seem to exist, but the writing is said to be quite popular in private correspondence.

The Gola alphabet, perhaps invented in the 1960's, remains undeciphered. It has about 30 characters and is written from left to right. It has been described as a secret script of the Poro Society of Liberia and Sierra Leone, which seems unlikely.

All the West African scripts discussed so far are in all likelihood derived from or influenced by the Vai syllabary. In an area somewhat farther east, Southern Nigeria and western Cameroun, writing systems have also appeared, but without any likely derivation from Vai.

In 1936, R. F. G. Adams [41] discovered an alphabetic script in South Eastern Nigeria, in Efik country. There are 32 letters and a few diacritics. The direction of writing is from left to right. Some of the letters apparently represent two consonants, e.g. **ks, sk, pt.** Although Adams states that all letters have both capital and small forms, in his accompanying table, seven letters lack distinctive capitals. However that may be, the mere existence of such a distinction suggests a stimulus of some sort from Roman writing, since this distinction occurs elsewhere only in European writing systems.

The script was used for writing the secret language of the Obɛri Ɔkaimɛ religious sect, a local deviant Christian group apparently founded in about 1928.

According to the followers of this sect, both the script and the language are the inspiration of Sɛminant "the Holy Spirit". At present the script appears to be little used. Kathleen Hau has tried to ascribe a considerable antiquity to Obɛri Ɔkaimɛ writing and seems to consider it related to nsibidi, the Benin carvings, the Nupe writing as mentioned by Frobenius, and ultimately to the as yet undeciphered Linear A script found in Crete. Her arguments are perforce superficial in that she seizes upon mere formal resemblances without establishing comparable functions or values. [42] A more impressive series of sound-shape comparisons can be made between Obɛri Ɔkaimɛ and Roman script; compare, for example: ⴌ z, š i, ५ y, ℓ 1, ꝡ f, ⸕ h, ⱱ v, ⸞ d, ⸿ (and its capital ⸚)e(E), ⸗ M, ⸒ B (cf. b).

Another "holy" alphabet used in a Yoruba sect, was derived between 1926 and 1928 by Josiah Oshitelu of Ogere (Western Nigeria). It was written from right to left and remains undeciphered. The script seems to have been used in writing a "revealed" language, never apparently Yoruba.

One of the most interesting of all the indigenous African writing systems is the Bamum script, used in southern Vameroun, and initiated and developed by King Nʒoya. [43] The most fascinating part about this script is the fact that by successive royal decrees an originally logographic system was changed into a basically aplhabetic one after passing through a syllabary stage. Bamum writing was probably first started about 1900, an unambiguous case of stimulus diffusion. Nʒoya knew of German and Arabic writing, although he apparently did not fully understand the system of either. He reportedly wanted to create his own system and called a group of elders together with instructions that each was to think up symbols for a number of common words; these symbols he later codified or rejected. Subsequent changes introduced into the system were largely a function of Nʒoya's increasing knowledge of foreign writing: he was tutored in writing at a German missionary school. The result was that Bamum writing eventually became what Gelb has called a syllabary "showing certain tendencies toward alphabetization". [44] In its final stage, the script employed some 70 signs. Writing was always from left to right whatever the stage of development. Apart from changes in the values of the signs used, their shapes were also modified and tended to become more and more abstract. Delafosse has illustrated such changes with the following example:

1900	1907	1911	1916	1918

Original meaning of the logograph: *king* [mfɔn]; present value of sign **f(u)**. The older logograph is now written with signs that can be transliterated as **m-fu-ɔ-n**.

Notes and References

1) Kathleen Hau, 1959, Evidence of the use of pre-Portuguese written characters by the Bini?, *Bulletin de l'Institut Français d'Afrique Noire* **21**: 109–154. Also (in the same journal), 1964, A royal title on a palace tusk from Benin (Southern Nigeria), **26**: 21–39; 1967, The ancient writing of Southern Nigeria, *ibid.*, **29**: 150–190.

2) As reported in Carl Meinhof, 1911, Zur Entstehung der Schrift, *Zeitschrift für ägyptische Sprache* **49**: 1–14.

3) D. Zahan, 1950, Pictographic writing in the Western Sudan, *Man* 50: 136–38.

4) Regina G. Twala, 1951, Beads as regulating the social life of the Zulu and Swazi, *African Studies* **10**.3: 113–123. She suggests on p. 115 that "sometimes beads stand for letters, threads of beads for words, then the pattern would stand for a sentence, a complete thought". It is not clear from her discussion that such is literally the case.

5) C. A. Gollmer, 1885, On African symbolic messages, *Journal of the Royal Anthropological Institute of Great Britain and Ireland*, **14**: 169–81. In the accompanying discussion (by Cust? p. 181) the name of the symbolic languages of the Yoruba is given as **a-ku**.

6) R. E. Dennett, 1966, *At the back of the black man's mind*, London, pp. 71ff.

7) Marcel Grianle and Germaine Dietereen, 1951, Signes graphiques soudanais, *Cahiers d'Ethnologie, de Geographie et de Linguistique* no. 3.

8) See J. K. MacGregor, 1909, Some notes on Nsibidi, *Journal of the Royal Anthropological Institute* **39**: 209–219; Elphinstine Dayrell, 1911, Further notes on "Nsibidi" signs with their meanings from Ikom district, Southern Nigeria, *Journal of Royal Anthropological Institute* **41**: 521–540; Percy Amaury Talbot, 1912, *In the shadow of the bush*, Appendix G.

9) R. F. G. Adams, 1947, Obɛri Ɔkaimɛ: a new African language and script, *Africa* **17**: 24–34. It is not known what sort of signs were actually used, however. Dayrell, 1911 (*op. cit.*), notes that some women wear nsibidi signs as tattoos (although in other areas, women are not allowed to know nsibidi at all). Talbot, 1912 (*op. cit.*), 320 says that among the Ekoi

"Young women and children are found of ornamenting their faces, especially their foreheads, with designs in various colours. ... The outlines are often filled in with Nsibidi writing, and sometimes a girl's whole life-history is proclaimed in this manner."

He adds that according to tradition the Ekoi learnt nsibidi from the monkeys that crowded round their camp fires (p. 305).

10) Holger Pedersen was apparently the first person to suggest that the Ancient Egyptian system was basically syllabic. See his *Sprogvidenskaben i det nittende Aarhundrede, Metoder og Resultater*, København (1924)–translated as *Linguistic science in the nineteenth century*, Cambridge (1931. See also W. F. Albright, 1934, *The vocalization of the Egyptian syllabic orthography*, New Haven. For a discussion of the theoretical issues and implication of the syllabic vs. alphabet interpretation, see I. J. Gelb, 1963, *A study of writing*, Chicago.

11) Absence of a vowel apparently is treated as a kind of (zero) vowel, so that $t^v m^v$ could actually be realized as **tam**, etc. See the discussion of Arabic script below. The crucial point seems to be that no word could begin with either a vowel or consonant cluster.

195

12) For a detailed discussion of Meroïtic writing, see E. Zylharz, 1930, Das meroitische Sprachproblem, *Anthropos* 25: 406–463. Also, Hans Jensen, 1935, *Die Schrift in Vergangenheit und Gegenwart*, Glückstadt and Hamburg, 54–57.

13) Kroeber, 1948, *Anthropology*, New York, 370–72.

14) See Gelb, 1963 (*op. cit.*), 122–3.

15) See, André Basset, 1948. Écritures libyque et touarègue (in Ch. Fossey, *Notices sur les caractères étrangers anciens et modernes*, 135–43); Carl Meinhof, 1931, *Die libyschen Inschriften* (Deutsche Morgenländische Gesellschaft, Abhandlungen für die Kunde des Morgenlandes, 19, 1). Also Jensen, 1935 (op. cit.), 106–111.

16) See Jensen, 1935 (op. cit.), 108–10.

17) In at least the Azjer subgroup, as reported in G. P. Murdock, 1959, *Africa: Its people and their culture history*, New York, 407.

18) E. Littmann, 1913, *Deutsche Aksum-Expedition*, vol. 4, p. 78.

19) As suggested in J. Friedrich, 1935, Einige Kapitel aus der inneren Geschichte der Schrift, *Archiv für Schreib- und Buchwesen* NF 2. 8–18.

20) The only printed example of this occurs in Lilani Alidina Somjee, 1890, *Guide to the Swahili language in Gujarati characters* (place?).

21) As cited in Frank R. Blake, 1940, The development of symbols for the vowels in the alphabets derived from the Phoenician, *Journal of the American Oriental Society* 60. 3. 410.

22) In some account he is called a native of Tyre, or a Turk; his name is also written Moripius.

23) The status of c in Swahili is a matter of some dispute; it may represent, in some sense, ki (or ky).

24) As reported in John Williamson, 1947, The use of Arabic script in Swahili, Supplement to *African Studies* 6. 4. 7 pp.

25) H. E. MacMichael, 1922 *History of the Arabs in the Sudan*. See also the review by Maurice Delafosse, 1932, in *Revue d'Ethnographie et des Traditions Populaires* 4: 106–6.

26) Enrico Cerulli, 1932, Tentativo indigeno di formare un alfabeta somalo, *Oriente Maderno* 12: 212–3.

27) Mario Maino, 1951, L'alfabeta "Osmania" in Somalia, *Rassegna di Studi Etopici* 10: 108–21.

28) I am indebted for most of the information in this paragraph to a personal communication from Professor B. W. Andrzejwski.

29) It is perhaps appropriate to add a footnote here about the conflicting reports of an indigenous form of writing used by the Galla, as reported by Antoine d'Abbadie in 1842. All his informants except one denied the existence of such writing, but the exceptional source volunteered the information without being asked. See, Extraits de deux lettres addressées à M. d'Avezac par M. Antoine d'Abbadie, *Bulletin de la Société de Geographie* 17: 123.

30) For a detailed account (with extensive examples and illustrations) of scripts from the westernmost portion of this area, see David Dalby, 1967, A survey of the indigenous scripts of Liberia and Sierra Leone: Vai, Mende, Loma, Kpelle and Bassa, *African Language Studies* 8: 1–51. A good deal of the discussion in the present chapter is based on information in Dalby's article.

31) 1931, *The Voice of Africa* 2: 368–9. Interestingly enough, Frobenius mentions that these "books" were bound in ivory covers, which is vaguely in line with Hau's contention about the Benin ivories.

32) The literature on the Vai script is quite extensive, and is covered in P. E. H. Hair, 1963, Notes on the discovery of the Vai script, with a bibliography, *Sierra Leone Language Review* 2: 36–49. Of particular importance are the following: S. W. Koelle, 1849, *Narrative of an expedition into the Vy country of West Africa, and the discovery of a system of syllabic writing, recently invented by the natives of the Vy tribe*, London;

A. Klingenheben, 1933, The Vai Script, *Africa* 6: 158–171.

33) Alfred E. Kroeber, 1948, *Anthropology*, 370.

34) The connection is suggested by Dalby in an interesting footnote to the article previously mentioned (p. 10).

35) See, for further details: J. Friedrich, 1938, Zu einigen Schrifterfindungen der neuesten Zeit, *Zeitschrift der deutschen Morgenländischen Gesellschaft*, 92 (NF 17). 189–208; David Dalby, 1966, An investigation into the Mende syllabary of Kisimi Kamara, *Sierra Leone Studies* NS 19. 119–123.

36) See J. Joffre, 1943, A new West African alphabet used by the Toma, French Guinea and Liberia, *Man* 43.85. 108–112; 1945; Sur un nouvel alphabet ouest-africain: le Toma *Bulletin de l'Institut Français d'Afrique Noire* 7: 160–73.

37) See A. Lassort, 1951, L'écriture guerzée, *Première Conférence Internationale des Africanistes de l'Ouest, 1945, Comptes Rendus* 2: 209–15.

38) See Th. Monod, 1958, Un nouvel alphabet ouest-africain: le bété (Côte d'Ivore), *Bulletin de l'Institut Français d'Afrique Noire* 20: 432–553 (including a copy of Buly-Bouabré's manuscript guide to the script).

39) See W. J. Pichl, 1966, L'écriture bassa au Liberia, *Bulletin de l'Institut Française d'Afrique Noire* 28: 481–4.

40) Dalby, 1967 (*op. cit.*), 34f.

41) R. F. G. Adams, 1947, Obɛri ɔkaimɛ: a new African language and script, *Africa* 17: 24–34.

42) For references, see note 1) of this chapter.

43) See Maurice Delafosse, 1922, Naisance et évolution d'un système d'écriture de création contemporaire, *Revue d'Ethnographie et des Traditions Populaires* 3: 11–19; I. Dugast and M. D. W. Jeffreys, 1950, *L'écriture des Bamum* (Mémoire de l'Institut Français d'Africa Noire), Cameron; A. Schmitt, 1963, *Die Bamum-Schrift*, Wiesbaden (3 vols.).

44) Gelb, 1963 (*op. cit.*), 209.

45) See L. W. G. Malcolm, 1920–21, Short notes on the syllabic writing of the Eɣap, Central Cameroons, *Journal of the Africa Society* 20: 127–9.

46) As mentioned by Delafosse, 1922 (*op. cit.*), 19f.

47) Gelb, 1963 (*op. cit.*), Chapter 6, pp. 190–205 (especially p. 205).

48) Discussed in d'Abbadie, 1842 (*op. cit.*). A facsimile of the entire letter is given opposite p. 160.

49) Marcel Cohen, 1932, Inscriptions arabes en caractères séparés recueillies en Mauritanie par. P. Boëry, *Hespéris* 14. 20.

50) See David Dalby, 1970, The historical problem of the indigenous scripts of West Africa and Surinam, in *Language and History in Africa* (D. Dalby, ed.), New York, 109–119.

Part Six   CONCLUSION

CHAPTER XVII

Policies and Proposals

Independence for African countries and the spread of Western education have brought with them many problems of language policy and planning.

The main problem is surely the enormous linguistic diversity in Africa, greater in several senses than in any other continent. For one thing, every sub-Saharan country has from 12 to over 100 languages spoken within its boundaries.[1] On an area less than one quarter of the total land mass of the planet, with a population less than one tenth the world total, perhaps one fourth of the world's languages is spoken. The nearly 300 million people in Africa speak something over 1000 languages—with only about 40 spoken by more than a million people.[2] Language communities with 1000 or fewer speakers are not rare, and at least 20 languages are reported with fewer than 100 speakers.[3]

A number of languages are known (or strongly believed) to be extinct, including Koptic, Guanche, Lenge, Old Mfengu and several presumably Khoisan languages such as /Kam-Ka-!ke. A great many other languages have probably disappeared without a trace. M. D. W. Jeffreys has recorded the death throes if not the actual death of a language (or dialect) called ŋkat spoken in the former British Cameroons. The last speaker was estimated as being 113 years old in 1944, and he was then unable to speak the language fluently.[4] Nadel reports that the Gbedegi, a group among the Nupe of Nigeria, spoke at least a special dialect some one or two generations before his study, but that it had disappeared without a trace.[5] Occasionally, however, predications on the early demise of this or that particular language or dialect prove to be greatly exaggerated. Golo, spoken in Sudan, was reported earlier in the century to be dying out, but Santandrea points out that since the tribal regroupings undertaken by the Sudan government in 1950, Golo has taken on a new lease on life. However, it seems clear that a number of languages with few speakers will disappear in a generation or two. In most of the language communities described as having fewer than 100 speakers, the younger generation is either bilingual in their own language and the language of a culturally more dominant group, or monolingual in the foreign language alone.

With all this linguistic diversity one might have expected language controversies, possibly even language riots, to equal anything reported from India or Ceylon. In point of fact, however, there has been almost no difficulty along these lines anywhere in Africa. The main reason for this seems to be that the language divergence in Africa is so great that no faction is generally in the majority and hence no native language has been set up as an official national language. The solution has usually involved maintaining the former colonial languages.

A few exceptions exist. In 1964, Swahili was declared to be the primary official language of Tanzania. In 1965, three countries followed a similar course: Rwanda (setting up Rwanda), Burundi (Rundi), and the Central African Republic (Sango). Togo has decided to make use of Ewe and secondarily also of Hausa alongside of French, but this decision seems not to have had any significant practical application. In North African states, Arabic is the official language, sometimes cojoined by French, as in Algeria, Morocco, and Mauretania. In Nigeria before the coup of 1966, the Northern Region had adopted both Hausa and English as co-equal official languages; simulaneous translation into either was provided for in the local legislative council. As a matter of fact some Nigerians, not necessarily native speakers of Hausa themselves, had come out in favor of Hausa as the national language of all of Nigeria, rather than English or some southern language. The Tiv, however, resisted Hausaization after Nigerian independence and this led to riots over the issue. The dissolution of the Northern Region as a political entity has left the future status of Hausa unresolved, but the possibility of Hausa as a national anguage is still discussed; the Mid-West has decreed it should be taught in Secondary Schools.

In Ethiopia, the official language is Amharic, and the use of other languages is officially discouraged. In Sudan, an Arabization policy is under way and Arabic is being forcibly spread in those areas of the south where it is not natively spoken. Resistance to this policy has resulted in a long term civil war, another one of the few instances in African history where what is at least partially language policy has resulted in bloodshed. An even more strident example has been charged to the Arab conquerors of Egypt, who at one point reportedly cut off the tongues of persons who spoke Koptic in public.

One might assume that basically monolingual countries would have no language problems to speak of. Somalia presents an extraordinary counter instance. Practically the entire population speaks Somali, but Somali has no legal status largely because no official spelling of it exists. Because of opposition by entrenched Muslim conservatives the use of a Roman script for Somali has been consistently blocked, and even a modification of Arabic script is apparently not .deemed suitable. The result: Arabic, Italian, and English are used officially although only a very small percentage of the population is fluent in any of these.

For the most part, the educational and linguistic policies of contemporary African states continue earlier colonial policies. France, Spain, and Portugal all decided on direct rule involving administration and education in the metropolitan language only. In Mozambique and Angola, for example, from the very first day a child goes to school he may not use his native language in class but is subject to Portugese even though he may not understand a word of it. In francophone areas, a similar policy is actually maintained even now after independence. But recently, owing to UNESCO recommendations, a campaign to eradicate adult illiteracy in the vernaculars has begun. With the exception of anglophone countries, literacy has meant literacy in the language of the colonial power. The English policy of indirect rule encouraged education in the native languages of the pupils and the translation of legal codes into the vernaculars. Of course, because of the largely arbitrary political units involved, crosscutting as they did ethnic and linguistic boundaries, even the English system required an élite who could speak the colonial language—often the major bond between political leaders from different areas within a country. The result in both direct and indirect rule is often the creation of a class, representing not more than 10% of the population, characterized and held together by the acquisition of a European language.

In Arabic speaking countries another kind of problem is encountered. In these areas the native language of the people—any of various colloquial Arabic dialects—is also not the official, written language; rather an elevated literary language, classical Arabic, spoken natively by no one is taken as the standard. The closest contempary European parallel is the situation in Greece, where everyone speaks some colloquial dialect but the official language is in effect almost the ancient Greek of the New Testament. The problem in both language communities is complicated by the fact that in certain formal situations, the elevated literary language really occurs in cultured speech, and its nonoccurrence would be considered boorish to say the least. Such a situation, where two related but grammatically and lexically quite distinct dialects are used by native speakers in different social settings is called DIGLOSSIA. The problems of such a situation are hardly of the same magnitude of that involved where a totally foreign language is used in the schools. But in many ways, the elevated language is for all practical purposes a foreign language.

The difficulties posed by the various situations considered can be solved only if we first specify our goals. If we believe that the expense of educating an underdeveloped or nonindustrialized society is so great that only an élite can be educated at all, then there is little need to modify existing methods or policies. Or if indeed we are actually opposed to modernization or industrialization, or view the essence of education as the ability to read (but not necessarily understand) religious texts or the like, the questions posed here become academic. But neither of these views represents the professed goal of any government in Africa, nor do I think that many people anywhere nowadays feel they should be. On the contrary, the most commonly professed goals are those of a population politically informed, technologically trained, able to produce literary, historical, and other cultural or scientific contributions for the benefit of the entire world.

In light of such aims, what are the most efficient language programs that should be attempted? I believe the following specific proposals are relevant and sound although not all linguists or language planners may agree.

A major point that must be made clear from the start is that *literacy and bi- (or multi-) lingualism involve entirely separate learning processes*. To inflict a child with both at once, to require (as is the normal procedure in large parts of Africa) that a child tearn to read and write a foreign language he has not mastered without having previously learned to read and write in his own is pedagogically monstrous. The results entail far too often a lack of genuine facility in either skill.

The implications of this axiom are many. Perhaps the most obvious is that learning to write should follow learning to speak and that, preferably, everyone should learn to be literate in his own language first if he is literate at all. Successful programs to bring this about cost a great deal, and the number of African languages lacking adequate analyses, orthographies, and pedagogical materials is staggering. Some have estimated a trained linguist must put in five years work to accomplish such a program and that expenses would probably run about $15,000 a year, or $75,000 per language. Expensive though this is, the human cost if such programs are not created is infinitely greater. Language is a tool. It is the instrument for conveying knowledge, traditions, aspirations. Language is clearly of overriding importance in human life; and for any given individual, it is his native language that usually occupies this vital position. Much can be said for maintaining that literacy in one's native language is—or should be—a fundamental human right.

On the other hand, modern governments must confront the threats to political unity within their borders that may be associated with such a policy. Along these lines we may note that detractors of the apartheit programs of the Republic of South Africa have suggested that that government's great interest in the development of native languages—which in other contexts would probably be hailed enthusiastically—constitutes a devisive tactic to fragment the various black African groups. And it has been alleged that practically every publication of a translation of the Bible into an African language has been accompanied by the formation of separatist sects.

Be that as it may, balkanization of Africa does not follow inelluctibly from my proposal. Indeed, anything approaching language suppression (as the Basque and Catalan experiences in Europe suggest) may well prove to be a political disaster. Nor need we insist that linguistic unity is a *sine que non* for political unity, as the Swiss examples has demonstrated for several centuries despite the cliché ideal of one nation one language. The adoption of widely spoken lan-

guages is obviously desirable and a national language is convenient if only because duplication of books and similar expenses can be avoided, and perhaps also
because it can help to override ethnic, tribal, or local factionalism. As for spreading and intrenching a national language, the best method is undoubtedly large
scale adoption of conversational methods recently developed. Radio and television will probably prove to be as important as formal classes in bringing about
a viable national language. Above all, literacy in this second language should
follow (or at first merely re-inforce) proficiency in speaking.

The decision as to what language to set up as a national language is another
matter. The situation is complicated by a number of considerations, mostly
practical, and not all rational. For example, throughout West Africa a form of
pidgin English is widely understood by peoples of diverse cultural and linguistic
backgrounds. Should the spread of pidgin be officially sponsored, however? Many educated West Africans feel that anything less than standard English
would be degrading. I myself think that one should seize upon all possibilities
for ways of communication with enthusiasm, and sponsor the spread of pidgin
by at least providing extensive reading materials in a standarized pan-West-Afri-
can orthography. Since pidgin is more often than not intelligible to speakers of
standard English, no insurmountable problems would be created for an eventual
acquisition of the standard. In North Africa, I suggest that whereas various forms
of colloquial Arabic must be adopted, classical Arabic should nevertheless be
retained as a second language (and taught conversationally, not in the traditional
manner): since it is the language of Arabic and Islamic culture, doing otherwise
would constitute an impoverishment.

A few proposals have been made for the adoption of one or more African
languages as a pan-African lingua-franca, e.g. Swahili. A suggestion of this sort
was adopted, for example, by the Second Congress of Black Writers and Artists
held at Rome in 1958. In all honesty, and with due respect to the notions and
proponents of *négritude*, such a proposal seems unlikely to meet any pressing
needs of Africans. What is necessary, no matter how distasteful to anticolonialist
sentiments it may be, is the wider dissemination of English or French. Since
more than 60% of all original scientific and technical publication occurs in
English, and an enormous amount of material is translated into it, English would
undoubtedly be the wisest choice for a second or third language. Even German
scholars, with one of the proudest traditions of scholarship in the world, have
taken to presenting their findings in English, so that no African should feel he is
"selling out" by advocating English. Cameroun has in fact decided on both English and French as official languages. The importance of policies of this sort is
obvious when one realizes that even with a knowledge of Arabic one would be
something on the order of 50 years behind the times in the scientific world.

Creating an adequate scientific and technical vocabulary is a problem many if not all African languages are caught up in. A variety of solutions are available but an extremely common one is wholesale indiscriminate borrowing from European languages—often to the consternation of purists. The Academy of the Arabic Language in Cairo together with other similar institutions in the Arab world demands the abandonment of foreign words in favor of terms invented from native roots using native methods of derivation. The results of such efforts should be sobering to all would-be language dictators: more often than not, the foreign word is retained in actual usage and the suggested "native" replacement is totally ignored. Another humbling example along somewhat different lines involves a proposed reform of the Yoruba number system. The traditional method of counting has a base of 40 rather than 10 and higher numerals often entail a highly involved derivation. In the early 1960's the linguist Robert Armstrong proposed a few minor structural changes that would permit the creation of a thorough-going decimal system. His proposals are almost universally regarded as reasonable. But the reform itself is almost a total failure in that hardly anyone uses it; older people keep the traditional system, the younger ones have by and large adopted English.[6]

Of course such organizations as the (now defunct) Swahili Committee or the Hausa Language Board are not without importance. They help to codify and stabilize existing usage and may be succesful in pushing through new forms or in tipping the balance in favor of one of a number of competing forms. An interesting suggestion with regard to borrowing has been made by Jan Knappert, who thinks that whenever possible Italianate or Neo-Latin forms for modern international vocabulary should be encouraged and borrowed as opposed to Arabic or even English or French forms. For languages such as Swahili or Hausa with a tremendous stock of Arabic words already, the results would be an extraordinarily rich basis for vocabulary building. Knappert's rejection of English or French forms stems largely from the fact that in native orthographics their international origin would be almost unrecognizable. For example, the word *culture* if borrowed into Swahili in line with its English pronunciation would be written as *kalcha*, but in an Italianate form as *kultura*. This suggestion is again eminently reasonable, I think, but unfortunately not likely to be followed.

A more realistic side to language planning is the creation of a single compromise orthography for the various dialects of a language. This should be done if only because the costs of printing are enormous and growing steadily, so that different dialect editions of the same publication should be avoided as much as possible. One solution common in the past was to recognize one dialect as "standard" and simply ignore the others. More recently, several attempts have been made to set up compromise standards (or "union" language) based on features common to a number of dialects, with occasionally arbitrary or morphophonemic spellings that can accommodate more than one dialect. The most succesful attempt reported in the literature seems to be that of Union Shona, created in 1929 and based on five of the six major dialects of Shona spoken in Rhodesia and Mozambique. Despite initial opposition, Union Shona has become well established. Union Igbo, on the other hand, has met with much less success and has been virtually abandoned. The reason for failure in this instance seems partially at least the fact that too ambitious a compromise was attempted, together with an unfortunate orthographic confusion brought about by a series of spelling reforms that were essentially independent of the Union Igbo scheme. Another example of a successful merger is that of Nandi and Kipsigis in Kenya the union form being called Kalenjin.

Something that must be avoided at all costs is the introduction of artificial distinctions that lead to language barriers of various sorts. Natural dialect differences pose a very great difficulty in standardization, but artificial distinctions sanctified by divergent writing conventions are sometimes even more tricky to get rid of later on. Several egregious errors of language planning must be blamed to missionary groups, who have tended to work independent of each other. In Swahili, for example, a considerable number of times (mostly proper names) introduced by missionaries in their Christianizing efforts, have had Protestant and Catholic variants.

CATHOLIC	PROTESTANT	
Kristu	Kristo	Christ
Enjili	Injili	Gospel
Karamu Takatifu	Ushirika Mtakatifu	Holy Communion
Dominika	Jumapili	Sunday
Paska	Pasaka	Easter
Bikira Maria	Mwanamwali Mariamu	The Virgin Mary
Maria Magdalena	Mariamu wa Magdala	Mary Magdalen
Yosef	Yusufu, Josefu	Joseph
Yoane, Yohani	Yohana, Yoana	John

[Yohana is a man's name among Protestants, a woman's name among Catholic.] For another East African language, Teso, Hilders and Lawrence say that

The divergence in word usage between Roman Catholics and Protestants ... is not, however, confined to religious words. Even the word for *he* is written and pronounced ŋesi by Protestants and **nesi** by Roman Catholics.[7]

More recently missionary groups have tended to collaborate among themselves and with local language committees to get rid of the existing differences and to avoid creating new ones in the future.

Another source of difficulty arises from the arbitrary breaking up of language groups by the colonial powers. The English tried to provide orthographies for the native languages spoken in the areas under their control. But it is only since independence that francophone countries have done the same. In a few instances two separate sets of orthographic rules are the result. This is true for example of Hausa. The newer spelling used in francophone Niger is considerably better than the older one long established in Nigeria—for one thing the newer one shows vowel length (unfortunately, a decision to mark tone was abandoned). But the inferior spelling is fairly well entrenched, and spelling reform is therefore very difficult at this time.

With regard to spelling, which often generates a remarkable amount of emotion, the following proposals are strongly urged. All languages should have an official spelling using Latin letters. Of course, any language may also use some other script for religious or other purposes, e.g. Arabic and Amharic; but the Roman form should be primary, taught first in school, and obligatory on public signs (street and traffic signs, and the like). Not adopting Roman script places an unjustified obstactle in learning most other African and European languages (and perhaps even one's native language—given the greater complexity of, say, Arabic script), and makes difficult the use of typewriters, the telegraph, printing in general, the production of books for the blind, among many other things. The argument that literature published in the older script will become inaccessible to the younger generation is hardly well-founded: the older script can be taught to those who need to know it for literary or historical reasons, and since new editions of older works will have to be published anyway, Romanized versions can quickly replace the traditional ones.

Furthermore, no make-shift Romanization should be used but rather the recommendations of the International African Institute or the International Phonetic Association should be followed. Some language planners have argued that languages spoken in francophone areas should use spelling conventions in line with official French rules, and similarly for anglophone and other areas. Thus, ʃ ʒ c j would be spelt ch j tch dj in former French territories, and sh zh ch j in English ones. So eminent an Africanist as Meinhof championed such a position, and for American Indian languages spoken in Latin American countries this sort of policy is adopted and encouraged by most linguists. It must certainly be rejected for Africa. Too many language communities are split up by political boundaries imposed originally by colonial powers: Ewe, Hausa, Kongo, Yao, for example, are broken up between English, French and/or Portuguese areas and more than one orthographic standard for each of these languages would be intolerable.

Despite the tradition of ignoring such features as tone and vowel length in the orthographics of African languages, they should regularly be indicated if phonemic. The spelling of European languages usually shows a great many distinctions not found in speech; such a system is difficult to learn to write but relatively easy to read once learnt because generally free of ambiguity. The spelling of African tonal languages shows far fewer distinctions than are found in speech. As a result the system is deceptively easy to learn to write but hard to read: the reader must supply or deduce more of the total context than is otherwise necessary and the whole process of reading is slowed down. Clearly tone and vowel length must not systematically be ignored merely because someone doesn't like accent marks or double vowels.

Throughout this discussion I have assumed that people are rational and that when reasonable proposals are offered they will not be rejected out of hand. Much of my discussion has focused on what is perhaps basically trivial from a linguistic view, but capable of generating a remarkable degree of heat. For example, it has been proposed that the Africa Alphabet (or some suitable alternative) be adopted for all African languages. This alphabet makes use of several letters not found in the current alphabets of European languages but necessary for the adequate and efficient writing of many other languages. Some language planners have dismissed the introduction of new letters without examining the case for their introduction. The technical difficulties involved are not insurmountable. A special adjustment called a Typit-Guide has been designed for typewriters so that extra keys, called typits, can be used; the letters ɛ ɔ ə ɲ ɓ ɗ ʃ ʒ and a number of others are already available. The Imperial Typewriter Company, IBM, and some other manufactures have produced phonetic keyboards and could well produce a "Pan African" typewriter. As for printing facilities, I suggest that one project that African governments interested in African unity can should realize—apart from such other low-level practical goals as establishing a right-hand drive throughout Africa before traffic and economic considerations make it even more difficult—is the establishment of a Pan-African printing company with strategically located branches and with type for all African languages and the facility for producing books in any language of the continent. A relatively small sum invested now in such a project would be of considerable value for the future.

Here then are some of the problems and prospects of languages in Africa. Much has been done, but still for all practical purposes everything remains to be done.

Notes and References

1) Jacob Orstein, 1964, Africa seeks a common language, *The Review of Politics* **26**. 205.
2) Amharic, Arabic, Ewe, Fulani, Galla, Hausa, Igbo, Ibibia-Efik, Kikuyu, Kimbundu, Lingala, Luo, Makua, Malagasy, Malinke-Bambara-Dyula, Mossi, Nyanja, Ruanda-Rundi, Somali, Sutho, Twi-Fante, Umbundu, Yoruba, Xhosa, Zulu.
3) Birked (almost extinct, Sudan), Boguru (few, Sudan), Bonεk (under 50, Cameroon), Demisa (100, South Africa), Fumu (almost extinct, Congo), Gule or Fungi (dying out, Sudan), Kaaloŋ or Mbɔŋ (c. 50, Cameroun), Kande (almost extinct, Gabon), Kooki (very few, Uganda), Leko (almost extinct, Zaïre), Mongoba (c. 50, Zaïre), li-Ngbee (c. 30, Zaïre), Ngbinda (few, Sudan), Sanye (fast disappearing in favor of Galla, Kenya), Togoyo (almost extinct, Sudan), !Kora (50?, South Africa), //ŋ!Ke (perhaps a few old people, South West Africa).
4) Jeffreys, 1945. The death of a dialect, *African Studies*, **4**: 37−40.
5) S. E. Nadel, 1942, *A black Byzantium*, London, 23.
6) Robert G. Armstrong, 1962, *Yoruba numerals* (*Nigerian Social and Economic Studies*, 1), London.
7) J. H. Hilders and J. C. D. Lawrance, 1958. An *English-Ateso and Ateso-English vocabulary*, Nairobi xi.

209

APPENDIX I

African Languages with a Million or More Speakers

Name	Affiliation	Where Spoken	No.of Speakers in millions
AMHARIC	AA:Semitic	Ethiopia	8
BERBER	AA:Berber	N.W. Africa	10
EFIK	NK:Benue-Kongo	E. Nigeria	1
EWE	NK:Kwa	Dahomey, Togo, Ghana	1.5
FULANI	NK:West Atlantic	Western Sudan	6
GALLA	AA:Kushitic	Ethiopia	5
GANDA	NK:Bantu	Uganda	2
HAUSA	AA:Chadic	Nigeria, Niger, Wester Sudan	14
IGBO	NK:Kwa	E. Nigeria	5
KANURI	NS:Saharan	Nigeria, Niger, Chad	2
KIKUYU	NK:Bantu	Kenya	1.5
KIMBUNDU	NK:Bantu	Angola	1
KONGO	NK:Bantu	Zaïre, Congo Angola	2
LINGALA	NK:Bantu	Zaïre, Congo	1
LUBA	NK:Bantu	Zaïre, Zambia	1.5
LUO	NS:Nilotic	Kenya, Tanzania	1
MAKUA	NK:Bantu	Mozambique	2
MALAGASY	MP:Malagasy Cluster	Madagascar	6
MALINKE-BAM-BARA-DYULA	NK:Mande	Western Sudan	4–6
MOSSI	NK:Voltaic	Upper Volta, N.Ghana, N.Togo	3
NYANJA	NK:Bantu	Malawi, Mozambique, Rhodesia, Zambia	1

RWANDA-RUNDI	NK:Bantu	Rwanda, Burundi, Zaïre	5—8
SANGO	NK:Adamawa-Eastern	Central African Republic	1.5
SENUFO	NK:Voltaic	Ivory Coast, Upper Volta, Mali, N.Ghana	1
SHONA	NK:Bantu	Mozambique, Rhodesia	1
SOMALI	AA:Eastern Kushitic	Somalia	3
SONGHAI	NS:Songhai	Mali, Upper Volta, Niger	1
SOTHO	NK:Bantu	Basutoland, South Africa	2—3.5
SWAHILI	NK:Bantu	Tanzania, Kenya, Zaïre, Uganda, Zambia	11—15
TIV	NK:Benue-Kongo	N.Nigeria	1
TWI-FANTE	NK:Kwa	Ghana	3
UMBUNDU	NK:Bantu	Angola	2
WOLOF	NK:West Atlantic	Senegal, Gambia	1.5
XHOSA	NK:Bantu	South Africa	3
YORUBA	NK:Kwa	W.Nigeria, Dahomey, Togo	5
ZANDE	NK:Adamawa-Eastern	Zaïre, Central African Republic	1
ZULU	NK:Bantu	South Africa	4

APPENDIX II

Greenberg's Classification

I. NIGER-KORDOFANIAN (or KONGO-KORDOFANIAN)

A. NIGER-KONGO

1) West Atlantic
    a) Northern (e.g. Wolof, Fulani, Serer-Sin, Serer-Non, Biafada)
    b) Southern (e.g. Temne, Gola)

2) Mande
    a) Western (e.g. Soninke, Malinke-Bambara-Dyula, Vai)
    b) Eastern (e.g. Dan, Busa)

3) Voltaic (or Gur) (e.g. Senufo, Mossi, Gurma)

4) Kwa (e.g. Bassa, Ewe, Gã, Twi-Fanti, Yoruba, Bini, Igbo, Ịjọ)

5) Benue-Kongo
    a) Plateau (e.g. Kamibari, Birom)
    b) Jukunoid (e.g. Jukun)
    c) Cross-River (e.g. Ibibio, Efik, Yakö)
    d) Bantoid (e.g. Tiv, the Bantu languages)

6) Adamawa-Eastern
    a) Adamawa (e.g. Mbum, Nimbari)
    b) Eastern (e.g. Zande, Gbaya, Ngbandi)

B. KORDOFANIAN

1) Koalib (e.g. Koalib, Otoro)
2) Tegali (e.g. Tegali, Tagoi)
3) Talodi (e.g. Talodi, Masakin)
4) Tumtum (e.g. Tumtum, Kadugli, Katcha)
5) Katla (Katla, Tima)

II. NILO-SAHARAN

A. SONGHAI (Songhai)

B. SAHARAN (Kanuri, Kanembu; Teda, Daza, Zaghawa, Berti)

C. MABAN (e.g. Maba, Runga, Mimi)

D. FUR

E. CHARI-NILE
  1) Berta
  2) Kunama
  3) Central Sudanic (e.g. Bongo, Bagirmi, Sara, Kreish, Moru, Lugbara, Ma'di, Mangbutu, Mangbetu, Lendu)
  4) Eastern Sudanic
     i)   Nubian
     ii)   Murle, Masongo, etc.
     iii)   Barya
     iv)   Ingassana [Tabi]
     v)   Nyima, Afitti
     vi)   Temein, Teis-um-Danab
     vii)   Merarit, Tama, Sangor
     viii) Dagu, Shatt, Njalgulgule, etc.
     ix)   Nilotic
            a) Western (e.g. Shilluk, Acoli, Lango, Luo, Dinka, Nuer)
            b) Eastern (e.g. Bari, Karimojong, Turkana, Maasai)
            c) Southern (e.g. Nandi, Päkot [Suk])
     x)   Nyangiya, Teuso [Ik^a]

F. KOMAN (Koma, Ganza, Uduk, Gule, Gumuz, Mao)

III. AFRO-ASIATIC

A. SEMITIC (e.g. Arabic, Amharic, Tigre, Tigrinya)

B. EGYPTIAN

C. BERBER

D. KUSHITIC
  1) Northern (Beja [Bedauye])
  2) Central (e.g. Kemant, Awiya)
  3) Eastern (e.g. Galla, Sidamo, Somali)

4) Western (e.g. Janjero, Wolamo)
5) Southern (Iraqw, Mbugu, Sanye, Burungi, Goroa, Alawa)

E. CHAD* (e.g. Hausa, Margi, Musgu, Somrai)

* Subclassification of the many Chadic languages has recently been revised by Newman and Ma.

IV. KHOISAN

A. SOUTH AFRICAN KHOISAN
1) Northern (e.g. Auen, !Kung)
2) Central (e.g. Naron, Hottentot, Hiechware)
3) Southern (e.g. /Xam, /Nu//En)

B. SANDAWE

C. HATSA

Bibliography

Most of the items cited in the text are listed here. Several other works of some importance not otherwise cited are also included. Needless to say, this bibliography is not exhaustive.

Adams, R.R.G., 1947, Obɛri ɔkaimɛ: a new African language and script, *Africa* 17:24–34.

Albert, Ethel M., 1972, Culture patterning of speech behavior in Burundi, in *Directions in sociolinguistics*, John J. Gumperz and Dell Hymes, eds., New York: Holt, Rinehart and Winston.

Albright, W.F., 1934, *The vocalization of the Egyptian syllabic orthography*, New Haven: American Oriental Society.

Alexandre, Pierre, 1967, *Langues et langage en Afrique noire*, Paris: Payot (English edition by Northwestern University Press, 1971).

Ansre, G., 1963, Reduplication in Ewe, *Journal of African Languages*, 2.2:128–132.

Appleyard, J.W., 1850, *The Kafir language*, King William's Town: Wesleyan Missionary Society.

Arewa, E. Ojo and Alan Dundes, 1964, Proverbs and the ethnography of speaking folklore, in *The ethnography of communication*, John J. Gumperz and Dell Hymes, eds., (American Anthropologist Special Publication 66.6.2:70–85).

Armstrong, L.E., 1941, *The phonetic and tonal structure of Kikuyu*, London: Oxford University Press.

Armstrong, Robert G., 1962, Glottochronology and African linguistics, *Journal of African History*, 3.3:283–290.

1962, *Yoruba numerals*, Nigerian Social and Economic Studies, 1, London: Oxford University Press.

1963, Vernacular languages and cultures in modern Africa, in *Language in Africa*, John Spencer, ed., Cambridge: University Press.

1964, *The study of West African languages*, Ibadan: Ibadan University Press.

Arnott, D.W., 1964, Downstep in the Tiv verbal system, *African Language Studies* 5:34–51.

Assirelli, O., 1950, *L'Afrique polyglotte* (translated by Denis-Pierre de Pedrals), Paris: Payot.

Bamgbose, Ayo, 1966, *A grammar of Yoruba*, West African Language Monographs 5, Cambridge: Cambridge University Press.

Bascom, W.R. and M.J. Herskovits, 1959, *Continuity and change in African cultures*, Chicago: University Press.

Basset, André, 1948, Écritures libyque et touarègue, in Ch. Fassey, *Notices sur les caractères étrangers anciens et modernes*, 135–43.

1952, *La langue berbère*, London: Oxford University Press.

Basset, René, 1913, Notes sur la langue de la Guiné au XVe siècle, Academia das Sciencias de Lisboa, Separata do Boletim da Segunda, Vol. 6, Coimbra.

Bearth, Thomas and Hugo Zemp, 1967, The phonology of Dan (Santa), *Journal of African Languages*, 6.1:9–29.

215

Beattie, John H., 1967, Consulting a Nyoro diviner: the ethnologist as client, *Ethnology*, 6:57–65.

Bendix, Edward H., 1970, Serial verb in Creole and West African [sic], unpublished paper read at the Annual meeting of the American Anthropological Association in San Diego, California, November 1970.

Berry, Jack, 1957, Vowel harmony in Twi, *Bulletin of the School of Oriental and African Studies*, 19:124–30.

Berry, Jack and Joseph H. Greenberg, eds., 1971, *Linguistics in sub-Saharan Africa*, Current Trends in Linguistics, Vol. 7, The Hague: Mouton.

Blake, Frank R., 1940, The development of symbols for the vowels in the alphabets derived from the Phoenician, *Journal of the American Oriental Society*, 60.3:410.

Blakney, Charles P., 1963. On "banana" and "iron", linguistic footprints in African history, *Hartford Studies in Linguistics* 13, Hartford.

Boas, F., O. Dempwolff, G. Panconelli-Calzia, A. Werner, and D. Westermann, eds., 1927, *Festschrift Meinhof*, Hamburg: Kommissionsverlag von L. Friederichsen and Co.

Brosnahan, L.F., 1965, A fifteenth century word list, *The Journal of West African Language*, 2.2.5.

Bryan, M.A., 1947, *Notes on the distribution of the Semitic and Cushitic languages of Africa*, London: Oxford University Press.

    1959, The T/K languages, a new substratum, *Africa*, 29:1–21.

    1968, The *N/*K languages of Africa, *Journal of African Languages*, 7.3:169–217.

Bryan, M.A. and A.N. Tucker, 1948, *Distribution of the Nilotic and Nilo-Hamitic languages of Africa*, London: Oxford University Press.

Burling, Robbins, 1970, *Man's many voices*, New York: Holt, Rinehart and Winston.

Calame-Griaule,, G. and P.F. Lecroix, 1969, Graphie et signes africains, *Semiotica*, 1:3:256–72.

Carnochan, J., 1960, Vowel harmony in Igbo, *African Language Studies*, 1:155–63.

Carrington, J.F., 1949, *Talking drums of Africa*, London: Harry Kingsgate Press.

    1953, Communication by means of gongs and other instruments in Central Africa, *Explorations*, 1:24–33.

Carroll, John B., ed., 1957, *Language, thought, and reality: selected writings of Benjamin Lee Whorf*, Cambridge, Mass.: MIT Press.

Centre National de la Recherche Scientifique, 1967, *La classification nominale dans les langues négro-africaines* (Acte du Colloque organisé á Aix-en-Provence, 3–7 juillet 1967), Paris: Editions du Centre National de la Recherche Scientifique.

Cerulli, Enrico, 1932, Tentative indigeno di formare un alfabeto somalo, *Oriente Moderno*, 12:212–213.

Chomsky, Noam and Morris Halle, 1968, *The sound pattern of English*, New York: Harper and Row.

Clarke, John, 1848, *Specimens of dialects: Short vocabularies of languages and notes of countries and customs in Africa*, Berwick-upon-Tweed: Daniel Cameron.

Cohen, Marcel, 1932, Inscriptions arabes en caractères séparés recueillies en Mauritanie par P. Boery, *Hesperis*, 14:20.

Cole, D.T., 1953, Fanagalo and the Bantu languages in South Africa, *African Studies*, 12:1–9.

    1957, *Bantu linguistic studies in South Africa*, Johannesburg, Witwatersrand University Press.

    1960, African linguistic studies, 1943–60, *African Studies*, 19:219–29.

Crabb, David W., 1965, *Ekoid Bantu languages of Ogoja, Eastern Nigeria*, Part I, West African Language Monograph Series 4, Cambridge: Cambridge University Press.

Crazzolara, J.P., 1933, *Outlines of a Nuer grammar*, Wien (Anthropos: Internationale Sammlung linguistischer Monographien, Bd. 13).

Cust, Robert Needham, 1883, *A sketch of the modern languages of Africa*, 2 Vols., London: Trubner and Co.

Dalby, David, 1966, An investigation into the Mende syllabary of Kisimi Kamara, *Sierra Leone Studies NS* 19:119–123.

1966, Levels of relationship in the classification of African languages, *African Language Studies*, 7:171–179.

1967, A survey of the indigenous scripts of Liberia and Sierra Leone: Vai, Mende, Loma, Kpelle and Bassa, *African Language Studies*, 8:1–51.

1968, The indigenous scripts of West Africa and Surinam: Their inspiration and design, *African Language Studies*, 9:156–97.

1969, Further indigenous scripts of West Africa: Manding, Wolof and Fula alphabets and Yoruba "holy" writing, *African Language Studies*, 10: 161–81.

1970, The historical problem of the indigenous scripts of West Africa and Surinam, in *Language and History in Africa, 1970*, D. Dalby, ed., New York: Africana Publishing Corporation, 109–119.

Dalby, David, ed., 1970, *Language and history in Africa*, New York: Africana Publishing Corporation.

Dalby, David and P.E.H. Hair, 1967, A West African word of 1456, *Journal of West African Languages*, 4:13–14.

Dayrell, Elphinstine, 1911, Further notes on "Nsibidi" signs with their meanings from Ikom district, Southern Nigeria, *Journal of the Royal Anthropological Institute*, 41:521–540.

Delafosse, Maurice, 1904, *Vocabulaires comparatifs de plus de 60 langues on dialectes parlés à la Côte d'Ivoire et dans les regions limitrophes*. Paris: E. Leroux.

1914, Mots soudanais du moyen age, *Mémoires de la Société Linguistique de Paris*, 18:281–8.

1920, Sur l'unité des langues négro-africaines, *Revue d'Ethnographie et des Traditions Populaires*, 1:123–128.

1922, Naissance et evolution d'un système d'écriture de création contemporaire, *Revue d'Ethographie et des Traditions Populaires*, 8:11–19.

1924, Les langues du Soudan et de la Guinée, in *Les langues du monde*, A. Meillet and M. Cohen, eds., pp. 463,560, Paris: E. Champion (Société de Linguistique de Paris, Collection Linguistique Vol. 16).

Dennelt, R.E., 1906, *At the back of the black man's mind*, London.

Doke, C.M., 1926, *The phonetics of the Zulu language*, Johannesburg,: University of Witwatersrand Press.

1931, *Report on the unification of the Shona dialects*, Hertford: Stephen Austin.

1935, *Bantu linguistic terminology*, London: Longmans.

1945, *Bantu: Modern grammatical, phonetical, and lexicographical studies since 1860*, London: Percy Lund.

1954, *The Southern Bantu Languages*, London: Oxford University Press.

Doke, C.M. and D.T. Cole, 1961, *Contributions to the history of Bantu linguistics*, Johannesburg: Witwatersrand University Press.

Drexel, A., 1921–5, Gliederung der afrikanischen Sprachen, *Anthropos*, 16/17.73–108; 18/19, 12–39; 20.210–243, 444–460.

Dugast, I. and M.D.W. Jeffreys, 1950, L'écriture des Bamum Cameroun, *Mémoire de l'Institut Français d'Afrique Noire*.

Du Toit, Brian M., 1966, Riddling traditions in an isolated South African community, *Journal of American Folklore*, 79:471–475.

Dyen, Isidore, 1956, Language distribution and migration theory, *Language*, 32:611–626.

Ehret, Christopher, 1967, Cattle-keeping and milking in eastern and southern African history: The linguistic evidence, *Journal of African History*, 8.1:1–17.

    1968, Sheep and Central Sudanic peoples in Southern Africa, *Journal of African History*, 9.2:213–221.

    1971, *Southern Nilotic History: Linguistic approaches to the study of the past*, Evanston, Illinois: Northwestern University Press.

Eichhorn, 1781, *Repertorium*, vii 161.

Evans-Pritchard, E.E., 1929, Some collective expressions of obscenity in Africa, *Journal of the Royal Anthropological Institute*, 59:311–332.

    1934, Imagery in Ngoh Dinka cattle names, *Bulletin of the School of Oriental and African Studies*, 7:623–628.

    1940, *The Nuer*, Oxford: Oxford University Press.

    1948, Nuer modes of address, *The Uganda Journal*, 12:166–171.

    1949, Nuer curses and ghostly vengence, *Africa*, 19:288–292.

    1956, Sangi, characteristic feature of Zande language and thought, *Bulletin of the School of Oriental and African Studies*, 18:161–180.

Ferguson, Charles A., 1956, Arabic baby Talk, in *For Roman Jakobson: Essays on the occasion of his sixtieth birthday*, Niels Fock, ed., The Hague, Mouton.

    1959, Diglossia, *Word*, 15:325–340.

Fodor, Istvan, 1966, The problems in the classification of the African languages, Budapest: Center for Afro-Asian Research of the Hungarian Academy of Sciences, *Studies on Developing Countries* No. 5.

Fortune, G., 1962, The contributions of linguistics to ethnohistory, in *Historians in Tropical Africa*, E.T. Stokes, ed., Salisbury.

Foulché-Delbose, R., 1897, *Voyage à la Côte occidentale d'Afrique*, Paris: Alphonse Picard et fils.

Friedrich, J., 1935, Einige Kapitel aus der inneren Geschichte der Schrift, *Archiv für Schreib-und Buchwesen, NF*, 2:8–18.

    1938, Zu einigen Schrifterfindungen der neuesten Zeit, *Zeitschrift der deutschen Morgenländischen Gesellschaft*, 92 (NF 17):189–208.

Frobenius, Leo, 1968, *The voice of Africa*, 2:368–9, New York: B. Blom (reprint of 1913 ed.).

Flück, Johann, 1955, Die arabischen Studien in Europa bis in den Aufang des 20, *Jahrhunderts, Leipzig*, 31–2.

Gardiner, A.H., 1915, The nature and development of the Egyptian hieroglyphic writing, *Journal of Egyptian Archaeology*, 2:61–75.

    1916, The Egyptian origin of the Semitic alphabet, *Journal of Egyptian archaeology*, 3:1–16.

Gairdner, W.H.T., 1917, *Egyptian colloquial Arabic*, Cambridge: W. Heffner and Sons Ltd.

Gelb, I.J., 1952, *A study of writing* (rev. ed. 1963), Chicago: University of Chicago Press.

Gleason, H.A., 1961, *An introduction to descriptive linguistics* (rev. ed.), New York: Holt, Rinehart and Winston.

Gluckman, Max, 1959, The technical vocabulary of Barotse jurisprudence, *American Anthropologist*, 61:743–759.

Gollmer, 1885, On African symbolic messages, *Journal of the Royal Anthropological Institute*, 14:169–81.

Goodman, Morris, 1970, Some questions on the classification of African languages, *International Journal of American Linguistics*, 36.2:117–122.

1971, The strange case of Mbugu (Tanzania), in *Pidginization and Creolization of Languages*, Dell Hymes, ed., London: Cambridge University Press, pp. 243–254.

Greenberg, J.H., 1947, Arabic loanwords in Hausa, *Word* 3.1:85–97.

1948, The tonal system of Proto-Bantu, *Word* 4.3:196–208.

1960, A survey of African prosodic systems, in *Culture in history: Essays in honor of Paul Radin*, Stanley Diamond, ed., New York: Columbia University Press.

1953, Historical linguistics and unwritten languages, in *Anthropology Today*, A.L. Kroeber *et al.*, Chicago: University of Chicago Press, 265–286.

1957, Nilotic,"Nilo-Hamitic",and Hamito-Semitic: a reply, *Africa* 27:364–378.

1958, The labial consonants of Proto-Afro-Asiatic, *Word*, 14.2/3:295–302.

1959, Africa as a linguistic area, in *Continuity and change in African society*, Bascom and Herskovits, eds., Chicago: University of Chicago Press, 15–27.

1959, A method for measuring functional yield as applied to tone in African languages, in *Report of the Tenth Annual Round Table Meeting on Linguistics and Language Studies*, Richard S. Harrell, ed., Washington, D.C.: Georgetown University Press.

1960, Linguistic evidence for the influence of the Kanuri on the Hausa, *Journal of African History*, 1.2:205–212.

1963, *The languages of Africa*, Bloomington (International Journal of American Linguistics 29.1.II.): Indiana University Press.

1963, The Mogogodo, a forgotten Cushitic people, *Journal of African Languages*, 2.1:29–43.

1965, Urbanism, migration, and language, in *Urbanism and migration in West Africa*, H. Kuper, ed., Berkeley: University of California Press, 50–9.

Greenberg, Joseph H., ed., 1963, *Universals of language*, Cambridge: Massachusetts Institute of Technology Press.

Gregersen, Edgar A., 1967, *Prefix and pronoun in Bantu* (Indiana University Publications in Anthropology and Linguistics, Memoir 21 of the International Journal of American Linguistics), Supplement to International Journal of American Linguistics, 33.3., July, Part 2.

1967, Linguistic seriation as a dating device for loanwords, with special reference to West Africa, *African Language Review*, 6:102–108.

1968, Words and things in African prehistory, *Anthropological Linguistics*, 10.3:1–4.

1973, Kongo-Saharan, *Journal of African Languages*, 11.1: 69–89.

Guinness, H. Grattan, 1882, *Grammar of the Congo languages as spoken in the cataract region below Stanley Pool* (translated from the Latin of Brusciotto), London: Hodder and Stoughton.

Guthrie, M., 1948, *The classification of the Bantu languages*, London: Oxford University Press.

1953, *The Bantu languages of Western Equatorial Africa*, London: Oxford University Press.

1962, Bantu origins: a tentative new hypothesis, *Journal of African Languages*, 1.1:9–21.

1962, Some developments in the prehistory of the Bantu languages, *Journal of African History*, 3.2:273–282.

1967–70, *Comparative Bantu* (4 Vols.), Farnborough: Gregg International Publishers.

Hagman, Roy, 1973, A grammar of Nama Hottentot (unpublished PhD dissertation, Columbia University, New York).

Hair, P.E.H., 1963, Notes on the discovery of the Vai script, with a bibliography, *Sierra Leone Language Review*, 2:36–49.

    1966, A note on de la Fosse's "Mina" vocabulary of 1479–80. *Journal of West African Languages*, 3:55–7.

    1967, Ethnolinguistic continuity on the Guinea coast, *Journal of African History*, 8:247–268.

Harries, Lyndon, 1961; Some grammatical features of recent Swahili prose, *African Language Studies*, 2:37–41.

Hau, Kathleen, 1959. Evidence of the use of pre-Portuguese written characters by the Benin, *Bulletin de l'Institut Français d'Afrique Noire*, 21:109–154.

    1964, A royal title on a palace tusk from Benin (Southern Nigeria), *Bulletin de l'Institut Français d'Afrique Noire*, 26:12–39.

    1967, The ancient writing of Southern Nigeria, *Bulletin de l'Institut Français d'Afrique Noire*, 29:150–190.

Herne, Bernd, 1970, *Status and use of African lingua francas*, New York: Humanities Press.

Herzog, G., 1945, Drum signaling in a West African tribe, *Word*, 1:217–38.

Hilders, J.H. and J.C.D. Lawrence, 1958, *An English–Ateso and Ateso–English vocabulary*, Nairobi: The Eagle Press.

Hiskett, M., 1965, The historical background to the naturalization of Arabic loan-words in Haussa, *African Language Studies*, 6:21.

Hjelmslev, Louis, 1963, *Sproget: En introduktion*, København: Berlingske Forlag.

Hodge, Careleton T., 1966, Hausa–Egyptian establishment, *Anthropological Linguistics*, 8.1:40–57.

Hoenigswald, H.M., 1963, Are there universals of linguistic change?, in *Universals of Language*, Joseph Greenberg, ed., Cambridge, Mass: MIT Press.

Hoffman, Carl, 1963, *A grammar of the Margi language*, London: Oxford University Press.

Hohenberger, Johannes, 1956, Comparative Masai word list, *Africa*, 26:281–9.

    1958, *Semitisches and hamitisches Sprachgut im Masai, mit vergleichendem Wörterbuch*, Sachsenmühle (Frankische Schweiz): Im Selbstverlag des Verfassers.

Homburger, L., 1939, Le serère-peul, *Journal de la Société des Africanistes*, 9:85–102.

    1941, *Les langues négro-africaines*, Paris: Payot.

Houis, Maurice, 1966, *Aperçu sur les structures grammaticales des langues négro-africaines*, Lyon: Faculté de Théologie.

Huber, Hugo, 1965, A diviner's apprenticeship and work among the "Bayaka", *Man*, 65:46–47.

Huntingford, C.W.B., 1956, The "Nilo-Hamitic" languages, *Southwestern Journal of Anthropology*, 12:200–222.

Hymes, D.H., 1960, Lexicostatistics so far, *Current Anthropology*, 1:3–44. ed., 1971, *Pidginization and creolization of languages*, London: Cambridge University Press.

Jakobson, Roman, 1940, Kindersprache, Aphasie and allgemeine Lautgesetze, Uppsala Universitets Arrskrift.

    1962, Why "mama" and "papa"? *Selected Writings I*, The Hague: Mouton.

    1962, *Collected Works*, The Hague: Mouton.

Jakobson, Roman and Morris Halle, 1956, *Fundamentals of Language*, The Hague: Mouton.

Jeffreys, M.D.W., 1945, The death of a dialect, *African Studies*, 4:37–40.

    1947, Speculative origins of the Fulani language, *Africa*, 17:47–54.

    1952, Corsali 1515 on Bantu and Sudanic languages, *African Studies*, 11:191.

Jensen Hans, *1935, Die Schrift in Vergangenheit und Gegenwart*, Gluckstadt and Hamburg. J.J. Augustin.

Joffre, J., 1943, A new West African alphabet used by the Toma, French Guinea and Liberia, *Man*, 48.85:108–112.

1945, Sur un nouvel alphabet ouest-africain: le Toma, *Bulletin de l'Institut Français d'Afrique Noire*, 7:160–73.

Johnston, Sir Harry H., 1919–22, *A comparative study of the Bantu and Semi-Bantu languages*, 2 Vols., Oxford: The Clarendon Press.

Kilger, P. Laurenz, 1935, Die ersten afrikanischen Katechismen im 17. Jahrhundert, *Gutenberg-Jahrbuch*, 257–264, Mainz.

Kim, Chin-Wu, and Herbert Stahlke, eds., 1971, *Papers in African Linguistics*, Edmonton: Linguistic Research Inc. (Current Inquiry into Language and Linguistics 1).

Kirk-Greene, A., 1964, The Hausa Language Board, *Afrika und Übersee* 47-187-203.

1966, The vocabulary and determinants of schoolboy slang in Northern Nigeria, *Journal of African Languages*, 5.1:7–33.

Klingenheben, A., 1923–4, Die Präfixklassen des Ful, *Zeitschrift für Eingeborenen-Sprachen* 14.

1933, The Vai script, *Africa*, 6:158–171.

1962, Influence of analogy in African Languages, *Journal of African Languages*, 1.1:30–42.

Koelle, S.W., 1849, *Narrative of an expedition into the Vy country of West Africa, and the discovery of a system of syllabic writing, recently invented by the natives of the Vy tribe*, London.

1854, *Polyglotta Africana; or A comparative vocabulary of nearly three hundred words and phrases, in more than one hundred district African languages*, London: Church Missionary House (reprinted 1963, Graz: Akademische Druck).

Köhler, Oswin, 1955, Geschichte der Erforschung der Nilotischen Sprachen, *Afrika and Übersee*, Beiheft 28.

1963, Observations on the Central Khoisan language group, *Journal of African Languages*, 2.3:227–234.

Kopoka, O.B. 1957–59, *Sarufi na ufasaha* (*A grammar of Swahili in Swahili*), Kampala: East African Swahili Committee.

Kroeber, A., 1948, *Anthropology*, New York: Harcourt, Brace.

Krumm, B., 1932, *Wörter und Wortformen orientalischen Ursprungs im Suaheli*, Hamburg: Friederichsen, De Gruyter.

Kunene, D.P., 1963, Southern Sotho words of English and Afrikaans origin, *Word*, 19: 347–75.

Labouret, H., 1923, Langage tambouriné et sifflé, *Bulletin du Comité d'Etudes Historiques et Scientifiques de l'Afrique Occidentale Française*, 120–158.

Ladefoged, Peter, 1964, *A phonetic study of West African languages*, Cambridge: University Press.

Langacker, Ronald, W., 1967, *Language and its structure*, New York: Harcourt, Brace and World.

Lasebikan, E.L., 1956, The tonal structure of Yoruba poetry, *Presence Africaine*, 18–19:45–50.

Lassort, A., 1951, L'écriture guerzée, Première Conference Internationale des Africanistes de l'Ouest, 1945, *Comptes Rendus* 2:209–15.

Leakey, L.S.B., 1961, *The progress and evolution of man in Africa*, London: Oxford University Press.

Lees, Robert B., 1953, The basis of glottochronology, *Language* 21:113–27.

Lenneberg, E.H., 1967, *The biological bases for language*, New York: John Wiley and Sons.

Lepsius, R., 1855, *Das allgemeine linguistische Alphabet*, Berlin.

    1880, *Nubische grammatik*, Berlin: Wilhelm Hertz.

Leslau, Wolf, 1946, *Bibliography of the Semitic languages of Ethopia*, New York: New York Public Library.

    1964, *Ethiopian argots*, The Hague: Mouton.

Littmann, E., 1913, *Deutsche Aksum-Expedition*, 4:78, Berlin.

Lukas, Johannes, 1937, *A study of the Kanuri language*, London: Oxford University Press.

Lukas, Johannes, ed., 1966, *Neue afrikanistische Studien*, (Hamburger Beiträge zur Afrika-Kunde, Band 5), Hamburg: Deutsches Institut fur Afrika-Forschung.

MacGregor, J.K., 1909, Some notes on Nsibidi, *Journal of the Royal Anthropological Institute*, 39:209–219.

MacMichael, H.A., 1922, *History of the Arabs in the Sudan*, Cambridge: Cambridge University Press.

Mafeje, Archie, 1967, The role of the bard in a contemporary African community, *Journal of African Languages*, 6.3:193–223.

Maino, Mario, 1951, L'alfabeto "Osmania" in Somalia, *Rassegna di Studi Etiopici*, 10:108–21.

Malcolm, L.W.G., 1920–21, Short Notes on the syllabic writing of the Eγap, Central Cameroons, *Journal of the Africa Society*, 20:127–9.

Manessy, G., 1962, Nom et verbe dans les langues Mande, *Journal of African Languages*, 1.1:57–68.

    1964, L'alternance consonantique initiale en Manya, Kpelle, Loma, Bandi et Mende, *Journal of African Languages*, 3.2:162–178.

    1966, Les substantifs à prefixe et suffixe dans les langues voltaïques, *Journal of African Languages*, 5.1:54–62.

Marsden, William, 1782, Remarks on the Sumatran languages, *Archaeologia*, 6:154–158.

Mbaga, K. and W.H. Whiteley, 1961, Formality and informality in Yao speech, *Africa*, 31:135–146.

Meek, C.K., 1960, The Niger and the classics: the history of a name, *Journal of African History*, 1.1:6.

Meinhof, Carl, 1899, Grundriss einer Lautlehre der Bantusprachen, Berlin, Deutsche Morgen-ländische Gesellschaft, Abhandlungen für die Kunde des Morgenlandes (trans., 1932 as Introduction to the phonology of the Bantu languages).

    1910, *Die moderne Sprachenforschung in Afrika*, Berlin (trans., 1915, as Introduction to the study of African languages).

    1911, Zur Entstehung der Schrift, *Zeitschrift fur agyptische Sprache*, 49:1–14.

    1912, *Die Sprachen der Hamiten* (Abhandlungen der Hamburger Kolonialinstitut, 9, Reihe B, Bd 6), Hamburg: L. Friederichsen.

    1919–20, Afrikanische Worte in orientalischer Literatur, *Zeitschrift für Eingeborenen-Sprachen*, 10:147–52.

    1931, *Die Libyschen Inschriften*, Leipzig, Deutsche Morgenlandische Gesellschaft, Abhandlungen fur die Kunde de Morgenlandes, *19.1*.

    1941/42, Entstehung und Gebrauch der Lokativendung in Bantusprachen, *Zeitschrift für Eingeborenen-Sprachen*, 32:161–165.

    1942, Pwani, *Zeitschrift für Eingeborenen-Sprachen*, 32:300–2.

    1948, *Grundzüge einer vergleichenden Grammatik der Bantusprachen* (2nd ed.), Hamburg: Eckardt und Messtorff.

Merlo, Ch. and P. Vidaud, 1967, *Unité des langues négro-africaines*, Paris: G.P. Maison-neuve et Larose.

Messenger, John C., Jr., 1960, Anang proverb riddles, *Journal of American Folklore*, 73: 225–235.

Monad, Th., 1958, Un nouvel alphabet ouest-africain: le bété (Côte d'Ivoire) *Bulletin de l'Institut Français d'Afrique Noire*, 20:432–553.

Mokarovsky, H., 1963, *Die Grundlagen des Ful und das Mauretanische*, Wien: Herder (Afro-Asiatisches Institut, Vienna, Wissenschaftliche Schiftenreihe, Bd. 1).

Murdock, George P., 1959, Cross-language parallels in parental kin terms, *Anthropological Linguistics*, 1.9:1–6.

1959, *Africa: its peoples and their culture history*, New York: McGraw-Hill.

Nadel, S.F., 1942, *A black Byzantium*, London. (published for the International Institute of African Languages and Cultures by the Oxford University Press).

1954, Morality and language among the Nupe, *Man*, 54:55–57.

Newman, Paul, 1970, *A grammar of Tera* (University of California Publications in Linguistics Vol. 57), Los Angeles: University of California Press.

1970, Historical sound laws in Hausa and in Dera (Kanakuru), *Journal of West African Languages*, 7.1:39.

Newman, Paul and Roxana Ma, 1966, Comparative Chadic: phonology and lexicon, *Journal of African Languages*, 5.3.218–251.

Nina Rodrigues, (?), 1932, *Os africanos no Brasil*, São Paulo.

Nketia, Joseph Hanson Kwabena 1963, *Drumming in Akan communities of Ghana*, Edinburgh: Thomas Nelson & Sons.

Olmsted, David L., 1954, Achumawi-Atsugewi non-reciprocal intelligibility, *International Journal of American Linguistics*, 20:181–184.

1957, Three tests of glottochronological theory, *American Anthropologist*, 59:839–42.

Orstein, Jacob, 1964, Africa seeks a common language, *The Review of Politics*, 26:205.

Painter, Colin, 1970, *Gonja: a phonological and grammatical study*, Bloomington: Indiana University Press.

Pedersen Holger, 1924, Sprogvidenskaben i det nittende Aarhundrede, Metoder og Resultater, Kjøbenhavn: (trans. 1931 as Linguistic science in the nineteenth century, Cambridge: Harvard University Press).

Pike, Kenneth, L., 1966, *Tagmemic and matrix linguistics applied to selected African languages*, Ann Arbor, Michigan (The University of Michigan Center for Research on Languages and Language Behavior).

Polomé, E.C., 1963, Cultural languages and contact vernacular in the Republic of the Congo, *Texas Studies in Literature and Language*, 4:499–511.

Practical orthography of African languages, revised ed., 1930, *Memorandum I*. International Institute of African Languages and Cultures, London.

Prost, R.P.A., 1956, *La langue Soñay et ses dialectes*, Dakar (Mémoires de l'Institut Français d'Afrique Noire, no. 47).

Pumphrey, M.E.C., Shilluk "royal" language conventions, *Sudan Notes and Records*, 20:319–321.

Rattray, R.S., 1922, The drum language of West Africa, *Journal of the Royal Asiatic Society of Great Britain and Ireland*, London, 22:226–36, 302–16.

Rice, Frank A., ed., 1962, *Study of the role of second languages in Asia, Africa, and Latin America*, Washington, D.C.: Center for Applied Linguistics of the Modern Language Association of America.

Richardson, I., 1959, *The role of tone in the structure of Sukuma*, London: School of Oriental and African Studies.

1961, Some observations on the status of Town Bemba in Northern Rhodesia, *African Language Studies*, 2:25–36.

Samarin, William J., 1962, Lingua francas, with special reference to Africa, in *Study of the role of second languages*, Frank Rice, ed., Washington, D.C.: Center for applied Linguistics, 54–64.

1965, The attitudinal and autobiographic in Gbeya dog names, *Journal of African Languages*, 4.1:57–72.

1969, The art of Gbeya insults, *International Journal of American Linguistics*, 35: 323–329.

Sapir, Edward, 1921, *Language*, New York: Harcourt Brace.

Schachter, Paul, 1961, Phonetic similarity in tonemic analysis with notes on the tone system of Akwopim Twi, *Language*, 37.2:231–238.

1966, A generative account of Hausa *Ne/Ce*, *Journal of African Languages*, 5:34–53.

Schmidt, P.W., 1926, *Die Sprachfamilien and Sprachenkreise der Erde*, Heidelberg.

Seitel, Sheila, 1969, Ethnography of communication in four African societies, in Working Paper no. 16, *Studies of Interaction*, Language Behavior Research Laboratory, University of California, Berkeley.

Shafer, Robert 1959, Phonétique comparée du Nigéro-Sénégalien (Mande). *Bulletin d'institut Français d'Afrique Noire*, 21:179–200.

Simmons, Donald C., 1958, Cultural functions of the Efik tone riddle, *Journal of American Folklore*, 71:133–138.

1960, Ibibio tone riddles, *Nigerian Field*, 25:132–4.

1960, Tonality in Efik signal communication and folklore, in Anthony F.C. Wallace, ed., *Men and cultures*, Philadelphia: University of Pennsylvania Press, 803–808.

1960, Tonal rhyme in Efik poetry, *Anthropological Linguistics*, 2.6:1–10.

Smith, M.G., 1957, The social functions and meaning of Hausa praise singing, *Africa*, 27:26–44.

Somjee, Alidina, 1890, *Guide to the Swahili language in Gujarati characters*.

Spencer, John, ed., 1963, *Language in Africa: Papers of the Leverhulme conference on universities and the language problems of tropical Africa, held at University College, Ibadan*, Cambridge: University Press.

Spencer, John, ed., 1971, *The English language in West Africa*, London: Longmans.

Stalke, Herbert, 1970, Serial verbs, *Studies in African Linguistics*, 1.2:60–99.

Stern, Theodore, 1957, Drum and whistle languages; an analysis of speech surrogates, *American Anthropologist*, 59:487–506.

Stokes, E.T., ed., 1962, *Historians in tropical Africa*, Salisbury.

Talbot, Percy Amaury, 1912, *In the shadow of the bush*, Appendix G, London: William Heinemann.

Torrend, J., 1891, *A comparative grammar of the South-African Bantu languages*, London: Kegan Paul.

Trigger, B.G., 1964, Meroïtic and Eastern Sudanic: a linguistic relationship?, *Kush*, 12: 188–194.

Tucker, A.N., 1929, *The comparative phonetics of the Suto-Chuana group of the Bantu languages*, London: Longmans, Green.

1936, African alphabets and the telegraph problem, *Bantu Studies*, 10.1:67–73.

1940, *The Eastern Sudanic languages*, vol. 1, London: Oxford University Press.

1957, Philology and Africa, *Bulletin of the School of Oriental and African Studies*, 20:541–554.

Tucker, A.N. and M.A. Bryan, 1956, *The non-Bantu languages of North-Eastern Africa*, London: Oxford University Press.

Tucker, A.N. and J. Tompo Ole Mpaayei, 1955, *A Maasai grammar*, London: Longmans, Green.

Turner, Lorenzo Dow, 1949, *Africanisms in the Gullah dialect*, Chicago: University of Chicago Press.

Twala, Regina G., 1951, Beads as regulating the social life of the Zulu and Swazi, *African Studies*, 10.3:113–123.

Voegelin, C.F. and F.M., 1964, Languages of the world: African fascicle one (*Anthropological Linguistics* 6.5).

van Ginneken, J., 1939, *La reconstruction typologique des langues archaiques de l'humanite*. Amsterdam: Verhandelingen der koninklijke Nederlandsche Akademie van Wetenschappen te Amsterdam.

von Warmelo, N.J., 1930, Early Bantu ethnography from a philological point of view, *Africa*, 3:31–48.

Weinreich, Uriel, 1953, *Languages in contact*, New York: Linguistic Circle of New York.

Welmers, William E., 1946, A descriptive grammar of Fanti, *Language*. (*Supplement*) 22 (3).

1964, The syntax of emphasis in Kpelle, *Journal of West African Languages*, 1.1:13–26.

1973, *African Language Structures*, Los Angeles.

Werner, Alice, 1904–5, The custom of "hlonipa' in its influence on language, *Journal of the Royal African Society*, 4:112–116.

1915, *The language families of Africa*, London: S.P.C.K. (2nd ed. 1925, published by Kegan Paul).

1930, *Structure and relationship of African languages*, London: Longmans, Green.

Wescott, Roger W., 1965, Speech-tempo and the phonemics of Bini, *Journal of African Languages*, 4.3:182–190.

1967, African languages and African prehistory, in Creighton Gabel and Norman R. Bennett, eds., *Reconstructing African culture history*, Boston: University Press, 45–54.

Westermann, D., 1927, *Die westlichen Sudansprachen und ihre Beziehungen zum Bantu*, Berlin: Walter de Gruyter (Mitteilungen des Seminars für Orientalischen Sprachen, Jahrgang 29, Beiheft)

1940, Afrikanische Tabusitten in ihrer Einwirkung auf die Sprachgestaltung, *Abhandlungen der Preußischen Akademie der Wissenschaften*, Jahrgang 1939, Philosophisch-historische Klasse, Nr 12.

1949, Sprachbeziehungen und Sprachverwandtschaft in Afrika, *Sitzungsberichte der Deutschen Akademie der Wissenschaften* Philosophisch-historische Klasse, Nr. 1, Berlin.

1952, African linguistic classification, *Africa* 22:250–256.

Westermann, D., 1927, *Die westlichen Sudansprachen und ihre Beziehungen zum Bantu*, guages (2nd ed. 1949), London: Oxford University Press.

Westermann, D. and M.A. Bryan, 1952, *Languages of West Africa*, London: Oxford University Press.

Westphal, E., 1962, A re-classification of Southern African non-Bantu languages, *Journal of African languages*, 1:1–8.

Whiteley, W.H., 1964, Problems of a lingua franca: Swahili and the trade-unions, *Journal of African Languages*, 3:215–225.

Williamson, John, 1947, The use of Arabic script in Swahili, *African Studies (Supplement)*, 6.4.

Williamson, Kay 1965, *A grammar of the Kolokuma dialect of Ijo*, Cambridge: Cambridge University Press (West African Language Monographs 2).

Wolff, Hans, 1959, Intelligibility and inter-ethnic attitudes, *Anthropological Linguistics*, 1.3:34—41.

1959, Subsystem typologies and area linguistics, *Anthropological Linguistics*, 1.79.

1962, Rara, a Yoruba chant, *Journal of African Languages*, 1.1:45—6.

Zahan, D., 1950, Pictographic writing in the Western Sudan, *Man*, 50:136—38.

Zylharz, E., 1930, Das meroitische Sprachproblem, *Anthropos*, 25:405—463.

1941—42, Das Land Punt, *Zeitschrift für Eingeborenen-Sprachen*, 32:302—311.

Index